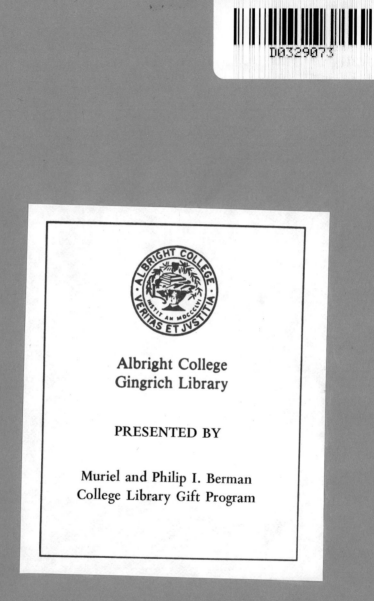

LEGENDS OF GALILEE, JORDAN, AND SINAI

LEGENDS OF

GALILEE, JORDAN, AND SINAI

THE SACRED LAND: VOLUME 3

ZEV VILNAY

The Jewish Publication Society of America
PHILADELPHIA

1978 · 5739

Copyright © 1978
by The Jewish Publication Society of America
All rights reserved
First edition
ISBN 0–8276–0106–9
Library of Congress catalog card number 73–168156
Manufactured in the United States of America
Designed by Sol Calvin Cohen

CONTENTS

List of Illustrations xix

GALILEE

I. HAIFA—THE GATEWAY OF ISRAEL

1. Why Was it Called Haifa? 3
2. The Pronunciation of the Jews of Haifa 5
3. Among the Rocks on the Haifa Seashore 5
4. Who Was Haifa's Bitterest Foe? 6
5. The Martyr of the Holy War 7

II. CARMEL—THE MOUNT OF ELIJAH

1. "Thy Head upon Thee Is like Carmel" 9
2. The Prophet Elijah on Mount Carmel 10
3. The Cavern of the Prophet Elijah 10
4. The Mad Maid in the Cave of Elijah 12
5. The Cave of Elijah and Jesus of Nazareth 13
6. The Altar of Elijah on Mount Carmel 14
7. Hiel Hid in the Altar of Baal 15
8. The Melons that Turned to Stone 17
9. The Magic Stone of Mount Carmel 18

vi § CONTENTS

10. The God of Carmel 19
11. Tabor and Carmel Envy Sinai 21
12. The Arrogance of Tabor and Carmel 22
13. The Temple Will Be Built on Carmel and Tabor . 22
14. The Wise Men of Mount Carmel 23
15. The Gorge of the Cyclamen 24
16. Reincarnation 25

III. THE SEA OF HAIFA

1. Zebulun Inherited the Sea of Haifa 27
2. The Sea of Haifa—a Silver Bowl 29
3. The Sea of Haifa in the Days to Come 30
4. The Discovery of Glass 30
5. The Sons of Zebulun Were Glassmakers 31
6. The Sand that Turns into Glass 31
7. How Purple Was Discovered 32
8. Zebulun Were Purplemakers 34
9. The Children of Zebulun Were Tradesmen 36
10. The Bond Between Zebulun and Issachar 37
11. The River Kishon—the Ancient River 38

IV. ACCO AND ITS SURROUNDINGS

1. Why Was It Called Acco? 40
2. Famous Sages of Acco 42
3. The Fate of Nakdimon's Daughter in Acco 43
4. Miriam the Daughter of Tanhum in Acco 43
5. The Synagogue of King Ahab in Acco 44
6. To Bring Fish to Acco 44
7. The Precious Treasure in the Mosque of Acco ... 45
8. The Spring of the Ox 45
9. The Spring that Observes the Sabbath 46
10. The River Naaman and the Wall of Acco 46
11. The River Naaman and the Serpents 47
12. Rock of the Three Continents 47
13. The Palm Groves of Acco 48
14. The Grave of Abu-Atabah 49

V. THE LADDERS OF TYRE

1. Abraham at the Ladders of Tyre 51
2. The Reviving of the Lion at the Ladders of Tyre 52
3. Alexander the Great in Rosh-Hanikra 52
4. The Cave of Sighs 54
5. King Solomon's Pools near Tyre 54
6. Hiram, King of Tyre, Built Him Seven Heavens . 56
7. "Tyre Is Thine" 57
8. Tyre and the Coming of the Messiah 59

VI. THE VALLEY OF JEZREEL (ESDRAELON)

1. The Western Valley of Jezreel Went to Zebulun . 60
2. The Central Valley of Jezreel Went to Issachar .. 61
3. The Sons of Issachar Were Men of Learning 63
4. The Temple in the Land of Issachar 64
5. Why Naboth Perished from the Earth 64
6. The Prophet Elisha in Shunem 65
7. Sheikh Abreik and the Healing Marsh 66
8. From Nahalal to Jerusalem 67
9. Rabbi Levi and the Inhabitants of Simonia 68
10. The Acacia Shrubs on the Hill of Shimron 69
11. The Humble Man from Havraya 69
12. The Town of Dobrath and the Prophetess
    Deborah 70
13. The Cave of the Traitress 71
14. Why the Teacher in Taberneth Was Dismissed .. 71
15. Tel Keimon—Joshua's Battlefield 72
16. Yokneam—the Mount of Cain 73
17. The Battle of Armageddon 76
18. Nebuzaradan in the Valley of Megiddo 77
19. Ein-Ibrahim—Spring of Abraham 77
20. Rabbi Pinhas and the River Ginnai 78
21. Ein-Harod—the Spring of Gideon 79
22. The Valley of Jezreel—the Battlefield of David
    and Goliath 81
23. The Hill of Moreh—Little Hermon 82

VII. THE VALLEY OF BEIT-SHEAN

1. Beit-Shean Is the Gate of Eden 84
2. The Paradisial Spring in the Valley of Beit-Shean 86
3. The Pronunciation of the Jews of Beit-Shean 86
4. If the Palms of Beit-Shean Should Disappear 86
5. Where Was Satan Banished to? 87
6. Where Did the Palace of Melchizedek Stand? ... 88
7. The Curse on Mount Gilboa 88
8. To Bring Hay to Ofraim 89
9. The Bridge of Meeting 90
10. The Rivers Jordan and Yarmuk 91
11. Who Built Hamat-Gader? 92
12. On a Rock of Hamat-Gader 92
13. A Custom Practiced in Govat-Shamai 93

VIII. NAZARETH AND TABOR

1. The Origin of the Name Nazareth 94
2. The Priestly Family in Nazareth 95
3. The Synagogue-Church of Nazareth 96
4. The Church that Sailed in the Air 97
5. The Column of St. Mary 99
6. The Leap of the Lord—Mount of the Precipice .. 99
7. Mensa Christi—Table of Christ 101
8. A Moslem Traveler in Nazareth 101
9. The Priestly Family in Kefar-Kanna 101
10. The Cave of Melchizedek on Mount Tabor 103

IX. ZIPPORI AND ITS VICINITY

1. The Town of Zippori 106
2. Prosperous Zippori 107
3. Rabbi Judah Ha-nasi in Zippori 108
4. Rabbi Yossi in Zippori 109
5. Priestly Families in Zippori 109
6. The Vendor of the Philter of Life in Zippori 110
7. The Fate of a Tailor from Zippori 110
8. Magicians in Ancient Zippori 111
9. Ruma—the Abode of Antoninus Caesar 111
10. Ruma—Where Messiah Will Appear 112

11. The Reaper in the Valley of Beit-Netofa 113
12. How Rabbi Joshua Dissuaded the Rebels 114
13. The Rock of Nails 115

X. LOWER GALILEE

1. The Two Galilees 116
2. Usha—the Seat of the Divine Providence 117
3. The Wondrous Cavern of Cabul 117
4. Why Was Cabul Destroyed? 118
5. The Fertility of Ancient Sikhnin 120
6. Why Was Sikhin Destroyed? 120
7. The Stone of Haninah 121
8. The Pious Women of Tiran 122
9. From Yama to Tigni (Tigna) 123
10. Why Is Beit-Keshet so Named? 123

XI. THE SEA OF GALILEE (KINNERET)

1. Why Is It Called Kinneret? 125
2. How the Sea of Galilee Was Created 126
3. The Taste of the Fish of Kinneret 127
4. Who Had Fishing Rights in Lake Kinneret? 128
5. The Well of Miriam in the Kinneret 128
6. The Merits of Miriam's Well 130
7. Miriam's Well Wanders in the Diaspora 131
8. The Bucket of Miriam 132
9. From the Holy of Holies to the Sea of Galilee ... 133
10. The Arch of the Covenant in Lake Kinneret 133
11. The Rock of the Ants 134
12. When Will Lake Kinneret Be Dried up? 135
13. The Miraculous Stream of the Jordan 136
14. The Blue Hearts of Galilee 136

XII. THE SHORES OF LAKE KINNERET

1. The Redemption of Israel Is Like the Morning
   Star 138
2. The Valley of Arbel in Olden Days 139
3. The Messiah in the Valley of Arbel 140
4. Why Was It Called Ginnosar? 141

5. The Fruit of Ginnosar and Jerusalem 141
6. Ginossar Was in the Land of Naphtali 141
7. Naphtali, Satisfied with Favor 142
8. Naphtali, a Hind Let Loose 142
9. Ein Kahal—the Hiding-Place of the Treasures ... 143
10. Napoleon and the Treasures in Ein Kahal 144
11. Job on the Shores of Lake Kinneret 145
12. The Miracle of the Loaves and Fishes 145
13. Capernaum on the Shore of Lake Kinneret 147
14. The Spring in Capernaum 148
15. Chorazim near Capernaum 148
16. Chorazim—Bethsaida—Capernaum 149
17. Bethsaida's Gift to Emperor Hadrian 150
18. Wherefore the Name Kursi? 151
19. Gog at the Shores of Lake Kinneret 151

XIII. TIBERIAS—ANCIENT RAKKATH

1. The Name Tiberias 152
2. Wherefore the Name Rakkath? 154
3. The Inhabitants of Rakkath—Lovers of Remains . 154
4. How Tiberias Was Purified 155
5. The Redemption Will Begin in Tiberias 157
6. The Messiah's Rod Is Concealed in Tiberias 157
7. The People of Tiberias Give Good Words 158
8. The Twelve Months in Tiberias 158
9. The Black Stones of Tiberias 159
10. Purim of Tiberias 159
11. The Holy Ari in Tiberias 161
12. When the Wall of Tiberias Is Rebuilt 161
13. The Emperor and Rabbi Judah the Prince 162
14. The Old Planter and the Emperor 163
15. The Miraculous Herb of Tiberias 164
16. What Did Daniel Do in Tiberias? 164
17. Early Tiberias and Late Zippori 165
18. From Tiberias to Sussita 166
19. Tiberias and Zefat Benefit from Each Other 166

XIV. THE HOT SPRINGS OF TIBERIAS

1. The Hot Springs Stream past Hell 168
2. Why Are There no Hot Springs in Jerusalem? ... 169
3. A Miracle at the Hot Springs of Tiberias 170
4. Steam Baths in Tiberias on the Sabbath 170
5. The Cure-Seekers at the Hot Springs 171
6. Who Heats the Springs of Tiberias? 172

XV. IN THE SURROUNDINGS OF TIBERIAS

1. The Palace of Berenice, Daughter of the King ... 174
2. The Palace of the Emperor's Daughter 175
3. The Blessing of the Rain in Migdal 176
4. The Priestly Family of Migdal-Nunia 176
5. Handicrafts in Ancient Migdal-Zovim 176
6. From Migdal-Zovim to Jerusalem 177
7. The Acacia Trees in Migdal-Zovim 177
8. Mazka—the Pleasant Hamlet 178

XVI. ZEFAT—THE MYSTIC CITY

1. The Name "Zefat" 179
2. Fire Signals on the Mount of Zefat 180
3. The Praise of Holy Zefat 182
4. Zefat Destroyed by an Earthquake 182
5. Zefat Shall Be Suddenly Rebuilt 183
6. The Holy Ari—Leader of the Zefat Cabalists 184
7. The Sephardic Synagogue of the Ari 185
8. The Synagogue of Elijah the Prophet 186
9. The Ari's Seat in the Synagogue 186
10. The Ashkenazic Synagogue of the Ari 188
11. The Field of Apples 189
12. The Abode of the Holy Ari in Zefat 190
13. Ostrich Eggs in the Synagogues of Zefat 191
14. The Ritual Bath of the Holy Ari 192
15. The Synagogue of Abuab in Zefat 193
16. The Citadel on Mount Zefat 194
17. Rabbi Abraham Halevy in the Streets of Zefat ... 194
18. A Descendant of King David in Zefat 196

19. "Tashlich Day" in Zefat 197
20. The Cavern of the Daughters of Jacob 197
21. The Study House of Shem and Ever 199
22. Zefat—the Birthplace of Queen Esther 199
23. How Fireflies Helped the Jews of Zefat 200
24. The Sultan's Prayer 201
25. The Rivalry Between Jerusalem and Zefat 201

XVII. MEIRON AND PEKIIN

1. On the Way to Ein-Zeitim 204
2. Where Do the Waters of Ein-Zeitim Flow from? . 205
3. The Cockerel Saint 206
4. The Spring in Nahal Hatahanot 206
5. "Like the People of Meiron" 207
6. The Lintel and the Messiah 208
7. The Tomb of Rabbi Shimon Bar Yohai 210
8. The Rebellious Rabbi Shimon 211
9. The Grave of Rabbi Eleazar 212
10. The Holy Ari and his Friends at Meiron 213
11. The Pilgrimage to Meiron 213
12. The Priestly Family in Meiron 215
13. The Cavern of the Priests near Meiron 216
14. The Throne of Elijah the Prophet 216
15. The Bath of the Prophetess Deborah 218
16. Tekoa Is First for Oil 219
17. How Was Tekoa Built? 220
18. Why Does Hanukkah Last Eight Days? 220
19. The Cave of Shimon Bar Yohai 221
20. The Prayer in the Cave of Rabbi Shimon Bar
    Yohai 222
21. Elijah at the Cave of Rabbi Shimon 224
22. How the Zohar Was Found 224
23. The Saint of the Mills 225

XVIII. ON THE HEIGHTS OF UPPER GALILEE

1. The Messiah Will Appear in Upper Galilee 227
2. The Praise of Galilee in the Olden Days 228
3. The Faulty Pronunciation of the Galileans 229
4. May a Lion Devour Thee! 229

5. What Caused the Ruin of Upper Galilee? 230
6. The Inheritance of Asher in Galilee 231
7. The Two Rival Villages 233
8. Do Not Bring Potters to Kefar Hananiah 234
9. The Affluence of Ancient Gush-Halav 234
10. What Did the Emperor Receive from
    Gush-Halav? 235
11. The Chain of King David at Gush-Halav 236
12. The Cavern of the Babylonians 236
13. The Strange Inscription in Kefar-Biram 237
14. The Wonder-Child of Kefar-Biram 238
15. The City of Refuge 239
16. What Did the Emperor Receive from Nizhana? . 240

XIX. IN THE VALLEY OF THE UPPER JORDAN

1. Ayelet-Hashahar—the Morning Star 241
2. Joseph's Pit in Upper Galilee 242
3. The Bridge of the Daughters of Jacob 243
4. The Tears of the Daughters of Jacob 244
5. Yesod-Hamaalah—Why Was It so Called? 245
6. Rabbi Meir in Kefar-Mamla 246
7. The Origin of the Name Hula 246
8. From Jerusalem to Hula 247
9. A Trade of the Sons of Naphtali 247
10. The Sources of the Jordan 248
11. Dan Was Formerly Named Leshem 249
12. The Symbol of Dan 250
13. Dan Is a Lion's Whelp 250
14. The Hill of the Judge 251
15. The Golden Calf in Dan 252
16. May the Waters of Panias Be Turned into Blood . 253
17. The Suffering of Panias 254
18. The Miraculous Statue in Banias 254

XX. ON THE HEIGHTS OF MOUNT HERMON

1. Mount Hermon 256
2. Mount Hermon—Snow Mount 257
3. The Angels on Mount Hermon 258

4. The Place of the Promise 259
5. The Snow-Capped Hermon 261
6. Moses and Mount Hermon 262
7. Jerusalem Will Be Built on Mount Hermon 263
8. The Hivites on Mount Hermon 263
9. Water Flows from Mount Hermon to Persia 264

JORDAN

XXI. ON THE HEIGHTS OF GOLAN

1. The Fortress of Nimrod 269
2. From Ram to Panias 271
3. Moses and the Tunnel of Caesarion 271
4. How the Lake of Ram Came into Being 272
5. The Big Eye of Ram 272
6. Where Was the Land of Tob? 273
7. The Tombs of the Israelites in Golan 274

XXII. IN THE LAND OF BASHAN

1. Edrei—the Capital of King Og 275
2. How King Og Fought the Israelites 276
3. The Land of the Prophet Job 277
4. Karnaim—the Birthplace of Job 278
5. Wherefrom Came the Wicked Haman? 280
6. Wherefore the Name Ashtarot-Karnaim? 280
7. The Stones on the Eastern Border of Eretz-Israel .. 281

XXIII. THE LAND OF GILEAD

1. The Inheritance of Gad 283
2. The Banner of Gad 284
3. Why It Was Called Mahanaim 284
4. King David in Mahanaim 285
5. The Flag of Reuben 286
6. In the Inheritance of Gad and Reuben 287
7. The Town of Refuge in the Land of Reuben 288
8. Beit-Geres—the Gate of Eden 289
9. The Origin of the Name Balka 289

XXIV. THE LANDS OF AMMON AND MOAB

1. Ammonites and Moabites in Jerusalem 291
2. The Clouds over Ammon and Moab 292
3. In the Wilderness of Ammon and Moab 292
4. Israel in the Desert of Ammon and Moab 293
5. Redemption Shall Begin in the Desert of Moab 294
6. The Israelite Victory in Transjordan 295
7. King Solomon in the Land of Ammon 296
8. The Theater of King Solomon in Rabat-Ammon . . . 297
9. When the Palm Trees of Rabat-Ammon Perish 298
10. The Pools of Heshbon 298
11. The Cave of Rakim 299
12. The Thorn-Palms of the Iron Mount Are Valid 300
13. Jacob at the Burning Waters 301
14. Baara—the Spring of Burning Waters 302
15. Who Heats the Hot Baths of Ibn Hammad? 303
16. The Sneezing Goats in the Mountains of Machor . . . 304

XXV. NEBO—BETH-PEOR—SHITTIM

1. Wherefore the Name "Mountains of Avarim"? 305
2. Moses on Mount Nebo 306
3. Through the Grace of Prayer 306
4. Moses Wished to Enter the Holy Land 307
5. Moses' Eye and the Temple's Portal 308
6. The Treasures Hidden on Mount Nebo 309
7. Moses, the Man of God, and Beth-peor 310
8. Wherefore the Name Beth-peor? 311
9. The Cult of Peor 312
10. Abel-Shittim—the Place of Folly 312
11. Why Was It Called Shittim? 314
12. The Fountain and the River of Shittim 314
13. Korah and his People at the River Shittim 315
14. Mattanah, Nahaliel, Bamoth, Hagai 315

XXVI. THE LAND OF EDOM

1. The Horites—the Ancient Edomites 317
2. The Boon of Rain on Mount Seir 318
3. In the Mountains of Gebal 318

 4. The Torah Was Offered to the Sons of Esau 319
 5. Moses and Aaron on Mount Hor 320
 6. The Shrine of Aaron the Priest 320
 7. The Spring of Moses in Edom 321
 8. Petra and Its Inhabitants 322
 9. The Treasure of Pharaoh in Petra 323
10. The Palace of Pharaoh's Daughter 325

S I N A I

XXVII. THE DESERT OF SINAI

 1. The Wilderness of Snakes and Scorpions 329
 2. Moses Set the Time for Meals 330
 3. The Manna—the Food of Israel 330
 4. The Manna-Carrying Tamarisk Bush 331
 5. The Quail in the Desert of Sinai 333
 6. In the Wilderness of Shur 334
 7. The Name "Desert of Shur" 336
 8. Israel in the Desert of Paran 336
 9. He Appeared on Mount Paran 337

XXVIII. STATIONS AND SITES IN SINAI

 1. Baal-zephon—a Station in the Wanderings 338
 2. Pi-hahiroth—a Station in the Wanderings 339
 3. Marah—a Station on the Way of Israel 339
 4. Mithkah and Marah 340
 5. Alosh—a Station in the Wanderings 340
 6. Rephidim of the Sinai Desert 341
 7. Tophel—Laban—Di-zahab 342
 8. El-Arish—the Capital of Sinai 343
 9. A Bigger Traitor than the Governor of El-Arish . 344
10. Rhinocorura—-Ancient el-Arish 344
11. Who Saved the Town Pelusion? 346

XXIX. SINAI—THE MOUNT OF GOD

 1. The Various Names of Mount Sinai 347
 2. Sinai Is also Named Bashan 348
 3. Wherefore the Name Sinai? 349

4. Wherefrom Came Mount Sinai? 350
5. Why Was the Law Given from Sinai? 350
6. Why Was the Holy Law Given in a Wilderness? . 351
7. Moses on the Heights of Mount Sinai 351
8. Sinai Unites Israel 353
9. How Did the Lord Appear on Sinai? 354
10. The Divine Presence Exalted Mount Sinai 354
11. A Voice from Mount Sinai 354
12. Israel's Reward on Mount Sinai 354
13. When Was the Torah Given? 355
14. Sinai and the Uprooter of Mountains 355
15. A Law from Mount Sinai 357
16. The Broken Pieces of the Holy Tablets 358
17. Where Did the Burning Bush Grow? 359
18. Moses—the Good Shepherd 360
19. The Cave of Moses and Elijah in Sinai 360
20. Korah Was Swallowed up in the Sinai Mountains 361
21. The Seat of Moses 362
22. The Healing Rock of Moses 363
23. The Rock that Spoke to Moses 364
24. A Stone from Sinai in Jerusalem 366

XXX. THE WONDERS AT THE RED SEA

1. How Israel Crossed the Red Sea 367
2. The Dividing of the Red Sea 368
3. The Miracles at the Red Sea 369
4. The Almighty on the Red Sea 371
5. The Prophet Jonah in the Red Sea 371

ILLUSTRATIONS

1. Haifa and Mount Carmel 4
2. Cavern of the Prophet Elijah on Mount Carmel 12
3. Elijah's offering 15
4. Offering of false prophets 16
5. "Melons of Elijah," Reyzen van Cornelius de Bruyn, 1681 18
6. Foot of "God of Carmel" 20
7. Cyclamen 25
8. Sailboat in Bay of Haifa 28
9. Bay of Haifa 29
10. Making of glass (1336). A page from "The Voiage and Trauile of Syr John Maundevile Knight" (Halliwell Edition), 1839 33
11. Ancient Syrian coin 34
12. Purple mollusks from Mediterranean Sea 36
13. Acco (1830). A drawing by W. H. Bartlett in J. Carne, *Syria, the Holy Land*, 1845 41
14. Palm tree near Acco 48
15. Rosh-Hanikra—Head of the Hollow (1880). From C. W. Wilson, *Picturesque Palestine*, 1882 53
16. Pools of Solomon near Tyre (1688), Reyzen van Cornelius de Bruyn 55

17. "Tomb of Hiram" 57
18. Tyre on Mediterranean Sea (1880). From P. Lortet, *La Syrie d'aujourd'hui,* 1884 58
19. Pictorial Map of the Valley of Jezreel. From Thomas Fuller, *A Pisgah Sight of Palestine,* 1650 62
20. Blind Lamech shoots at Cain. From a sixteenth-century map of the Holy Land 74
21. Blind Lamech shoots at Cain. A twelfth-century mosaic in Monreale, Sicily 75
22. Fountain of Gideon (1910) 80
23. Arab building in Zarin 82
24. Mound of ancient Beit-Shean (1850). A painting by W. Tipping in Josephus, *Jewish Wars* (ed. Traill), 1851 85
25. Bridge of Meeting (1835) 91
26. Nazareth about the year 1660. From J. Jansonius, *Illustriorum Hispaniae Urbium,* 1660 95
27. Synagogue-Church in Nazareth 97
28. Church of the Annunciation in Nazareth. An eighteenth-century bas-relief now in the Museum of Cluny, Paris 98
29. Church of "Mensa Christi"—Table of Christ ... 100
30. Kefar-Kanna—Cana of Galilee 102
31. Mount Tabor (1842). From J. T. Bannister, *A Survey of the Holy Land,* 1844 104
32. Medieval fort on the ruins of Zippori 107
33. Sea of Galilee and snow-capped Hermon 126
34. Well of Miriam (1859). From a printed sheet of illustrations of the Holy Places, prepared by Rabbi Haim Abulafia 129
35. Rock of the Ants in Sea of Galilee 134
36. Valley of Arbel 139
37. Rocks of the Five Loaves (1838). From J. d'Estourmel, *Journal d'un Voyage en Orient,* I, 1844 ... 146
38. Ruins of Synagogue of Chorazim 149
39. Tiberias Surrounded by Mountains of Galilee (1839). From D. Roberts, *The Holy Land,* 1842. Drawings made on the spot 153
40. Hot Springs of Tiberias (1850). A painting by W. Tipping in Josephus, *Jewish Wars* (ed. Traill),

1851 169
41. Zefat (c. 1914). From a sheet of colored pictures of sacred cities and sites of the Holy Land 181
42. Cabalists in Zefat. A folk painting by S. Moscovitz, an inhabitant of Zefat referred to as *"Der Zeigermakher"*—the Watchmaker—because of his profession. The painting is in the museum of Heichal-Shelomo, Jerusalem 187
43. Central gate of the ancient synagogue of Meiron
.... 209
44. "Throne of Elijah the prophet" 217
45. Village of Pekiin 222
46. Ancient synagogue of Kefar-Biram 237
47. Ayelet-Hashahar 242
48. Mound of ancient Dan 248
49. Snow-capped Hermon 257
50. Place of our Father Abraham 260
51. Pool of Ram 270
52. Job on the Dunghill. An illustration from a twelfth-century manuscript Bible 279
53. Door socket. Found in Hierokonpalis about 3,000 B.C.E., and now in the museum of the University of Philadelphia 309
54. Acacia tree (Acacia spirocarpa) 313
55. Petra—Roman Theater (1828). From L. de Laborde, *Voyage de l'Arabie Pétrée*, 1830 323
56. Petra—*El-Khazne* (1828). From L. de Laborde, *Voyage de l'Arabie Pétrée*, 1830 324
57. Manna-carrying tamarisk 332
58. Quail 334
59. Palm grove of El-Arish 345
60. Moses with the Tablets of the Law. An illustration from the fourteenth-century Passover Haggadah of Sarajevo, Yugoslavia 352
61. Moses with the Tablets of the Law. From the Hebrew Book of Customs, *Sefer Haminhagim*, printed in Amsterdam 353
62. The Israelites in front of Mount Sinai. From a Mahzor (prayer book for the Feast of Shevuot, printed in Prague, 1854 356
63. Seat of Moses 363

64. Moses strikes the Rock. An illustration from *Zena va-Rena,* the Yiddish translation of the Pentateuch 364

65. Moses strikes the Rock. A section of an ancient mosaic, from *Liber Annus,* XVII, 1967, p. 267 . 365

66. Opening of the Red Sea. From a fresco on the wall of the ancient synagogue of Dura-Europos, third century 369

67. Israelites and Egyptians in the Red Sea. From a modern Passover Haggadah printed in Amsterdam 370

GALILEE

I
HAIFA—THE GATEWAY OF ISRAEL

Haifa, Israel's third largest city and its main harbor, is built around the large bay of the Cape of Carmel, which protrudes into the Mediterranean Sea.

Across the Valley of Zebulun, with its historical connotations, Haifa faces the Mountains of Galilee, whose many peaks and folds hold memories of some of the most portentous events ever to have shaped the course of Western culture.

1 / WHY WAS IT CALLED HAIFA?

Haifa is mentioned for the first time in the third century, in the Talmud. The origin of the name and its meaning are unknown. One fourteenth-century scholar surmised that it came from the Hebrew *hof*, which means "shore." Today, people choose to say that Haifa is a contraction of the two words *hof yafe*—beautiful shore. Indeed, situated on a rounded bay, at the meeting place of mountain, valley, and sea, Haifa does enjoy magnificent scenery.

In medieval times, the Christian pilgrims called the town "Caifa"—a name derived from the Hebrew *caif,* meaning "rock"—because of the dark boulders strewn along the coast.

Others called the city "Caiaphas," because they believed that it had been built at the time of Caiaphas, the High Priest of Jerusalem in the days of Jesus of Nazareth.

In the fourteenth century, this last version was cited by Sir John Mandeville, who wrote: "Hylle of Carmelyn, where Helyas the prophet dwellede. And at the Fote of this Hille was sometyme a gode Cytee of Cristene Men, that Men cleped Cayphas; for Cayphas first founded it; but it is now alle wasted."[1]*

FIG. 1. HAIFA AND MOUNT CARMEL
An artist's impression, middle of the nineteenth century.

---

* Superior numerals refer to Sources of the Legends.

2 / THE PRONUNCIATION OF THE JEWS OF HAIFA

Numerous Greek tradesmen lived in the district of Haifa in time gone by. Apparently, through their exposure to this foreign influence, the Jewish inhabitants neglected to maintain in their speech the different gutturals of the Hebrew language. This failure to enunciate clearly caused them to mispronounce many words, and thus corrupt their meaning. The same was said of the people of Tivon nearby and of Beit-Shean.

They all interchanged the letters "H" and "Ch," and the soft "A" with the guttural "A," and so distorted the meaning of the text of the Holy Scriptures. For instance, instead of reading: "And that they profane not [in Hebrew, *velo ye-CHalelu*] My Holy Name," they would read *"velo yeHalelu,"* which means, "And that they praise not My Holy Name." And instead of reading the verse from the prophecy of Isaiah, "And I will wait [in Hebrew, *veCHikiti*] for the Lord, that hideth His face," they read *"veHikiti,"* which means, "And I will beat." So instead of blessing and praising, they, by the laxity of their tongues, unwillingly insulted and abused the Holy Name.

Because of this, their priests were not allowed to officiate in the synagogues or to hold services.[2]

3 / AMONG THE ROCKS ON THE HAIFA SEASHORE

Tradition tells that in the days to come, the Almighty will build the Eastern Gate of the Temple out of a single pearl. A very pious man was found worthy to foresee this in a vision.

The man was walking among the rocks on the Haifa seashore. He was thinking, Can the Holy One, blessed be He, construct out of a single pearl the Eastern Gate of the Temple, together with its two small side gates?

Thereupon, a divine voice was heard, saying, "Were the

man not such a perfect saint, judgment would already have smitten him. The whole world was made in six days; should it be difficult to make the Eastern Gate and two side gates of the Temple out of a single pearl?"

The man at once besought mercy, saying, "Lord of the Universe! Though I thought it, I never uttered it with my lips!"

Suddenly, a miracle occured: The sea parted before him and he saw the ministering angels concealed therein. They were planing and polishing, and they said to him, "This is the Eastern Gate of the Temple that we are preparing, with its two side gates, all out of one pearl."[3]

4 / WHO WAS HAIFA'S BITTEREST FOE?

In ancient times, next to Jewish Haifa there stood a townlet named Castra, a Latin word meaning "fortress." Its gentile inhabitants were hostile to their Hebrew neighbors.

"As a lily among thorns, So is my love among the daughters," said Solomon of his beloved. This verse, say the sages, illustrates the situation of the people of Israel, who were surrounded by numerous enemies as are rose blooms among thorny boughs.

And on the verse of Lamentations: "The Lord hath commanded concerning Jacob, That they that are round about him should be his adversaries," it was commented: "As Castra to Haifa."

Castra, near Haifa, is undoubtedly the Samaritan settlement of the same name mentioned by a Christian pilgrim of the year 570 C.E. Today, it is a ruin known by the Arabic name *a-Samir*, situated at the foot of Mount Carmel, south of Haifa, on the Mediterranean seashore.[4]

5 / THE MARTYR OF THE HOLY WAR

In the railway station at Haifa, beside the train rails, there can be found a green monument, marking the grave of a Moslem martyr named Al-Mujahid—the Martyr of the Holy War. The Arab inhabitants of Haifa used to go there to pray, to make their offerings, and to kindle little lamps of oil.

In 1908, the Turkish Government dispatched an engineer to Haifa to supervise the construction of a railway then being built between Haifa and Damascus. According to the plans of the engineer, the lines were to run over the shrine of the Holy Martyr. At the beginning of the work, he instructed his men to level the tomb and to build the railway lines over it. The Moslem inhabitants of Haifa cried out in protest against such desecration, but in vain.

When the railway was completed, all the great men of the land gathered together to celebrate its opening. A special parlor car was prepared for the guests of honor, with the engineer as their host. The parlor car moved along, amidst the cheers of the onlookers. As it passed over the spot where the shrine of the Holy Martyr had stood, the earth trembled so violently that the parlor car almost overturned. The passengers shook with fear, and, turning to the engineer sitting in their midst, they asked him what it meant. Shamefaced, the engineer could not say a word.

The rails were examined, and everything was found to be in perfect order. As the parlor car returned over the same spot, however, the earth trembled with even greater violence, and the directors of the railway were very angry with the engineer who had seemingly failed in his task.

The engineer returned home sad and humiliated, and could find no peace within his soul. That night, he had a dream in which the spirit of the Holy Martyr appeared, saying, "Be it known unto you, it was I who caused the parlor car to shake, and had it not been for the innocent people with you I would have overturned it and killed you. Remember, therefore, if you do not remove the train rails from above me and rebuild my tomb your end will be a bitter one."

The next day, the engineer ordered his men to alter the course of the line, to rebuild the tomb, and to raise the monument that exists to this day. Since then, all trains have passed peacefully by.[5]

II

CARMEL–THE MOUNT OF ELIJAH

1 / "THY HEAD UPON THEE IS LIKE CARMEL"

Fair and fruitful Mount Carmel, whose luxuriant green head stands out clearly above the wide expanse of the sea, was the symbol of beauty in ancient times.

The poet of the Song of Songs praised his beloved thus: "Thy head upon thee is like Carmel,/And the hair of thy head like purple."

Legend expounds "Thy head upon thee is like Carmel" to mean: Your heads (leaders) are as dear to Me as Elijah, who went up Mount Carmel. "And the hair of thy head like purple" suggests Mount Carmel, too, for in the olden days purple dye was prepared at the foot of the mountain from the mollusks collected from the sea in its vicinity.*6

* See legend III:8.

2 / THE PROPHET ELIJAH ON MOUNT CARMEL

"The Almighty God said: I gave . . .
on the Carmel salvation to Elijah."

The prophet Elijah dwelt a long time on Mount Carmel.
Here the Archangel Michael appeared, and disclosed to him
all that will be wrought in the end of time. These secrets are
revealed in the book called *Midrash Eliyahu Hanavi*—"The
Homiletics of the Prophet Elijah."

The Scriptures tell how, in a drought year, from the summit of Carmel, the holy man once saved the people: "And
Elijah went up to the top of Carmel; and he bowed himself
down upon the earth, and put his face between his knees.
And he said to his servant: 'Go up now, look toward the sea.'
And he went up, and looked, and said: 'There is nothing.'
And he said: 'Go again seven times.' And it came to pass at
the seventh time, that he said: 'Behold there ariseth a cloud
out of the sea, as small as a man's hand.' . . . And it came to
pass in a little while, that the heaven grew black with clouds
and wind, and there was a great rain."

Mount Carmel is known to the Arabs as *el-Karmel*—the
Carmel. The Christians among them call it *Jabal Mar Elias*
—the Mount of Saint Elijah. The monks whose order was
founded there are called Carmelites, and Elijah is their pa-
tron.

The Arabs nickname Elijah *"el-Khadr"*—the Green One—
because his memory is alive and ever green in the tradition
of the people.[7]

3 / THE CAVERN OF THE PROPHET ELIJAH

On the side of Carmel's cape, facing the Mediterranean
Sea, within the boundaries of Haifa, there is a cavern hewn
into the rock and known in Jewish tradition as *Mearat*

Eliyahu ha-Navi—the Cavern of Elijah the Prophet. Jews often come to the cavern to pray and to kindle lights, as they are wont to do in their holy shrines.

On the Sunday following Sabbath *Nahamu,* when the chapter of Isaiah, "Comfort ye [*nahamu,* in Hebrew] My people," is intoned in the synagogue, a great pilgrimage is made to the cavern. Women measure it with string, and afterward use the string for wicks in the Sabbath candles.

Many virtues are attributed to the cave; it is especially famous for curing the mentally ill. These unfortunate people are brought from all parts of the country in the hope of recovery. Then, too, women who desire to give birth to a male child come and spend several days in the coolness of its rocky walls.

A Jewish pilgrim of the year 1742 wrote: "And we went to Carmel, which is a wonderful mountain, large and very, very high; its head reaching to the skies, and there is a big cave, and when we entered there the spirit of God rested upon us and our souls were enlightened very abundantly. And inside the cave there is a small cave, and it is said that here sat Elijah, his memory be blessed. And if ever anyone impure enters this cave, small currents of water immediately flow from its far corners, and the soul cleanses itself. And that is the sign that an unclean one was there. That we saw once on the Day of Atonement. And in front of the cave there is a small cistern which fills with rainwater. And in the summer days there is no water in it; it is dry. And people entreat: 'Elijah, our master, give us water!' And the next day it is filled with water. Many are the benefits bestowed upon the visitor, and indeed, when one enters there, one's soul is filled with the Holy Spirit, and one's hair stands on end from awe, [as it is said] 'How full of awe is this place!' "

Another Jewish pilgrim who visited the Cavern of Elijah about the year 1835 related: "And we found there many Jews. And when I started to pray, the prayer streamed by itself out of the mouth and my eyes were filled with tears, for I never prayed thus. And then I knew that I was standing on holy ground."[8]

FIG. 2. CAVERN OF PROPHET ELIJAH ON MOUNT CARMEL

4 / THE MAD MAID IN THE CAVE OF ELIJAH

In the middle of the nineteenth century, the Hebrew Jerusalemite newspaper *Columns of Awe* printed the following story:

"Last year, a young orphan maid, well-learned and of good breeding, thirteen years of age, was suddenly possessed by an evil spirit. She uttered the most terrible imprecations and blasphemous words against all that is holy to God and men, may the Almighty the Merciful save her soul!

"In her lucid moments, the poor girl complained that two stray spirits had taken hold of her. Sometimes she would faint, and sometimes her whole body would be convulsed by great spasms, while her voice came out in a coarse and vulgar tone.

"Once she was heard to say in her anguish that only Elijah could relieve her of her suffering. Her relatives bound her up and conveyed her to that grotto called after the great prophet, where it is customary to house the insane for three consecutive nights in the hope of achieving a cure.

"In the darkness preceding dawn, an old man followed by a young attendant appeared to her in her sleep. (Dream-diviners declared these undoubtedly to be the hallowed Elijah and his disciple Elisha.) The two holy men told her to dip herself into the sweet waters of the Sea of Galilee.

"This was speedily done, and the young maid recovered her health and returned home in the full bloom of her fair adolescence."[9]

5 / THE CAVE OF ELIJAH AND JESUS OF NAZARETH

Legend tells that Jesus of Nazareth learned the "Ineffable Name of the Lord," which was carved on the Holy Rock in the Great Temple of Jerusalem.

Jesus then went to the cave of Elijah on Mount Carmel to hide himself.

When he entered the cave, he uttered the "Name," and the entrance of the cave shut behind him.

Rabbi Judah Gannana (the Gardener) came to the cave and said, "Cave, Cave, open thyself, because I am the messenger of the Living God!"

When the cave heard these words, it opened, and Jesus escaped and abided on Mount Carmel.*[10]

6 / THE ALTAR OF ELIJAH ON MOUNT CARMEL

"The One who answered the prayer of Elijah the prophet on Mount Carmel . . . shall hearken to your prayer today."

On a high summit of the Carmel range, which commands a large view over the Valley of Jezreel, Samaria, and Galilee, there stands a Carmelite chapel. The monks believe that it is built on the site where Elijah put up his altar when he met the prophets of idolatry in the time of Ahab, King of Israel.

"The prophet said to the king: '. . . gather to me all Israel unto mount Carmel, and the prophets of Baal four hundred and fifty . . .' And Ahab . . . gathered the prophets together unto Mount Carmel. And Elijah came near unto all the people, and said: 'How long halt ye between two opinions? If the Lord be God, follow Him; but if Baal, follow him!' . . . . 'And he repaired the altar of the Lord that was thrown down. And Elijah took twelve stones, according to the number of the tribes of the sons of Jacob . . . and with the stones he built an altar in the name of the Lord . . . and he put the wood in order and cut the bullock in pieces, and laid it on the wood. . . . Then the fire of the Lord fell, and consumed the burnt-offering, and the wood, and the stones, and the dust, and licked up the water that was in the trench. And when all the people saw it, they fell on their faces; and they said, 'The Lord, He is God; the Lord, He is God.'

"And Elijah said unto them: 'Take the prophets of Baal; let not one of them escape.' And they took them . . . and Elijah

* See *Legends of Jerusalem*, p. 8: "The 'Name' on the Stone."

went up to the top of Carmel; and he bowed himself down upon the earth, and put his face between his knees."

The revelation of God to Elijah has been sanctified by Jewish tradition and also by Christians and Moslems. Mount Carmel is named by the Arabs, for the prophet, *Jabal Mar Elias*—the Mount of Saint Elijah. The above-mentioned chapel they call *"Mukhraka,"* i.e., "The Place of Burning." The brook Kishon, which flows at the foot of the Monastery, is known in Arabic as *Al-Mukatta;* some say from the Arabic *katta,* which means "to cut down," referring to the priests of Baal who were put to death on this spot.[11]

7 / HIEL HID IN THE ALTAR OF BAAL

Hiel the Bethelite built Jericho during the reign of Ahab, king of Israel, despite the malediction of Joshua son of Nun.

FIG. 3. ELIJAH'S OFFERING
On the altar, on Mount Carmel, is the accepted sacrifice in the midst of flames. At the left are probably the false prophets of Baal. On the right is probably Elijah, with four attendants.

Of Hiel it is written: "He was both great and rich and his father was of the tribe of Ephraim, and when he saw that which Ahab had done, incited to it by his wife Jezabel, daughter of Etbaal, he denied the Holy One, blessed be He, and the Law of Moses, and built [Jericho]. He gave himself over to the worship of idols which Jezabel had set up atop Mount Carmel to anger Elijah, who prayed to God on the mountaintop.

"What did Hiel do? He confronted the prophets of Baal and said to them: 'Be strong and stand up against Elijah, and I will make it seem that Baal is sending you fire.'

FIG. 4. OFFERING OF FALSE PROPHETS
On the altar, without flames, is the rejected sacrifice. Within the altar are Hiel and the snake, as told in the legend. On either side are the disappointed false prophets of Baal. These two illustrations are wall-paintings in the third-century synagogue of Dura-Europos (now Syria).

"He took two stones and a tow of flax and, entering the hollow of [the altar of] Baal, he rubbed the stones one against the other to light the tow. But Elijah, with the aid of the Holy Spirit, immediately divined his presence, and prayed: 'Master of the Universe . . . I pray You to destroy the villain in the hollow of [the altar of] Baal.'

"Whereupon the Holy One, blessed be He, commanded a snake to bite [Hiel's] heel, and he died. And so it is written, in the words of the prophet Amos: 'And though they hide themselves in the top of Carmel,/I will search and take them out thence.' "[12]

8 / THE MELONS THAT TURNED TO STONE

When Elijah the Prophet dwelt on Mount Carmel, he often forsook the lonely cave in which he lived and wandered amid the hills to seek his God and pray to Him. Sunk in thought, he would stray for days and nights along the paths and by-ways, his hair shaggy and his appearance wild. For he was very wroth with the prophets of Baal, and in his heart burned the zeal of the God of Hosts. He never took food with him, for he trusted in the Almighty, and he always chanced upon plants of the field or fruit of the trees, which were his food and which restored his spirit.

One evening, Elijah came to a field of ripe sweet melons. He was weary after a full day's journey, and his spirit was weak from hunger and thirst, so he approached the owner of the field and asked for a melon. But the man laughed at the queer shaggy wayfarer and said, "Those are not melons but stones, scattered in the field." Elijah became enraged and said, "God grant that your words become true!"

As soon as the prophet had spoken, the melons turned into round stones strewn over the ground. So if you find smooth round stones upon one of the spurs of Mount Carmel, you will know that they are the melons which the prophet cursed in his wrath and which have remained stones unto this day.

F. Goujon, a French pilgrim in the year 1671, told the story, in French, of the Garden of Melons—*Le Jardin des Melons.* He added that he had brought back with him a specimen that proved beyond doubt "the authenticity of the miracle."[13]

FIG. 5. "MELONS OF ELIJAH" (1681)

9 / THE MAGIC STONE OF MOUNT CARMEL

The Italian pilgrim Antoninus Martyr, who came to the
Holy Land in 570 C.E. when it was under Byzantine rule, told
of his visit to Mount Carmel and to the monastery atop its
headland. This site is dedicated to Saint Elijah, who on this
spot met the woman whose son he brought back to life.

The pilgrim added: On Mount Carmel is found a round
stone of small size, which, when struck, resounds, because it

is solid. This is the virtue of the stone: If it be hung on a woman, or on any female animal, she will never miscarry.

This story brings to mind the "preserving stone"—in Hebrew, *even tekumah*—about which the rabbis of the third century ruled: "One may go out with a preserving stone on the Sabbath, and not only when one has miscarried, but even [for fear] that she miscarry."[14]

10 / THE GOD OF CARMEL

Mount Carmel was renowned for its fertility. In ancient times, it was covered with vineyards; hence its name, which is a contraction of the Hebrew *kerem-El*—vineyard of God.

The beautiful green head of Carmel was sacred to many ancient cults. In an Egyptian hieroglyphic record of the fifteenth century B.C.E., it was called *"Rosh Kodesh"*—"Holy Headland."

In later times, there stood there an altar to the God of Carmel, and when Vespasian, then commander-in-chief of the Roman legions, came to subdue the Jewish revolt of 66 C.E., he went up the steep slopes to offer his prayers.

Tacitus, the Roman historian of the time, records this incident: "Carmel," he wrote, "this is the name given both to the mountain and to the divinity. The god has no image or temple—such is the rule handed down from father to son. There is only an altar and the worship of the god. When Vespasian was sacrificing there and thinking over the secret hopes in his heart, the priest Basilides, after repeated inspection of the sacrificial victim's vitals, said to him, 'Whatever you are planning, Vespasian—whether to build a house, or to enlarge your holdings, or to increase the number of your slaves—the god grants you a mighty home, limitless bounds, and a multitude of men.' "

A large marble foot was found on the top of the promontory of Carmel, on the site today forming the courtyard of the

Carmelite monastery. It carries the following Greek inscription, probably of the second or third century: "[Dedicated] to Heliopolitan Zeus [god of] Carmel [by] Gaius Julius Eustychas colonist [of] Caesarea."

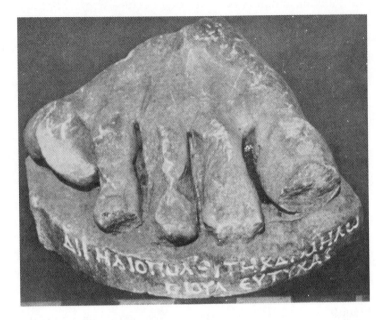

FIG. 6. FOOT OF "GOD OF CARMEL"

The sages of Israel too mention the pagan rites practiced on the top of Carmel by tree-worshiping cults. They record "three Asherot in the Land of Israel," and continue: "What is an Asherah? A holy tree which is venerated and preserved by the Gentiles, but its fruit is forbidden to the worshipers." And one of them was "the sycamore on the headland of Carmel."

Sycamore trees were very common in this area; indeed, for

many centuries, the town situated at the foot of the Carmel was called "Shikmona," from the Hebrew *shikma*—sycamore tree.[15]

11 / TABOR AND CARMEL ENVY SINAI

When the Lord was about to give the Torah to Israel on Mount Sinai, all the mountains, including Tabor and Carmel, rushed to Him in anger, exclaiming, "From my slopes alone should the Law be given unto Israel!"

And the Lord, blessed be He, answered them and said, "On your slopes idolaters have worshiped, but never on Mount Sinai; therefore have I chosen it."

Whoever rambles over the heights of northern Galilee and over the mountains of Gilead in the east can distinguish from the distance the rounded top of Mount Tabor, and whoever roams over Upper Galilee in the vicinity of Zefat (Safed) can discern from afar the dome of Tabor among the mountains, and the cape of Mount Carmel, which penetrates into the sea. Both are outstanding features of the landscape.

The prophet Jeremiah knew these two mountains well and he exclaimed: "Surely like Tabor among the mountains, / And like Carmel by the sea."

In the same vein, the medieval Hebrew poet Itshak Hakatan compared the justice of the Almighty, blessed be He, to Mount Tabor, which stands clearly revealed among the mountains, against wide horizons; in his hymn dedicated to the close of the holy Sabbath day, he says: "May He who maketh a distinction between holy and profane / Pardon our sins. / Thy righteousness is like Mount Tabor, / Let them be as yesterday which is past."[16]

12 / THE ARROGANCE OF TABOR AND CARMEL

When the Lord Almighty wished to give the Torah to the children of Israel, both Mount Tabor and Mount Carmel came to Him.

First Tabor spoke, saying proudly, "I am Tabor, and on me should rest the Divine Presence, for I am the loftiest mountain, and the waters of the deluge did not cover me."

Then Carmel said arrogantly, "I am Carmel, and on me should rest the Divine Presence, for when You divided the waters of the Red Sea, it was I who placed myself there so that the children of Israel could pass over me."

The Lord, blessed be He, replied, "Just because of your pride and your arrogance, I cannot countenance your claims. My wish is for Sinai, because it is humbler than all you mountains"; and He added, "Because you put yourselves to trouble for My honor, I shall give you a reward. Behold, in the time of Deborah I shall give deliverance to the children of Israel upon Mount Tabor . . . and also I shall give deliverance to Elijah upon Mount Carmel."

When did Tabor and Carmel come to the Lord? When they heard the sublime voice of the Lord from the heights of Mount Sinai saying, "I am the Lord, thy God!"

And the mountains shook and the hills quaked![17]

13 / THE TEMPLE WILL BE BUILT ON CARMEL AND TABOR

In the days to come, the Lord will bring the mountains Sinai, Carmel, Tabor (and Hermon) together, and Jerusalem shall be placed on their slopes and the Temple on their summits.

How do we know this? Because the prophet Isaiah said: "And it shall come to pass in the end of days,/That the mountain of the Lord's house shall be established as the top of the mountains,/And shall be exalted above the hills;/And all nations shall flow unto it."

Rabbi Hanina said: "Moreover, God will sing and all the mountains will respond with singing and chanting."[18]

14 / THE WISE MEN OF MOUNT CARMEL

Two men of Mount Carmel were taken captive and driven into exile. Their captor walked behind them. In front of the two men, a camel was carrying two full goatskins, one on each side.

Said one man to the other, "This camel which goes before us is a female and is blind in one eye; also, in one goatskin there is wine and in the other oil."

Their captor, greatly astonished, said to them, "Ye children of a stiff-necked people, how do ye know all this?" And the two men answered, "That the camel is a female we can tell by her legs. That she is blind in one eye is clear from the way she eats grass. She eats only on one side of the road—the side on which she can see the grass—and on the other side where she cannot see, the grass remains untouched."

"And how do you know that one goatskin contains wine and the other oil?" asked the captor.

"Because," answered the men, "we watch the drops as they fall from the goatsksins. The drops of wine sink into the ground, while the drops of oil remain on the surface."

Thereupon the captor kissed the two men, brought them to his house, and made a great feast for them. Raising his hands in prayer to God, he said, "Blessed be He who chose the children of Abraham and imparted to them some of His wisdom."[19]

15 / THE GORGE OF THE CYCLAMEN

The numerous gorges running through the Carmel are ablaze in spring with the blossoms of a great variety of plants. One of the most picturesque falls southward from the heights where the altar of Elijah was erected; it is known as *Nahal Rakefet*—the Gorge of the Cyclamen—for the many clumps of this lovely flower that cling to its rocky sides and peep out of the crevices.

The flower of the cyclamen is shaped like a crown but, unlike most blooms, it does not stand upright on its stem but seems to bend its lovely head. Thereby lies the following story:

When King Solomon was about to be crowned, an angel of God appeared in front of him and said: "Noble Prince, thou art soon to be anointed as the undisputed suzerain of the Land of Israel. Like all kings, thou must wear a crown. Go out, and from among all the beautiful flowers that adorn thy gardens chose the one in whose shape thy crown will be wrought."

The king went out into his gardens, and walked through all their lanes and paths, peering intently at the luxuriant exotic blooms around him. All were beautiful, but none seemed to retain his attention until he noticed, in a corner, between two rocks, a delicate and small flower, exquisite in shape and fashioned like a light, graceful crown. The king's choice was made on the spot.

At that time, the cyclamen blooms grew straight on their long stems, and, proud of the king's preference, they stood more upright and erect than ever.

But after many long years, when the enemy destroyed Jerusalem and its Temple and pillaged its treasures, at the precise moment when the crown of the kings was carried over the border all the cyclamen drooped their blooms in shame and sorrow and they vowed: "Never again shall we lift our heads until the crown is returned and shines again on the brow of the Chosen One of Israel."[20]

FIG. 7. CYCLAMEN
The Hebrew name is *rakefet*.

16 / REINCARNATION

The villages of the Druze are set among the hills, but their small farmsteads are in the valley, among the fields. In these farms the villagers live during harvest, afterward returning to their homes in the mountains. But it is very hard to take their working implements back and forth with them up and down the hills, so they hide them amid the rocks and ruins in the valley.

It is told of the Druze that they believe in the transmigration of souls. Benjamin of Tudela, a pilgrim of about the year

1175 (the first to mention the Druze), said of them: "They say that the soul of a virtuous man is transferred to the body of a newborn child, whereas that of the vicious passes into a dog or some other animal." And as conclusive proof of this assumption the following tale is told:

Near Hermon, there lived a very wicked Druze; he told no one where he hid his tools. And this Druze died without telling even his son where his sickles and other implements were concealed. The son was very upset, for he had no money to buy new tools. He himself was a very bad fellow, as his father had been and, still worse, he did not believe in the transmigration of souls.

Once, when he went hunting, he met a wolf and raised his rifle to shoot the animal. But the wolf opened its mouth and cried out, "Stop! Do not shoot, for if you kill me you kill your own father, whose spirit has passed into me!" The huntsman trembled with fear, then, recovering his courage, said, "If you speak the truth, tell me where you hid the sickles and the other tools!" And the wolf answered, "Amid the rocks, near such and such a brook, and in such and such a ruin."

The Druze went there and found the sickles, and ever after was a fervent believer in the transmigration of souls.[21]

III
THE SEA OF HAIFA

1 / ZEBULUN INHERITED THE SEA OF HAIFA

"Zebulun shall dwell at the shore of the sea,
And he shall be a shore for ships."

Along the shore of the Mediterranean Sea, between Haifa
in the south and Acco (Acre) in the north, stretches the Valley
of Zebulun, named after the tribe that inherited these parts.
In the olden days, it was known as the territory of Acco.

And how was the Land divided among the tribes? Through
the oracular power possessed by the High Priest when wearing the Urim and Tumim—the ceremonial breastplate.

And how was this power manifested? "Eleazar was wearing the Urim and Tumim, while Joshua and all Israel stood
before him. An urn [containing the names] of the tribes and
an urn [containing] descriptions of the boundaries were
placed before him. Animated by the Holy Spirit, he gave
directions, exclaiming, 'Zebulun is coming up and the boundary of Acco is coming up with it!' [Thereupon] he shook well
the urn of the tribes and Zebulun came up in his hand.
[Likewise] he shook the urn of the boundaries and the
boundary lines of Acco came up in his hand."

FIG. 8. SAILBOAT IN BAY OF HAIFA
The sailboat was the emblem of Zebulun.

The sages of Israel tell that the High Priest of Israel wore a breastplate inlaid with twelve different precious stones; each one symbolizing a tribe of Israel. The stone of Zebulun was the diamond; its flag was white, picturing a ship in its middle. Therefore Jacob the Patriarch blessed Zebulun, saying, "And he [Zebulun] shall be a shore for ships."[22]

2 / THE SEA OF HAIFA—A SILVER BOWL

"Haifa rests in the bosom of the Sea."

The beautifully rounded Bay of Haifa was within the territory of Zebulun.

When the Tabernacle was completed by the tribes of Israel wandering in the desert on their way to Canaan, the chieftains brought their offerings to it. "On the third day [came] Eliab the son of Helon, prince of the children of Zebulun; his offering was one silver dish."

The sages of Israel say, "Zebulun engaged in commerce, therefore his gift was a silver bowl, which is like the sea [the Bay of Haifa] in the portion of Zebulun."[23]

FIG. 9. BAY OF HAIFA

3 / THE SEA OF HAIFA IN THE DAYS TO COME

Moses, the Law-Giver, blessed Zebublun and his descendants in these words, "For they shall suck the abundance of the seas."

This, says legend, refers to the sea of Haifa, which was part of Zebublun's inheritance. "For there is no ingot of silver and gold and no vessel shipwrecked in the deep that shall not be shifted and thrown into the Sea of Haifa, which is the depository of the Great Sea, and whose treasures are preserved for the Righteous at the end of Time."*[24]

4 / THE DISCOVERY OF GLASS

On the banks of the river Naaman, which flows near Acco and was known to the Greeks as Belus, glass was first discovered.

Some Phoenicians were sailing from Egypt along the sea-coast of Palestine. In their ships they carried a cargo of large lumps of natron. As they approached Phoenicia, a great storm arose. Fearful, the sailors headed for the sandy shore close to the river Belus, and landed there.

The sailors wanted to prepare some food but along this vast stretch of sand they could find no stones on which to place their cooking pots in their campfire. So they brought from their boat some lumps of natron, and placed their pots on these, lighting the fire around them. When they had finished cooking, they saw, to their astonishment, that the natron had melted in the heat of the fire and had combined with the sand, creating a new material which was clear and transparent. It was glass.[25]

*See legend III:2.

5 / THE SONS OF ZEBULUN WERE GLASSMAKERS

Along the coast of Zebulun lies a strip of clean, white sand from which the sons of Zebulun soon learned to prepare glass; they became skilled artisans in that medium. Even today, on the border of the same sand strip stands the largest glass factory in Israel.

Moses, blessing Zebulun on his deathbed, mentions "the hidden treasures of the sand." "The sand—that means the white glass," explain the sages.

Legend relates that when the land was divided between the tribes of Israel, and the barren sands fell in Zebulun's share, he was angry, and complained bitterly before the Almighty: "Lord of the Universe! Upon my brethren Thou hast bestowed beautiful land, and to me Thou hast given this sea! Upon my brethren Thou hast bestowed fields and vineyards, and to me hast Thou given this barren sand!" The Lord replied to him: "As I live forever! Verily, Israel shall be in need of thee because of the glass that thou shalt make out of thy sand!"[26]

6 / THE SAND THAT TURNS INTO GLASS

In the first century, Josephus Flavius mentioned the river Belus (Naaman of today), which flows near Acco. Belus is a Greek corruption of "Baal," the chief god of the Phoenicians who dwelled along this coast. According to the Roman historian, there stood on the bank of the river the statue of Memnon—in Greek mythology, he was the son of Eos (the Roman Aurora), the goddess of the dawn. The Greeks in Egypt attributed to Memnon the two monumental statues of the Pharaohs erected beside the Nile in Upper Egypt. The soft wind blowing at the dawn of day into the crevices of the statues produced the "voices of Memnon," which the people believed to be oracles.

Josephus wrote: "The very small river Belus runs by it [the city of Acco] at the distance of two furlongs, near which there is Memnon's monument. Near it, there is a place no larger than a hundred cubits which deserves admiration, for the place is round and hollow, and affords such sand as glass is made of; which place, when it hath been emptied by the many ships there loaded, is filled again by the winds, which bring into it, as it were on purpose, that sand which lay remote, and was no more than bare common sand, while this mine presently turns it into glassy sand; and, what is to me still more wonderful, that glassy sand which is superfluous, and is once removed of the place, becomes bare common sand again. This is the nature of the place we are speaking of."[27]

7 / HOW PURPLE WAS DISCOVERED

How did man discover that the mollusk yields a beautiful purple dye? Once upon a time, a hunter went forth with his dog to shoot seafowl. As the bird fell, the dog brought it to his master. On one occasion, the dog came back with a peculiar kind of liquid dripping from his mouth. His master wiped it off with a handkerchief. After some time, when he took his handkerchief out of his pocket, the hunter noticed that it was stained a bright color. For a moment he thought that blood had been running from the dog's mouth, but on further examination, he found that the stain was not the color of blood.

The next day, on returning to the shore with the dog, he watched him and noticed that the dog was eating a certain kind of mollusk. His jaws dripped with a juice that looked exactly like that which the hunter had wiped off with his handkerchief the day before. Then he understood that it was the juice of the mollusk that had stained his handkerchief that brilliant shade we know as purple.

A variation of this tale is repeated by G.W. Tyron: "It is

clept Scalle of Thires, is 100 Furlonges. And beᷠ
syde the Cytee of Akoun renneth a lytille Ryvere,
that is clept Belon. And there nyghe is the Fosse
of Mennon, that is alle round ; and it is 100 Cu-
bytes of largenesse, and it is alle fulle of Gravelle,
schynynge brighte, of the whiche Men maken fair
Verres and clere. And Men comen fro fer, by
Watre in Schippes, and be Londe with Cartes, for
to fetten of that Gravelle. And thoughe there
be nevere so moche taken awey there of, on
the Day, at Morwe it is as fulle azen as evere
it was. And that is a gret Mervaille. And there
is everemore gret Wynd in that Fosse, that sterethe
everemore the Gravelle, and makethe it trouble. And zif ony Man do thereinne ony maner
Metalle, it turnethe anon to Glasse. And the

Glasse, that is made of that Gravelle, zif it be don
azen in to the Gravelle, it turnethe anon in to Gra-

FIG. 10. MAKING OF GLASS (1336)
In this description by Sir John Mandeville, the illustration shows the
river Naaman, formerly Belus (Belon), near the city of Acco
(Akoun).

related that the discovery of the dye is due to the dog of a Tyrian nymph which, crushing some of these shells [Murex trunculus] in its teeth, its mouth became stained with purple. To be exact, this event occurred in 1500 B.C.E. The color was so beautiful that the fair nymph expressed to her lover Hercules her desire to have a robe of similar hue. Hercules, of course, gratified her."

In all such stories, the discovery of purple is associated with the dog. The reason is perhaps the similarity between the Hebrew word *keleb*—dog—and the Syriac *kilab*—dyer.

An ancient Phoenician coin, preserved in the British Museum, pictures a dog and a purple mollusk much enlarged.[28] (See fig. 11)

FIG. 11. ANCIENT SYRIAN COIN
At the bottom, a dog and a purple mollusk.
A similar coin is preserved in the British Museum, London.

8 / ZEBULUN WERE PURPLEMAKERS

On the shores of the Mediterranean Sea, there are various kinds of mollusks from whose bodies the richest of purple and blue dyes can be produced.

Since ancient times, fishermen along the coastline of Haifa caught the mollusks from which purple was prepared. In medieval times, Haifa or one of its suburbs was known by the name Porphyreon, from the Greek *porphyra,* meaning "purple." The Phoenicians who lived along this coast in the olden days acquired their name from the Greek *phoinos,* meaning "scarlet."

Purple played an important role in the ritual of the Israelites. They dyed their prayer shawls with it. Complying with God's wish, they also adorned with this brilliant hue the tabernacle, when it was put up in the desert of the wanderings.

For God said to Moses, "Thou shalt make the tabernacle with ten curtains: of fine twined linen, and blue, and purple, and scarlet. . . . And thou shalt make a veil of blue and purple and scarlet. . . . And thou shalt make a screen for the door of the Tent, of blue, and purple, and scarlet. . . . And they shall make holy garments for Aaron thy brother, and his sons. . . . And they shall take the gold and the blue and the purple. . . ."

As for the blessing of Moses to Zebulun, "For they shall suck the abundance of the seas, and the hidden treasures," the sages interpreted "the hidden treasures" as referring to the mollusks that are concealed in the depths of the sea.

After the division of the Land of Canaan among the tribes of Israel, Zebulun inherited the territory around Haifa, and he came before the throne of the Almighty and said, "Lord of the Universe, upon my brethren You have bestowed fertile land, while I have inherited only seas and rivers." And the Lord answered Zebulun, saying, "As I live forever, all the tribes of Israel shall look to thee for the mollusk to give them the sacred purple."

The sons of Zebulun occupied themselves with the work of collecting the mollusks and preparing purple from them.

In Jeremiah's description of the destruction of the land at the hands of the Babylonians, one reads, "But Nebuzaradan the captain of the guard left of the poorest of the land to be vinedressers and husbandmen [Hebrew, *hayogvim*]."

"Hayogvim," says legend, "were the hunters of the purple mollusk."[29]

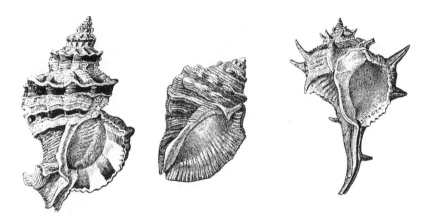

FIG. 12. PURPLE MOLLUSKS FROM MEDITERRANEAN SEA
At the left, *Mures trunculus.* In the middle, *Purpurea hameastostoma.* At the right, *Murex brandaris.*

9 / THE CHILDREN OF ZEBULUN WERE TRADESMEN

Since they dwelled on the shore of the Great Sea, the sons of Zebulun were navigators and tradesmen. According to the testimony of the ancients, Zebulun imported wares from beyond the seas and distributed them among his brother-tribes.

The blessing that Moses, the man of God, bestowed upon Zebulun: "Rejoice, Zebulun, in thy going out," was interpreted thus: Zebulun was a middleman between his brothers and the outside world, buying from his brothers and selling abroad, buying from abroad and selling to his brothers.

Another interpretation is: When Zebulun goes out to war, he is ever victorious and returns amid rejoicings.[30]

10 / THE BOND BETWEEN ZEBULUN AND ISSACHAR

On the border of the inheritance of Zebulun, which spreads through Lower Galilee and along the seashore, stretched the territory of Issachar, mostly in the Valley of Jezreel.

The sons of Zebulun were mainly tradesmen, rich in wordly goods. The sons of Issachar were mostly farmers and shepherds, and remained poor. But, tradition says, they devoted themselves to the learning of the Torah and acquired spiritual riches.

Legend tells of Zebulun that he was strongly attached to the Torah and that he donated freely to Issachar's maintenance. Thus Issachar was freed from material worries and could devote himself to the study of the Torah.

Wherefore Moses blessed them both together in these words: "Rejoice, Zebulun, in thy going out,/And, Issachar, in thy tents."

Why did Moses, the Law-Giver, see fit to honor Zebulun first, although he was the younger of the two? The sages explain: "Zebulun and Issachar made a covenant; Zebulun went out to sea and provided Issachar with sustenance. And Issachar studied the Torah. And whence did all this greatness come to Issachar? From Zebulun, who engaged in trade and supported Issachar, who was devoted to the Torah. Wherefore Zebulun deserved to be mentioned first."

The Book of Proverbs praises the Holy Torah in these words: "She is a tree of life to them that lay hold upon her,/And happy is everyone that holdeth her fast." The sages explain: "Them that lay hold upon her"—that is the tribe of Issachar. "Everyone that holdeth her fast"—that is the tribe of Zebulun.[31]

11 / THE RIVER KISHON—THE ANCIENT RIVER

The Children of Israel who lived at the time of the Exodus were men of little faith. When they saw the six hundred chariots of the Egyptians drawn into the sea, they did not believe that they had been destroyed. They still feared them and said to God, "Just as we came out on the other side, so will they come out."

Then God said to the Ruler of the Sea, "Let the sea cast forth the six hundred dead Egyptians onto the dry land, so that all Israel may see them." And the Ruler of the Sea answered, "Lord of the Universe! Is it right for the master to demand the return of the gift He has bestowed upon His slave? Why then should I return the dead Egyptians?" And the Lord replied, "The day will come when I shall give you half as much again. In place of the six hundred, you shall receive nine hundred." And the Ruler of the Sea answered, "Can the servant make demands upon his master? How then shall I be able to claim it from you?" And the Lord replied, "The river of Kishon shall be My pledge." The Ruler of the Sea agreed, and immediately he cast forth onto the land the bodies of the Egyptians. "Thus the Lord saved Israel that day out of the hand of the Egyptians, and Israel saw the Egyptians dead upon the seashore."

After several generations, when Israel dwelt securely in his land, the Canaanites led by Sisera, came upon it. Sisera was wont to pay his soldiers regularly, but now they went to him and said, "We will serve you without pay, for we long to fill our bellies with the waters of Israel." For this reason the prophetess Deborah sang: "The kings came, they fought;/- Then fought the kings of Canaan,/In Taanach by the waters of Megiddo;/They took no gain of money."

And thus it was that Sisera came with nine hundred chariots to overrun the Valley of Jezreel. The Canaanites were armed each with a long iron spear, and when the Lord saw them, he diverted the stars from their courses in order to draw them closer to the Canaanites. The heat of the stars warmed the spears till they glowed, and the Canaanites could not seize hold of them. Therefore they went to the waters of the Kishon to cool both themselves and their spears.

At that moment, the Lord said to the ancient river of Kishon, "Do you remember the pledge that I gave for you, when the children of Israel crossed the Red Sea? Go and fulfill that pledge to the Ruler of the Sea."

Immediately, the waters of the Kishon rose, swallowed up the Canaanites, and delivered them into the great sea.

When the Ruler of the Sea beheld this great sight, the fish opened their mouths and said, "Righteous is the Lord forever. Praise be unto Him." And the prophetess Deborah in her song of triumph said: "Hear, O ye kings; Give ear, O ye princes. . . ./They fought from heaven,/The stars in their courses fought against Sisera./The brook Kishon swept them away,/That ancient brook, the brook Kishon."[32]

IV
ACCO AND ITS SURROUNDINGS

1 / WHY WAS IT CALLED ACCO?

The city of Acco, one of the oldest towns of the Land of Israel, lies on the shore of the Mediterranean Sea. When the tribes of Israel conquered the land, Acco was already a fortified city.

The origin and the meaning of the name Acco are unknown, but explanations are numerous and varied.

According to the Greeks, the name is derived from *ake,* which signifies "healing" in their language. They related that the great Hercules, seeking a cure for his wounds, collected on the banks of a river in that vicinity an herb that restored his health. In memory of this incident, the city erected on the site was called Acco—the Cure.

In the gardens of Acco, there grew a plant whose botanical name was *Colocasia,* and whose edible roots were a favorite food of the inhabitants.

In the third century B.C.E., Acco was an important city ruled by Egyptian kings who named it Ptolemais, after their own dynasty.

The Crusaders restored the ancient name, amending it to

"Acre," and since the city was in the charge of the Knights of St. John, it became known as St. John of Acre. It was the main port of the Kingdom of Jerusalem throughout its existence.

In the beginning of the eleventh century, the Crusader historian William of Tyre mentioned the two names Acco and Ptolemais, attributing them to two brothers who allegedly fortified the city.

FIG. 13. ACCO (1830)
An engraving showing Acco's fortified wall along the seashore.

Moslem pilgrims, who knew the town by its Arabic name *Akka,* credited the founding of the city to a mythical santon, and even displayed what they said was his tomb. A Persian traveler in the year 1047 wrote, "I went and visited the tomb of Akka, who is the founder of the city of Akka. [He was] a very pious and great personage." A century later, another wayfarer refers again to "the tomb of Akk or Akka, for whom the neighboring city is named."

A final explanation can be found in the Hebrew legend that relates how the Great Sea flooded the earth twice in the history of mankind.

The second time, the waters reached the shore of Acco and stopped there. This is hinted in the words of Job: "Thus far [Hebrew, *ad po*] shalt thou come, but no further;/And here shall thy proud waves be stayed." *Ad po* can be also read *Ad co*—"till here." The name Acco would originate from the contraction of these two words.[33]

2 / FAMOUS SAGES OF ACCO

Acco had a large Jewish community in the second and third centuries. Some of its learned men are mentioned in the talmudic literature.

It is told of Rabbi Abba that he used to kiss the very rocks of Acco because of his great love for the land of his forefathers.

The Greek immigrants who settled in Acco built a bath adorned with statues of Aphrodite, the goddess of beauty and love. The Jews looked with disfavor on this worship of idols which the foreigners had introduced to Eretz-Israel—the holy abode of the One and Only God.

There is a tale that Proklos, the son of Philosophos, asked Rabban Gamliel, while he was bathing in the Bath of Aphrodite in Acco, "Why dost thou bathe in the Bath of Aphrodite?"

He replied, "One may not make answer in the bath!" (He meant that it is forbidden to speak words of the Law while naked.)

But when he came out, he said, "I came not within her limits; she came within mine!"[34]

3 / THE FATE OF NAKDIMON'S DAUGHTER IN ACCO

Nakdimon was one of the most wealthy men in Jerusalem. It is related of Miriam, the daughter of Nakdimon, that the rabbis allowed her five hundred gold dinars daily to be spent on her store of perfumes.

At the destruction of the Holy City, the family of Nakdimon lost all its riches and was dispersed throughout the country.

Rabbi Eliezer said, "I did see her gathering barley from beneath horses' hoofs in Acco, and I quoted this verse from the Song of Songs: 'O thou fairest among women,-/Go thy way forth by the footsteps of the flock/And feed thy kids.' "

Said Rabbi Eliezer, "Do not read 'thy kids' [Hebrew, *gediyotayich*] but read *naveyotayich*—'thy fair ones.' "[35]

4 / MIRIAM THE DAUGHTER OF TANHUM IN ACCO

It is related of Miriam that she was taken captive and was ransomed at Acco.

The people bought her a shift, and when she went to wash it in the sea, a wave came and carried it away. They bought her another, and when she went to wash it in the sea, a wave came and carried it away. They wished to buy her still another, but she said to them, "Leave the Collector to collect His debt."

When she sought a remission of the heavenly decree against herself, the Holy One, blessed be He, gave word to the sea, which then restored her garments to her!

She was forgiven because she admitted she must have done something wrong to be punished in such a way.[36]

5 / THE SYNAGOGUE OF KING AHAB IN ACCO

When the famous Rabbi Haim Ben Attar visited Acco in the year 1742, he was accompanied by a pupil of his who wrote of the occasion: "And outside the wall of Acco there is a large and tall synagogue. In the past, when the town was young, this building stood within its precincts. Now that the city is destroyed it [the synagogue] is outside the wall. And it has twelve windows [the number of the tribes]. And it was called the synagogue of Ahab and is still named thus, for here the king was wont to pray."

The ancients mention "the well of Ahab [which is] ritually pure." Apparently it was situated in the northern section of Eretz-Israel.[37]

6 / TO BRING FISH TO ACCO

Acco was so famous for its abundance of fish that it became proverbial; if wares were brought to a place which was already plentifully supplied, people of Israel used to say, "You are bringing fish to Acco."

The ancients declared that the fish of Acco tasted different from the fish of Sidon, although these two towns are situated on the same coastline. "Everything," they said, "is blessed [by rain]."

It once happened at Acco that a fish was caught and judged to weigh three hundred pounds, yet when they weighed it, it was only two hundred. An old fisherman who was present said to them, "That is because rain has not fallen." After rain fell they caught a fish and estimated it at two hundred pounds, yet on weighing it they found it to be three hundred![38]

7 / THE PRECIOUS TREASURE IN THE MOSQUE OF ACCO

The old city of Acco prides itself on a large and beautiful mosque whose green dome and slender minaret stand out conspicuously above the houses. It was built in 1871 by the famous ruler of Acco, Ahmed Jazzar Pasha, and still bears his name.

The floor of the spacious prayer hall is covered with Oriental carpets. In one corner of the balcony built all around the hall, at some height from the ground, a small box wrapped in green cloth is preserved. It contains a few hairs. According to Arab tradition, they are hairs from the beard of Mohammed, the Prophet of Islam. Once a year, during the fast held in the month of Ramadan, the hairs are displayed with great pomp to the Moslem worshipers, who prostrate themselves with great reverence and awe in front of the precious relic.*[39]

8 / THE SPRING OF THE OX

To the east of Acco, there is a little spring that the Arabs call *Ain el-Sitt*—the Spring of the Lady. It is related that at this spring Adam found the ox with which he first ploughed his fields. It was therefore formerly named *Ain el-Bakr*—the Spring of the Ox.

It is also said that its waters flow from one of the four fountains of the Garden of Eden, and whoever drinks thereof is relieved of all pain.

In medieval times, this spring was sacred to Jews, Moslems, and Christians alike, who came to it in pilgrimage and eagerly drank its waters.

A Persian traveler, Nasir Khosrau, who passed through Acco in the year 1047, wrote, "Outside the eastern gate, and on the left hand, there is a spring to which you descend by

* See *Legends of Jerusalem*, p. 21.

twenty-six steps before reaching the water. This they call *Ain el-Bakr*—the Spring of the Ox—recalling that Adam, peace be upon him, discovered this spring and gave his oxen water therefrom; whence its name.

"The Court of the Mosque [of Acco] is partly paved with stone and partly sown with herbs, for, they say, it was here that Adam first practiced husbandry."

A Turkish voyager of the seventeenth century praised highly the Spring of the Ox. "Adam," he wrote, "used to pray here in a cell cut out of a stone standing amidst green fields. In this spring several prophets bathed; thus its waters acquired special virtues, and whoever bathes in it finds a speedy cure for his ailments. It is customary to bring to this fountain lean and sickly cattle. After drinking from its waters on seven consecutive days, they recover their health and quickly grow fat. Therefore, the people call anyone who is fat, clumsy, and lazy by the Arabic nickname *tor Acco*—ox of Acco."[40]

9 / THE SPRING THAT OBSERVES THE SABBATH

Hebrew folklore has it that not only do Jews observe Sabbath as their resting day but so do their rivers and springs.

The pilgrim Rabbi Petahia, who visited Acco in the year 1187, told: "In Acco a spring flows during all six days of the week, but on the Sabbath not even one drop of water is to be found in it."

He was probably referring to the Spring of the Ox mentioned previously—the only spring around Acco.[41]

10 / THE RIVER NAAMAN AND THE WALL OF ACCO

The river Naaman flows at the northern limits of the Valley of Zebulun, near the city of Acco. It is most likely the Shihor-Libnath mentioned in the Bible as being within the borders of the territory of Asher. To the whiteness of the sand through which it streams toward the Mediterranean Sea it owes its name "Libnath," derived from the Hebrew *laban*—white.

The Arabs tell that the Prophet Mohammed once came to the river and wished to cross but was prevented by the powerful current. Mohammed said, "Peace unto you, O River! May I cross over you?" And the river replied, in Arabic, "*Naaman,*" meaning, "yes." It is, therefore, called Naaman to this very day.

The river Naaman empties into the Mediterranean Sea, near the wall of Acco. At times it strays, emptying closer to or farther from the wall.

Legend has it that when the outlet approaches the gate of the city, it will herald the redemption of the world.

Once, when the Naaman flowed close by the wall of Acco, the people of the city came out joyfully and sacrificed lambs, saying, "Now redemption approaches!"[42]

11 / THE RIVER NAAMAN AND THE SERPENTS

In 1350, the German pilgrim Ludolphus of Suchem recorded a curious local superstition concerning the river Naaman: "There is likewise another river near Acre, on one side of which no serpent or venomous thing can live, though they can well do so on the other side; and it has been proved that serpents cast across this river die straightaway."[43]

12 / ROCK OF THE THREE CONTINENTS

In his record of the crusade led by Richard the Lion-Hearted, Geoffrey de Vinsauf describes the city of Acco (Acre of the Crusaders), around the year 1200. He has a tale repeated by no other traveler about the nearby river Belus: "Not far from the river, near the city, a low rock stands out, at which, it is said, the three divisions of the world—Asia, Europe and Africa—meet; and though the place contains the other separate parts of the world, in itself it is dependent on none, but is distinct from and independent of all three."[44]

13 / THE PALM GROVES OF ACCO

Around Acco grow beautiful palm groves—remnants of larger woods that shaded these parts in medieval times.

FIG. 14. PALM TREE NEAR ACCO

Palmarea, a settlement in their midst, was named after them.

The palms around Acco grow in various ways. Some stand erect and slim, lifting their proud green heads to the clear sky; others are bent down by the wind blowing from the sea; still others lie full length on the ground, under the burden of years.

Legend has it that because the palms of Acco are praying to the Lord of the Universe they adopt these different attitudes of prayer—some standing, some bowing low, and some prostrating themselves in utter humility.[45]

14 / THE GRAVE OF ABU-ATABAH

In the neighborhood of Acco, there stands a small building with a white dome enclosing the tomb of Abu-Atabah, a santon revered by the Moslems. Inside the dome, close to the tomb, there is a square pillar, shaped like a vertical threshold, which in Arabic is called *"atabah."* Therefore the tomb is known as *Abu-Atabah*—the Father of the Threshold.

A few generations back, when Napoleon Bonaparte, at the head of the French army, besieged the fortress of Acco, the Moslem inhabitants went out secretly to prostrate themselves before the tomb of Abu-Atabah. Thanks to their prayers, Allah came to their aid, and the French army could not break through their ramparts.

When this became known to Napoleon, he commanded his forces to remove the pillar from the tomb of Abu-Atabah and take it on board ship to France. The men carried out the order in spite of the opposition of the inhabitants. But then a miracle happened: When the ship reached the French shore and the sailors went to fetch the stone, to their great astonishment it was nowhere to be found.

With the help of Allah, the Merciful, and owing to the

holiness of Abu-Atabah, the stone had flown from the ship back to its own rightful place, where it is to be seen to this day.*

A similar story is told about the grave of Eliezer ben Arach, in Alma, near Zefat, as repeated by an anonymous Jewish traveler of the year 1522: "On this grave there is a great stone, and it is told that forty years ago the Arabs came and took it to use as a millstone. They employed many people to carry it to a far place, but the next day the stone was found once more on the grave!"[46]

*Flying stones are well-known in the folklore of the Holy Land. See *Legends of Judea and Samaria*, p. 218.

V
THE LADDERS OF TYRE

1 / ABRAHAM AT THE LADDERS OF TYRE

"And the Lord appeared unto Abram, and said:
'Unto thy seed will I give this land.'"

To the north of Acco, the mountains of Galilee protrude into the Mediterranean Sea, forming a high promontory. The road from Acco to Tyre, in Lebanon, travels over these heights along the seacoast. The way is so steep and uneven that it is like going up and down a ladder, and thus from ancient times the place was named *Sulamot de-Zor*—Hebrew for the Ladders of Tyre.

It is said of Abraham that in his wanderings over many lands, he came to Aram Naharayim (Mesopotamia), where he saw the inhabitants wasting their time in eating and drinking and in all forms of frivolity. Therefore he said, "May I never have a share in any of these lands."

When he came to the Ladders of Tyre and arrived at Eretz-Israel, he saw the inhabitants of the land ploughing and tilling the soil at the proper time, and sowing and reaping in due course. Therefore he said, "This is the land that I would ask of the Lord as my portion."

And the Lord said to him: "Unto thy seed have I given this land!"[47]

2 / THE REVIVING OF THE LION AT THE LADDERS OF TYRE

The story is told of a man who was traveling from Eretz-Israel to Babylonia. Once, while he was resting and eating his bread, he saw two birds quarreling with each other. One fell dead, and the other flew away speedily and after a while returned carrying some unfamiliar herb, which he applied to the beak of his dead companion. The dead bird arose, restored to life!

The man carefully collected the herb, which had fallen from the bird's beak, and he decided forthwith to devote his life to the resurrection of the dead.

When he reached the Ladders of Tyre, he found the body of a dead lion thrown across his way. He applied the herb to its powerful jaws and brought it back to life. Whereupon the lion jumped up and devoured him.[48]

3 / ALEXANDER THE GREAT IN ROSH-HANIKRA

The southern part of the Ladders of Tyre is called *Rosh-Hanikra*—Head of the Hollow. In medieval times its Arab name was *An-Nawakir*—the Hollows, or Cuttings. A Moslem geographer of the thirteenth century explains the reason thus:

"They say that Alexander wished to travel by the coast road to Egypt, and it was said to him, 'This mountain is a barrier between thee and the coast, and 'tis necessary that thou shouldst go round it.'

"But he commanded the hill to be pierced so that the road would pass through it; and for this reason it is called 'the Cuttings.' "

North of the Cuttings there is a ruin called "Iskandaruna" after the Macedonian conqueror; in the olden days it was an important way station on the way from Lebanon to Eretz-Israel.[49]

FIG. 15. ROSH-HANIKRA—HEAD OF THE HOLLOW (1880)

4 / THE CAVE OF SIGHS

The cape of the mountain *Rosh-Hanikra*—the Head of the Hollow—penetrates into the Mediterranean, and its white rocks stand out brightly above the sea. The waves and breakers that lap at its base have hollowed out many caves and crannies in the rocks.

In former times, where the modern highway runs today to Beirut, the capital of Lebanon, a steep and crooked path once wound its way up to Rosh-Hanikra, and thence to the Ladders of Tyre. Walking, and, far worse, riding on this track was very dangerous. The Arabs in the district tell of a terrible accident which happened here.

Once, a bride from Acco whose bridegroom dwelt in Tyre was being led up the path upon a gaily caparisoned mare. Following the bride came a great assembly of relatives and friends, all dancing joyfully to the sound of drums and cymbals. The throng came to Rosh-Hanikra and was advancing along the narrow winding way when suddenly the mare's forelegs slipped, and the bride was sent hurtling into the sea.

And when one nears one of the caves in the lower parts of Rosh-Hanikra, one hears a soft noise like that of heartbreaking sighs. People say it is the quiet sobbing of the unfortunate bride and so, to this day, the cave is called *Magharat an-Nauh*—the Cave of Sighs.[50]

5 / KING SOLOMON'S POOLS NEAR TYRE

South of the town of Tyre, which today is part of Lebanon, gushes forth a large spring called in Arabic, *Ras el-Ain*—the Head of the Spring. From here, in olden days, a channel was drawn to the town to supply its inhabitants with water. Pools were built around the spring to store water for drinking and for irrigation.

A medieval legend attributed the pools to King Solomon,

whose name they bear. Solomon, it was said, built them as a gift to King Hiram of Tyre in return for the Cedars of Lebanon which he had contributed to the building of the Great Temple in Jerusalem.

It is thought that King Solomon was referring to this fountain in the passage from the Song of Songs: "Thou art a fountain of gardens,/A well of living waters,/And flowing streams from Lebanon."

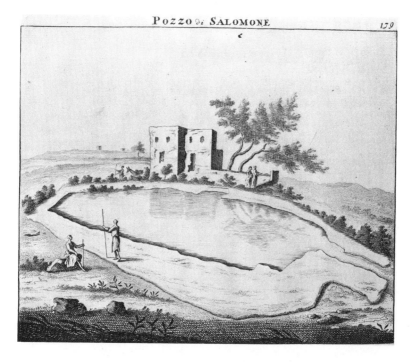

FIG. 16. POOLS OF SOLOMON NEAR TYRE (1688)

6 / HIRAM, KING OF TYRE, BUILT HIM SEVEN HEAVENS

"Nine entered the Garden of Eden alive:
One was Hiram, King of Tyre."

Legend relates of Hiram, King of Tyre, that he built seven heavens, and in them, flashes, thunder, and lightning.

"The first heaven he made of glass, and in it he put the sun and the moon, the stars and the planets.

"The second he made of iron.

"The third heaven was made of tin, studded with oval jewels, which collided one with the other and made a sound like thunder.

"The fourth heaven was of lead, the fifth of copper and the sixth of silver.

"The seventh heaven he made of gold studded with precious stones, and fixed in it a throne with beasts and stars, as he had seen King Solomon had.

"And Hiram made himself a golden bed, with four rubies, one in each corner, the like of which was not to be found in all the world. When he mounted it and sat upon it, shaking himself, he created lightning and flames. And as the stones beat one against the other, they made a sound like thunder. And all men would come and bow down before him."

Rabbi Haim Horowitz (about 1835) said: "When one hears thunder in Zefat, may it be built and stand firm, two days distance from Tyre, one does not immediately utter the prescribed blessing lest he be hearing only the thunder in the seven heavens built by Hiram, King of Tyre.

"Another view is that the sounds may be just the waters of the sea bursting through the bushes and into the caves along the shore.

"But when it is clear that what one hears is the thunder of God's glory—the blessing is recited!"[52]

FIG. 17. "TOMB OF HIRAM"

7 / "TYRE IS THINE"

When Alexander the Great invaded the Near East, he rode along the Mediterranean seashore, overrunning all opposition along his way until he reached the strongly fortified city of Tyre, lying on an island off the mainland.

Alexander put the town under heavy siege, well aware that the success of his campaign depended on its conquest.

One night, at the beginning of the blockade, a satyr appeared to him in his dream. Very much disquieted, he inquired of his wise men as to the meaning of this vision. They heartened his spirit by saying it was a good omen, for the name satyr is composed of the two Greek words *Sa Tyr*— Tyre is Thine![53]

FIG. 18. TYRE ON MEDITERRANEAN SEA (1880)

8 / TYRE AND THE COMING OF THE MESSIAH

In the days to come, when the time of the Messiah of Israel will be nearing, many wars will be waged, many towns will be destroyed, and scores of people will lose their lives. According to the legend, at that time the town of Tyre too will bear many ordeals: Israel will come and besiege Tyre for forty days, and at the end of the forty days, the men of Israel will stand up and chant, "Hear O Israel, the Lord, our God, the Lord is One."

And the walls of Tyre will fall, and the town will be conquered by Israel. Its inhabitants will run away, leaving behind all their silver and all their gold.

And from Tyre, Israel will proceed to Rome to fetch the vessels of the Temple which are kept there. And the Messiah, the King Nehemiah (the Consoler) will lead them to Jerusalem.[54]

VI

THE VALLEY OF
JEZREEL (ESDRAELON)

1 / THE WESTERN VALLEY OF
JEZREEL WENT TO ZEBULUN

When the Promised Land was divided among the Israelites, three tribes—Zebulun, Issachar, and Menashe—were given parts of the Valley of Jezreel in their portions. Zebulun inherited the western part of the valley to the shore of the sea, Issachar received the central plain, and Menashe the southeastern section to the banks of the Jordan.

On his deathbed the patriarch Jacob blessed every one of his sons in the order of their birth, starting from his firstborn Reuben, and terminating with Benjamin, his youngest. He made only one exception to this rule—after Judah, he called Zebulun, although it was Issachar's turn.

Legend wonders: Why did Jacob see fit to give his benediction to Zebulun *after* he had blessed Judah, though Issachar was older and deserved to be honored first? Because foreseeing the events of the future, the wise patriarch saw Jerusalem in ruins and the Sanhedrin—the Supreme Court of Israel—uprooted from its seat in Judah and removed to the inheritance of Zebulun. Therefore he blessed Zebulun immediately after Judah, going over the head of Issachar.

Indeed, when Jerusalem fell to the enemy, the Sanhedrin wandered to the cities of Beit-Shearim, Usha, and Shefaram, all three situated within the territory of Zebulun.[55]

2 / THE CENTRAL VALLEY OF JEZREEL WENT TO ISSACHAR

*"The fourth lot came out for Issachar . . .
And their border was Jezreel."*

The sons of Issachar inherited the central plain of Jezreel, good and rich soil, today the site of Afula and the villages around it.

Issachar's satisfaction in his portion is expressed in Jacob's blessing: "Issachar is a large-boned ass,/Crouching down between the sheep-folds./For he saw a resting-place that it was good,/And the land that it was pleasant;/And he bowed his shoulder to bear,/And became a servant under taskwork."

Why should Issachar have been singled out for such a comparison?—questioned the sages of Israel. The answer given is: "Because the shape of the territory of the tribe of Issachar resembles the back of an ass. As the back of an ass slopes on either side and the backbone is raised, so too is the territory of Issachar, which slopes into valleys on either side with a mountain rising between them in the middle. The valley on the one side stretches from Afula to the village of Jezreel, and the other valley stretches out between the mountains of Tabor and Nazareth. The mountain which divides the valleys is called 'Givat ha-Moreh' and rises like the backbone of an ass above that part of the Valley of Jezreel which was the inheritance of the tribe of Issachar." Wherefore, says one tradition, an ass was pictured on the flag of Issachar.

Issachar's great love for the Torah and his devotion to the

study of the holy books have given rise to a different interpretation of Jacob's blessing:

"Issachar is a large-boned ass" because as the bones of an ass stand out on his body, so did the knowledge of the Torah stand revealed in all the ways of the children of Issachar.

"Crouching down between the sheepfolds" refers to the rows of students sitting in the house of study.

"For he saw a resting-place that it was good"—that is the Torah.

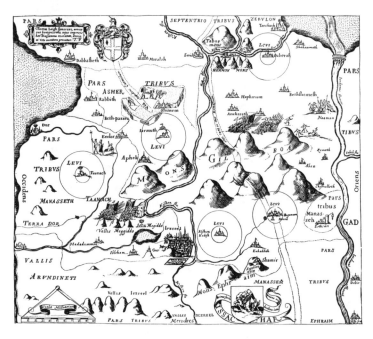

FIG. 19. PICTORIAL MAP OF THE VALLEY OF JEZREEL
This seventeenth-century map depicts, among other sites, Mount Tabor, Mount Gilboa, Jezreel, Megiddo, and Beit-Shean.

"And he bowed his shoulders to bear" represents the blessed burden of learning the Torah. Others say that it could be the beloved task of reclaiming the Land of Israel.

"And he became a servant under taskwork" refers to the two hundred men of Issachar who served in the great Sanhedrin, the Supreme Court of Israel.

"For the children of Issachar exceeded all the tribes in their love of the Torah. And whoever erred in the interpretation of the Law would ask the members of Issachar and they would explain it to him."[56]

3 / THE SONS OF ISSACHAR WERE MEN OF LEARNING

In the Book of Chronicles it is stated: "And of the children of Issachar, men that had understanding of the times, to know what Israel ought to do; the heads of them were two hundred; and all their brethren were at their commandment."

The symbol-stone of Issachar, which the High Priest carried on his breastplate, was a sapphire, and his flag pictured the sun and the moon on a black background, for it is written: "Issachar, men that had understanding of the times."

One commentator takes this to mean that "they were versed in the movements of the sun and the moon and were able to establish the first day of the month and fix leap years."

Legend adds that the great Sanhedrin, the Supreme Court of Israel, will in the future be in the land of Issachar.

And the great Beth-Hamidrash—the House of Study—will in the future be in the land of Issachar.[57]

4 / THE TEMPLE IN THE LAND OF ISSACHAR

Moses, the Law-Giver, blessed Issachar, saying:
"Rejoice . . . Issachar, in thy tents.
They shall call peoples unto the mountain;
There shall they offer sacrifices of righteousness."

This means, says legend, that the holy man of God deemed Issachar worthy to carry the Temple, the chosen House of the Lord. This may be in reverence for his learning and for his love of the Torah; it may also refer to Mount Tabor, which stands out beautifully over the portion of Issachar. The sages of Israel mention Tabor as one of the mountaintops on which the Temple will be built in a time to come.*⁵⁸

5 / WHY NABOTH PERISHED FROM THE EARTH

"If thy voice is pleasant,
Arise and honor God with thy voice."

In the central part of the Valley of Jezreel, near Afula, lies the site of the ancient city of Jezreel, from which the whole valley derives its name.

Jezreel was the winter capital of Ahab, King of Israel. Close to his palace grew the vineyard of Naboth the Jezreelite. The king wanted the vineyard but Naboth refused to relinquish his heritage.

After Naboth had been put to death at the king's order, the wicked ruler entered the vineyard and there met the prophet Elijah, who cried out in wrath: "Hast thou killed and also taken possession?"

Legend has another explanation for Naboth's bitter end. Naboth, it is said, was endowed with a pleasant voice, and

*See legend II:11.

when he went up to Jerusalem for the festivals all Israel would gather to hear him.

He failed once to fulfill the holy commandment and to make the pilgrimage to Jerusalem at the appointed time. "Then the children of Belial bore witness against him and he perished from the earth."

And that befell him because he did not go to Jerusalem as he should have, in awe of God, to honor His Name with the pleasant voice which He had bestowed upon him.

The Christian pilgrim Burchardus de Monte Sion, who visited the Holy Land in 1232, wrote of the town of Jezreel: "Before its gate there is still shown the vineyard of Naboth the Jezreelite."

Today, Jezreel, a flourishing settlement, stands on a hill rising close to the site of the ancient city. The small spring trickling at its foot was named after Naboth, and its soft murmuring waters perpetuate the memory of the unfortunate Jezreelite of the sweet voice.[59]

6 / THE PROPHET ELISHA IN SHUNEM

In biblical times, Shunem was an important town in the portion of Issachar. Today, in its place in the Valley of Jezreel, near Afula, stands an Arab village called Sulam, an obvious variation of the ancient name. In his wanderings, the prophet Elisha, the disciple of the great Elijah, used to visit Shunem, as the Book of Kings relates:

"And it fell on a day that Elisha passed to Shunem, where was a great woman; and she constrained him to eat bread. And so it was, that as oft as he passed by, he turned in thither to eat bread. And she said unto her husband: 'Behold now, I perceive that this is a holy man of God, that passeth by us continually. Let us make, I pray thee, a little chamber on the roof; and let us set for him there a bed, and a table, and a stool, and a candlestick; and it shall be, when he cometh to us, that he shall turn in thither.' And it fell on a day that he came thither, and he turned into the upper chamber and lay there."

And how did the woman find out that Elisha was a holy man of God? One answer is, "Because she did not see even one fly on his table while he ate the bread she gave him."

That explanation gave rise to the following commentary: "This proves that the woman has better discernment concerning the guests than the man."

Indeed, flies are a very common pest in the East, and no ordinary man escapes their importuning.

It was in Shunem that Elisha revived the son of the same Shunammite woman. "Because the Shunnamite provided Elisha with food, she merited the resurrection of her son," said the ancients.

Rabbi Ashtori ha-Parhi, who lived in the town of Beit-Shean in this vicinity during the Middle Ages, wrote about Shunem, in 1322: "A fountain springs from the northern rock in the middle of the city. And atop the fountain I saw a [deserted] house inhabited by many spirits. And I said unto myself, Verily, this is the house of the Shunammite in which Elisha, may he rest in peace, had his chamber."[60]

7 / SHEIKH ABREIK AND THE HEALING MARSH

On the mound of the historic Beit-Shearim, there is the grave of a holy man named Sheikh Abreik. According to one tradition, he is none other than Barak son of Abinoam, who, with Deborah the Prophetess, defeated the Canaanites in the neighboring fields of Jezreel and on the banks of the river Kishon.

The Arabs, on the other hand, maintain that Sheikh Abreik is the name of a holy man who never parted from the pitcher (*abreik,* in Arabic) that he always carried with him for his ablutions before prayer.

Near the grave of Sheikh Abreik, bordering on the nearby village of Sede-Yaacov, there flows a fountain surrounded by a marsh called by the Arabs *Almatbaah*—the Place of Immersion. Arabs from near and far were wont to visit it to immerse their bodies in its waters—sometimes up to the neck—believing it to be a reliable remedy for all kinds of ailments. Barren women, too, would come, hoping that the waters of the swamp would make them fruitful.

Arab legend has it that Almatbaah, the swamp of healing, was created for the sake of Sheikh Abreik. He was a day laborer, working in the nearby fields, but he spent most of his time in ablutions and prayers. His master secretly broke his pitcher, thinking that without the water the sheikh would be unable to perform his ablutions and prayers and would work more industriously, wasting less time.

When the sheikh prepared to wash before the midday prayer, he noticed that his pitcher was broken. Greatly grieved, he smote the ground with his staff, whereupon water flowed on the spot, forming in due course a small swamp, a place of healing for all time, a testament to the merit of the holy sheikh.[61]

8 / FROM NAHALAL TO JERUSALEM

Next to the village of Nahalal, there stood in ancient times a small town of the same name within the territory of Zebulun, as is told in the Book of Joshua: "And the border turned about it on the north to . . . Nahalal."

It is agreed that the name "Nahalal" derives from the Hebrew *nahel,* meaning "to lead the flocks to the water," as mentioned in Psalms: "He leadeth me [Hebrew, *inahaleni*] beside the still waters," and also in the verse of Isaiah: "Even by the springs of water will He guide them [Hebrew, *inahalam*]."

In the talmudic period, Nahalal was replaced by Mahalul and the sages identify the two as Nahalal-Mahalul.

One of the inhabitants of Mahalul, a man named Tartori, gained fame through his great piety, for he used to go up to Jerusalem every Sabbath eve to make his devotions at the Great Temple. And no one rose earlier than he to pick the fruit from the fig trees.[62]

9 / RABBI LEVI AND THE INHABITANTS OF SIMONIA

Near the village Nahalal, on the hill of Shimron, which rises above the highway from Haifa to Nazareth, there stood in biblical times the city of Shimron within the tribe of Zebulun, and in the talmudic age a Jewish village called Simonia.

Once, when Rabbi Judah-ha-Nasi (the Prince), who lived in the neighboring town of Zippori, was passing Simonia, its inhabitants came to meet him, saying: "My lord, appoint for us a man who will read to us the Written Law and will teach us the Oral Law, so that he may act as a judge in our midst."

Rabbi Judah appointed Rabbi Levi, son of Sisi, who came to Simonia. The people built for him a high pulpit upon which he could stand, and many questions did they put to him, but he could not reply. Rabbi Levi was so sorely troubled by his failure that he rose early the following morning and returned to Rabbi Judah, who asked him, "What have the people of Simonia done unto you?" Rabbi Levi answered, "Do not remind me of my troubles. They asked me three questions, not one of which I could answer."

"Why did you not answer them?" asked Rabbi Judah.

Rabbi Levi replied, "They built for me a high pulpit and placed me upon it. My heart became so filled with pride that the words of the Law disappeared from my mind."

It is written that when Roman troops surrounded the city of Rabbi Levi ben Sisi, "He took the Scroll of the Law and ascended to the roof. He said: 'Lord of the Universe! If I have violated one word of the Scroll of the Law, let the troops enter and plunder! And if I have fulfilled all that is written within it, let them disperse!'

"The troops immediately dispersed and withdrew."[63]

10 / THE ACACIA SHRUBS ON THE HILL OF SHIMRON

White acacia shrubs, rarely found in the country, grow wild on the Hill of Shimron, near the village of Nahalal. Arab legend accounts for their growth there by the following tale:

Many generations ago, the tribe of Hilal, famous for its wars and wondrous exploits, emigrated from Arabia and wandered throughout Eretz-Israel and the neighboring countries. They once made their camp on the Hill of Shimron *(Tel Simoniya)* and pitched their tents there.

Some time later, they decided to make a pilgrimage to the holy city of Jerusalem. They packed their tents and went on their way, but they forgot to remove several tent-pegs from the ground. In the course of time these pegs took root, and sprouted forth branches, and those are the acacia bushes growing there to this day.

Near the hill of Shimron, in the village of Malul, there are ruins of an ancient building called by the Arabs, *Kasr al-Zir* —the Palace of Zir. Amir Zir was one of the great warriors of the sons of Hilal. To the north of the village stretches a plateau called *Maidan al-Zir*—the Race-course of Zir. Here on this mountain the Amir Zir always appeared mounted on his noble steed and all the onlookers marveled at his skillful riding.[64]

11 / THE HUMBLE MAN FROM HAVRAYA

On the border of the Valley of Jezreel, next to the settlement Beth-Lehem of Galilee, stands a small ruin named, in Arabic, *Hawara*—that is, the White (Place)—because of the paleness of the ground around it. This is, in all probability, the site of the ancient Jewish townlet of Havraya, also named for the whiteness of the earth of the vicinity.

Havraya was the home of Rabbi Osheya Zeira. He was called Zeira (the Small), to distinguish him from a famous scholar, Rabbi Osheya Rabba (the Great), who was also a native of Galilee.

In later times the place name "Havraya" was mistakenly confused with its homonym "Hevraya," meaning "company." This error gave rise to a custom whereby rabbis wishing to emphasize their humbleness often added to their name the words, *"Zeira demin Hevraya"*—"the Small One of the Company [of Scholars]."[65]

12 / THE TOWN OF DOBRATH AND THE PROPHETESS DEBORAH

Dabburiye, a Moslem village at the foot of Mount Tabor, has preserved in Arabic form the name of the biblical city of Dobrath, whose site it occupies.

Dobrath was in the inheritance of Zebulun as it is told: "And the third lot came up for the children of Zebulun . . . and their border . . . went out to Dobrath."

Today, a new settlement established opposite the ancient site has been given the name Dobrath in its original form.

Dobrath is derived from the Hebrew *dober,* meaning "pastureland." The word occurs in the prophecy of Micah: "I will surely assemble, O Jacob, all of thee; I will surely gather the remnant of Israel. . . . As a flock in the midst of their pasture [*dober*]." Indeed, some of the best pastureland of Israel can be found on the slopes of the mountains in this vicinity.

Christian pilgrims in times past assumed that the appellation "Dabburiye" originated from the name of the Prophetess Deborah, who gathered the tribes of Israel on the top of neighboring Mount Tabor to repulse the Canaanite invaders in the Valley of Jezreel.[66]

13 / THE CAVE OF THE TRAITRESS

Not far from the Arab village of Iksal, the ancient Chesulloth of the tribe of Issachar, there runs amid the mountains of Nazareth a ravine in which there is a small cave. This cavern, which is in parts natural and in parts carved and built by man, once served as the refuge of hermits. The lintel over the entrance, still in position, has a cross carved upon it; several more crosses are to be found within the cavern.

Originally, there were yet more crosses, painted in red, but they have been defaced by Arab shepherds. Nowadays they look as if they had been marked in blood, and of them the Arabs tell this tale:

The sheikh of Iksal had a most beautiful daughter who was loved by one of the young men of Daburiyah, which lies below Mount Tabor. But there was a feud between the sheikh and the men of Daburiyah, and he would not let his daughter marry the youth. The girl, however, ran away and married her beloved.

One night, the girl's brother seized her, brought her to this cave, and murdered her. Then, dipping his hands in her blood, he went forth and made the stains on the lintel, saying, "Let the maidens of my folk learn that they must have their families' consent ere they wed."

Since this time the cave has been called: *Magharat el-Mathumeh*—the Cave of the Tainted Woman.[67]

14 / WHY THE TEACHER IN TABERNETH WAS DISMISSED

In the Valley of Jezreel, alongside the Afula–Haifa railroad tracks, there stands a ruin known by its Arabic name of Tarbanah, which in Talmudic times was the town of Taberneth, the scene of the following incident:

Rabbi Shimon was a teacher in Taberneth. While teaching the children, he would read so quickly that they were unable to follow him. The inhabitants of Taberneth came to him and asked that when reading the Torah to their children he pause between passages, in order to enable the students to read with him.

But Rabbi Shimon was obstinate and refused to listen to them. He went to Rabbi Hananiah in Zippori and told him the entire story.

Rabbi Hananiah said to him: "Even if they threaten to cut off your head do not listen to them! For the Law is deep and the children must hasten to learn it and know it."

Rabbi Shimon returned to Taberneth and continued to teach as was his custom. The inhabitants of Taberneth were angered and dismissed him.

Rabbi Zura, a third century sage, said: "If that scribe, Rabbi Shimon, had lived in my day, I would have appointed him a scholar."[68]

15 / TEL KEIMON—JOSHUA'S BATTLEFIELD

On the margin of the plain of Jezreel, close to the foot of the mountains of Carmel and Samaria, there is a beautiful hill upon which stood Yokneam, a royal city of the Canaanites that which was taken by Joshua son of Nun, and given to the tribe of Zebulun. Now it is a forsaken mound called Tel Keimon, next to the new settlement of Yokneam.

The Samaritans recount the war which was fought here between Joshua son of Nun and king Shaubak son of Hamam. Shaubak, desiring to avenge the death of his father, who had been killed in battle with the children of Israel, entered into a league with the neighboring kings. They all joined forces in Keimon. Joshua and his men came from Mount Gerizim to fight with them. Suddenly, Joshua and all his followers found themselves enclosed by seven iron walls, called into existence by the magic of the enemy. At Joshua's prayer, a dove appeared by which Joshua sent a message to Nabih son of Gilead, king of the two-and-a-half tribes of Israel which had remained in the territory east of the Jordan. Nabih hastened with a great army to Keimon, and Shaubak was defeated. At the shouting of Nabih's soldiers the walls around Joshua disappeared, and Joshua and his men were freed.[69]

16 / YOKNEAM—THE MOUNT OF CAIN

On the margin of the Valley of Jezreel, near the townlet of Yokneam, rises the hill Tel Caimon, on which stood the ancient town of Yokneam.

In medieval times, a city by the name of Caymont stood on this site. It is thought that this name is a contraction of the two words Cayn and Mount—the Mount of Cain—because here, presumably, Cain met his death.

After Cain had killed Abel his brother, God cursed him: "And Cain said unto the Lord: 'My punishment is greater than I can bear . . . I shall be a fugitive and a wanderer in the earth . . . whosoever findeth me will slay me.' And the Lord said unto him: 'Therefore whosoever slayeth Cain, vengeance shall be taken on him sevenfold.' And the Lord set a sign for Cain, lest any finding him should smite him."

Cain, carrying on his forehead the mark, in the shape of a horn, used to wander around this mountain. One of his descendants, called Lamech, was a blind man, and his son used to hold his hand and lead him to the hunt. When the son saw an animal he would say: "I see an animal!" And his father would draw the bow and kill his prey. Once, when Lamech and his son went hunting, they came to a hill, and the son, seeing the horn of Cain, who was among the bushes, mistook him for a deer and exclaimed: "I see an animal!" Lamech shot an arrow and killed Cain. When his son went to fetch in the prey, he found Cain dying, and said: "Alas! That is my grandfather!" Lamech was in great agony, and when he came to his wives, he said: "Adah and Zillah, hear my voice,/Ye wives of Lamech, hearken unto my speech,/For I have slain a man for wounding me/And a young man for bruising me,/If Cain shall be avenged sevenfold,/Truly Lamech seventy and sevenfold."

Sir John Mandeville too mentioned this tale. He wrote: "And seven miles from Nazareth is Mount Cain, and underneath it is a well where Lamech slew Cain with an arrow, supposing he had been a wild beast."[70]

FIG. 20. BLIND LAMECH SHOOTS AT CAIN

In the center, on the height, is Yokneam (called "Cain" on the map). Below is the Fount of Cain (Fons Cain). In the upper right-hand corner is the town of Beit-Shean (Bethsen).

TRAHES·LAMEC·ARCV·SVO·ITFEC·CAYM·

FIG. 21. BLIND LAMECH SHOOTS AT CAIN
A twelfth-century mosaic found in a church in Monreale, Sicily.

17 / THE BATTLE OF ARMAGEDDON

At the foot of the Mountains of Samaria, flanking the entrance to the Valley of Jezreel, rises a hill marking the place
of the ancient town of Megiddo, one of the most famous cities
of the Holy Land.

Situated at a highly strategic spot, it played a part in most of the wars waged in this area from the dawn of history until the birth of the State of Israel in our day.

Here, in 1479 B.C.E. Thutmose III, Pharaoh of Egypt, defeated and subjugated the Canaanites. About three hundred years later, in the period of the Judges, the Prophetess Deborah and Barak son of Abinoam destroyed the Canaanite forces irrupting from the sea coast, ". . . in Taanach by the waters of Megiddo."

In Megiddo again, two kings of Judah—Ahaziah and Josiah —lost their lives in battle.

In modern history, Megiddo was the site of a major breakthrough by the British fighting the Turks and Germans in Palestine during the First World War. Field Marshal Edmund Allenby, Commander-in-Chief of the British troops and architect of this victory, was awarded the title of Lord Allenby of Megiddo, or Armageddon, as the place is called in the New Testament. Armageddon is a contraction of the Hebrew *Har Megiddon*—Mount Megiddon.

Because of the many wars fought through history in its vicinity, Megiddo became, in Christian tradition, the symbol of all battlefields, and the site of the decisive fight to be waged between good and evil at the end of time. The Book of Revelation describes that fierce battle in detail:

"To gather them to the battle of that great day of God Almighty. . . . And he gathered them together into a place called in the Hebrew tongue Armageddon. . . . And there were voices, and thunders, and lightnings, and there was a great earthquake, such as was not since men were upon the earth."

Wherefore the ultimate conflict among the nations is often designated "Armageddon."[71]

18 / NEBUZARADAN IN THE VALLEY OF MEGIDDO

The second Book of Kings records: "Now in the fifth month, on the seventh day of the month . . . came Nebuzaradan the captain of the guard, a servant of the King of Babylon, unto Jerusalem. And he burnt the house of the Lord, and the king's house; and all the houses of Jerusalem, even every great man's house, burnt he with fire."

Joshua son of Levi, a sage of the second century, related: "An old man told me: 'In the valley of Megiddo Nebuzaradan killed two million two hundred and ten thousand Israelites. And in Jerusalem he killed nine hundred and forty thousand Israelites.' "

Another version says, in the Valley of Megiddo, two million one hundred and ten thousand Israelites; in Jerusalem, nine hundred and ten thousand.[72]

19 / EIN-IBRAHIM—SPRING OF ABRAHAM

At some distance from the biblical Megiddo, on the highway leading from Afula to Haderah, is the Arab village Ein-Ibrahim—Spring of Abraham, named, according to local tradition, after the patriarch who, they say, rested here on one of his numerous journeys.

In the Middle Ages, in the nearby village of Lejjun, which was situated opposite Megiddo, there gushed a spring, of which a Moslem geographer of the year 903 says: "Just outside Al-Lajjun, there is a large stone of round form over which is built a dome called the Mosque of Abraham. A copious stream of water flows from under the stone, and it is reported that Abraham struck the stone with his staff, and there immediately flowed from it enough water to suffice for the personal needs of the people of the town and also for the irrigation of their lands. This spring continues to flow to the present day."[73]

20 / RABBI PINHAS AND THE RIVER GINNAI

The Arab town of Jennin, in the southern corner of the Valley of Jezreel, is perpetuating, in a slightly corrupted form, the name of the biblical Ein-Gannim—Spring of Gardens—which occupied this site in the past. In the days of the Second Temple, it was known as Ginnah and as it does at the present time, it lay on the highway from Galilee to Judah and Jerusalem.

Within the town there emerges a spring whose waters run under a bridge and into a tributary of the River Kishon. Before the bridge was built, it was dangerous to cross this brook in the rainy season, for it usually overflowed its banks. The stream may have been the Ginnai, mentioned in the following tale of the third century:

Once, when Rabbi Pinhas, the son of Yair, was traveling on an errand of charity, he arrived at the tributary of the Ginnai at a time when it was in flood, and he said to it: "Ginnai, Ginnai, divide thy waters so that I may pass over thee," and the rivulet answered him: "Thou art about to carry out the command of thy Creator, to bring charity to the people, and I too am carrying out the command of my Creator, to flow to the sea. But thou canst not say for certain if thou wilt succeed, whereas I am already succeeding."

Whereupon Rabbi Pinhas said: "If thou dost not divide thy waters now for me, thou shalt become dried up and never again have waters to divide."

The rivulet grew afraid, and divided its waters.

With Rabbi Pinhas there was another man who had with him wheat, which he was carrying to distribute amongst the poor for Passover. Rabbi Pinhas turned to the rivulet and said: "Divide also thy waters for this man, who is engaged upon an errand of charity." And the rivulet again divided its waters.

Finally, there was an Arab who accompanied them, and for whom Rabbi Pinhas demanded of the rivulet that it divide its waters so that it could not be said: "Is this the way you treat the stranger within your land?" And the rivulet once again divided its waters.[74]

21 / EIN-HAROD—THE SPRING OF GIDEON

When the Sons of the East and the Midianites from the desert invaded the fields of the Valley of Jezreel, Gideon collected his men to drive them back. The Book of Judges relates:

"Then Jerubaal, who is Gideon, and all the people that were with him, rose up early and pitched beside En-harod.

"And the Lord said unto Gideon: 'The people that are with thee are too many for Me to give the Midianites into their hand, lest Israel vaunt themselves against Me, saying: Mine own hand hath saved me. Now therefore make proclamation in the ears of the people, saying: Whosoever is fearful and trembling, let him return and depart early from Mount Gilead.' And there returned of the people twenty and two thousand; and there remained ten thousand.

"And the Lord said unto Gideon: 'The people are yet too many; bring them down unto the water, and I will try them for thee there.' . . . So he brought down the people unto the water; and the Lord said unto Gideon: 'Everyone that lappeth of the water with his tongue, as a dog lappeth, him shalt thou set by himself; likewise every one that boweth down upon his knees to drink.' And the number of them that lapped, putting their hand to their mouth, was three hundred men; but all the rest of the people bowed down upon their knees to drink water. And the Lord said unto Gideon: 'By the three hundred men that lapped will I save you.' "

Why did Gideon choose the men who lapped the water and not those who bowed down to drink? It is said because the latter thus revealed that they were used to prostrate themselves in front of idols. And God would not deliver the victory into the hands of the worshipers of false gods.[75]

FIG. 22. FOUNTAIN OF GIDEON (1910)
This is the biblical spring of Ein-Harod.

22 / THE VALLEY OF JEZREEL—THE BATTLEFIELD OF DAVID AND GOLIATH

In the Valley of Jezreel there flows a spring which in biblical times was called Ein-Harod. The new village nearby bears its name. On this site, the Judge Gideon chose the men who defeated the Midianites.

According to an old tradition, the battlefield of David the Shepherd and Goliath the Philistine was also situated near the spring of Ein-Harod. The anonymous pilgrim from Bordeaux, France, who visited the Holy Land in the year 333 C.E., mentioned the city of Jezreel—Stradela—located not far from the spring of Harod, and he added: "Here reigned King Ahab and here also Elijah prophesied. This is the field in which David slew Goliath."

A Jewish scholar, Rabbi Ashtori ha-Parhi, who lived in Beth-Shean, in this vicinity, wrote, around the year 1322, "Eastward from the city of Jezreel, there is a spring flowing from Mount Gilboa and called by the Arabs *Ain Jalut*—the Spring of Goliath. They say that a fight took place there between David and Goliath."

A similar tradition exists in the folklore of the Jews of Kurdistan, a country in the hilly region bordering on ancient Mesopotamia (today Iraq). It is reflected in the first lines of a popular song which Jewish newcomers from Kurdistan have brought to Jerusalem entitled "The Story of David and Goliath," and thus reads the first stanza: "Hear now all you friends,/Listen all you dear ones,/To the story of David and Goliath/In battle in the fields of Megiddo."*[76]

---

* Biblical sources clearly indicate that the actual fight between David and Goliath took place in the Valley of Elah in the hills of Judea. See: *Legends of Judea and Samaria*, p. 133.

FIG. 23. ARAB BUILDING IN ZARIN
This village is the ancient Jezreel, which was the capital of the
Kingdom of Israel.

23 / THE HILL OF MOREH—LITTLE HERMON

In the very middle of the Valley of Jezreel rises the Hill
of Moreh, whose steep summit overlooks a wide horizon. Opposite stands Mount Tabor, with its beautiful rounded
top.

In the Middle Ages, the Christian pilgrims called the Hill
of Moreh by the name "Little Hermon" to differentiate be-

tween it and Big Hermon on the northern border of the Holy Land.

They attributed to Little Hermon the words of the psalmist: "The north and the south, Thou has created them;/Tabor and Hermon rejoice in Thy name."[77]

VII
THE VALLEY OF BEIT-SHEAN

1 / BEIT-SHEAN IS THE GATE OF EDEN

The Valley of Beit-Shean stretches from the Valley of Jezreel down to the banks of the River Jordan. In its midst is the town Beit-Shean.

The Tribe of Manasseh inherited Beit-Shean and its surroundings.

When blessing his children, the Patriarch Jacob said to Joseph, the father of Ephraim and Manasseh: "Joseph is a fruitful vine,/A fruitful vine by a fountain. . . ./And by the Almighty, who shall bless thee,/With blessings of heaven above,/Blessings of the deep that coucheth beneath."

The sages of Israel commented: "The blessings of the deep" refers to Beit-Shean and its fruitful valley, with its abundance of water and its good earth where many villages flourished. The ruins of some of them, attesting to a prosperous Jewish life and including among them remains of ancient synagogues, have been brought to light through the years.

When conversing about the Garden of Eden, Resh Lakish, a well-known scholar of the third century, stated with final-ity: "If the Garden of Eden is in the Land of Israel, its gate is at Beit-Shean."

The many wars waged in the Valley of Beit-Shean brought ruin and desolation to its villages. The springs that once irrigated and fertilized the land were later abandoned by man, and this turned the fields and plantations into vast malarial swamps. The Gate of Eden became the Gate of Gehenna.

Today, with the Jewish revival, the Valley of Beit-Shean flourishes again, and many new villages have been established next to the remains of ancient sites.[78]

FIG. 24. MOUND OF ANCIENT BEIT-SHEAN (1850)

2 / THE PARADISIAL SPRING IN THE VALLEY OF
BEIT-SHEAN

Mohammed, the prophet of the Moslem world, describes in the Koran, the holy book of Islam, the paradise that awaits his believers: "And for him who fears to stand before his Lord are two gardens. In both of them two fountains flow. In both of them two springs gush forth."

Moslem tradition holds that one of these two springs emerges in the Valley of Beit-Shean. The Arabs call it *Ein Umm-el-Felus*—Spring of the Mother of Money. And he who drinks from its water will be spared the pains of the next world.[79]

3 / THE PRONUNCIATION OF THE JEWS OF BEIT-SHEAN

The Jewish inhabitants of ancient Beit-Shean suffered from the same defective diction as the Jews of Haifa and of Tivon.

They did not pronounce clearly the gutturals of the Hebrew alphabet and thus corrupted the meaning of the Holy Texts.

Wherefore their priests were pronounced unfit to perform in the synagogues.*[80]

4 / IF THE PALMS OF BEIT-SHEAN SHOULD DISAPPEAR

In bygone days, the Valley of Beit-Shean was famed for its luxuriant palm groves. Travelers of the tenth century still praised them highly. By the thirteenth century, they had largely disappeared through neglect, and Yakut, the Arab geographer of that period, noted:

"Beisan was celebrated for the number of its palms, but I, Yakut, who have been there many times, never saw more than two palm trees there, and these of the kind that give

* See legend I:2.

dates one year and no more. This, they say, is a sign of the coming of the Antichrist [in Arabic, *Ad-Dajjal*]."

Various signs will announce the coming of the Antichrist, and one of them is the disappearance of the palms of Beit-Shean.

The story is told of a man who was thrown by a storm onto a faraway island; there he found the Antichrist waiting for his time to appear on earth. And when he met this man, the Evil One asked him, "What doeth the palms of Beit-Shean?"

And the man replied, "The people thereof gather the fruits."

So the Antichrist knew that his time had not yet come.

Today, the palm groves of Beit-Shean have regained all their past splendor, and the advent of Ad-Dajjal seems more remote than ever.[81]

5 / WHERE WAS SATAN BANISHED TO?

The Moslem traveler al-Masudi, who visited the Land of Israel in 943 C.E., when the country was under Arab rule, dealt with the fate of Adam and Eve after they were driven out of the Garden of Eden, and also of Satan and the Snake, who were with them. They were all exiled to various places in the world, each located very far from the other. Al-Masudi wrote: "Adam, to Sarnadib; Eve, to Djeddah; Satan [Iblis], to Beit-Shean; and the Snake, to Ispahan."

Sarnadib is situated in Ceylon in the Indian Ocean. Djeddah is on the shore of the Red Sea, the most important port of Saudi Arabia to this day. Even now there is shown in the town the grave of Eve, or, as the Arabs call her, *Umna Hawa* —Our Mother Eve. Ispahan, formerly the capital of Persia (Iran), is still an important city.[82]

6 / WHERE DID THE PALACE OF MELCHIZEDEK STAND?

On the edge of the Valley of Beit-Shean, in its southern-most section near the bank of the River Jordan, there rises a prominent mound that covers the remains of some ancient city today forgotten. The Arabs call it *Tel-Radagha*—Mound of Mire.

It is usually presumed to be the site of ancient Salim, in the vicinity of the spring of Aenon, where St. John, the precursor of Christ, baptized the followers of Jesus, as told in the New Testament: "And John also was baptizing in Aenon near to Salim, because there was much water there: and they came, and were baptized."

In the fourth century, Eusebius, one of the Fathers of the Church, mentions "Salim, eight miles south of Beit-Shean." It is also pictured in the famous sixth-century mosaic map of Madaba.

The Christian woman pilgrim, St. Silvia, passed this way about the year 385, when the country was ruled by the Byzantines. She told of the village Sedima, probably a corruption of the name Selima—ancient Salem—and described its green fertile valley in the following terms: "When I saw the pleasant place, I inquired what it was, and I was told: This is the city of King Melchizedek, formerly called Salem. The building which you see at the summit of that little hill, in the center of the village, is a church, which is now called in the Greek language *Opu Melchisedech,* for there Melchizedek offered pure victims to God—that is, bread and wine, as it is written."[83]

7 / THE CURSE ON MOUNT GILBOA

On Mount Gilboa, whose slopes overlook the Valley of Beit-Shean, the great war between Israel and the Philistines was fought, in which Saul, the first annointed king of Israel was slain.

The Bible relates: "Now the Philistines fought against Israel, and the men of Israel fled from before the Philistines, and fell down slain in mount Gilboa. . . . And the battle went sore against Saul. . . . Then said Saul to his armor-bearer: 'Draw thy sword, and thrust me through therewith; lest these uncircumcised come and thrust me through, and make a mock of me!' But his armor-bearer would not; for he was sore afraid. Therefore Saul took his sword and fell upon it. . . . So Saul died, and his three sons, and his armor-bearer, and all his men, that same day together."

When David heard of the tragic death of Saul and Jonathan, his son, he lifted up his voice in great lamentation: "Thy beauty, O Israel, upon thy high places is slain!/How are the mighty fallen! . . . /Ye mountains of Gilboa,/Let there be no dew nor rain upon you,/Neither fields of choice fruits;/For there the shield of the mighty was vilely cast away,/The shield of Saul, not anointed with oil. . . . /Saul and Jonathan, the lovely and the pleasant/In their lives, even in their death they were not divided. . . . /How are the mighty fallen,/And the weapons of war perished!"

Legend tells that since the curse of David no dew and no rain have fallen on the mountains of Gilboa, and they are barren and desolate. And so indeed they remained for many centuries.

In our day, the mountains of Gilboa are covered in part with newly-planted forests of pine and carob trees and, at long last, these historic slopes have been redeemed from the curse of the poet-king.[84]

8 / TO BRING HAY TO OFRAIM

Ofraim was a small Jewish town in the northern part of Eretz-Israel. Its precise location is unknown, but it probably stood near the Valley of Beit-Shean, on the site of the Arab village of Taybe, in the vicinity of the Jewish settlement Benei-Brith (Moledet).

Since, to an Arab, the name Ofraim is suggestive of the word *afrit* meaning "devil," the Arab village which succeeded the Jewish town relinquished the name Ofraim, and chose to call itself Taybe—the Good (Site).

Ofraim was situated among rich cornfields where hay was found in large quantities. Therefore, if wares were brought to a place where they were already plentiful the people of Israel used to say, "You are bringing hay to Ofraim."[85]

9 / THE BRIDGE OF MEETING

The tribe of Beni Sakher came from the edge of the desert and encamped south of the Sea of Galilee, beyond the Jordan. Now the Beni Sakher had renowned warriors in their midst, and their maidens were famed for their grace and beauty. Most famous was Halima, daughter of the emir of the tribe. And tidings of her loveliness came to all the tribes who dwelled in Kedar.

So a certain emir of the tribes of Beer-Sheba went seeking Halima, and he wandered through the length of the land asking for the camping place of the Beni Sakher, till he came to a bridge built over the Jordan. From this bridge paths and tracks led in all directions, and the emir did not know whither to turn. So he sat on the bridge waiting for a wayfarer whom he might ask.

He had just seated himself when he saw another emir from Gilead; he too sought the tribe of Halima and did not know which way to go, and he too sat waiting his lot.

In a few minutes came a third emir, and a fourth, and a fifth, all seeking the camp of the Beni Sakher to ask for the hand of Halima; and none of them knew whither to turn, so they all sat down to wait.

When they began to speak to each other, they found that they who had met on the Jordan bridge all sought the same prize.

Since then this bridge is called by the Arabs *Jisr el-Majame*

—the Bridge of Meeting—in memory of those bedouin emirs who went to woo Halima, most beautiful of the daughters of Arabia.[86]

FIG. 25. BRIDGE OF MEETING (1835)

10 / THE RIVERS JORDAN AND YARMUK

In the Book of Psalms, King David gave praise to the Lord: "The earth is the Lord's, and the fullness thereof;/The world, and they that dwell therein./For He hath founded it upon the seas,/And established it upon the floods."

The sages of Israel comment: These are the seven seas and the four rivers that encompass the Holy Land.

Among the seven seas mentioned are the Sea of Tiberias (Kinneret), the Sea of Sodom (the Dead Sea), the Sea of Sumcha (Lake Hula) and the Great Sea (the Mediterranean).

Among the four rivers mentioned are the Jordan and the Yarmuk. The Yarmuk flows from Transjordan between the

mountains of Golan and Gilead, and falls into the Jordan
south of the Sea of Galilee (Kinneret).

The power station built at the junction of the rivers Jordan
and Yarmuk is therefore called in Hebrew *Naharayim*—Two
Rivers.[87]

11 / WHO BUILT HAMAT-GADER?

The hot springs of Hamat-Gader, issuing in the Valley of
the Yarmuk, were known from antiquity; they are mentioned on several occasions in ancient literature.

A traveler of the year 570 C.E. calls them *Thermae Heliae*
—the Hot Springs of Elijah—after the prophet.

They appear in Arabic writings of the Middle Ages as *El-
Hamme*—the Hot Baths. In the thirteenth century, the Moslem geographer Yakut mentions El-Hamme and the remains
of the large edifice that had stood there, and he adds: "It is
told that this old building was put up by Solomon, the son of
King David, and it is like a palace, and in front of it the waters
flow from twelve springs: each one for the cure of a particular
disease; and every man finds here a remedy for his ills, with
the help of Allah the Merciful and the Compassionate."[88]

12 / ON A ROCK OF HAMAT-GADER

On the margin of the Jordan Valley, in the narrow gorge
of the river Yarmuk, stream the hot springs of Hamath-
Gader, *El-Hamme*—"Hot Baths," in Arabic. The place is
named after the town of Gader, or Gadara, which was situated on the ridge of the surrounding range of hills. Today, the
small village of Um-Keis stands in its place, beyond the frontier, in Transjordan.

A winding path, following the remains of an ancient road,
leads up the steep slope to Gader. The ascent of the mount
is strewn with many large and high rocks.

Hebrew legend has a tale about Hadrian, the Roman emperor who quelled the Jewish rebellion of Bar-Kokhba with great cruelty.

It is said that once, when Hadrian was traveling up the ascent to Hamath-Gader, he saw a young girl on the top of a cliff. He asked her, "Who art thou?"

She answered, "I am a daughter of Israel!"

Immediately, he alighted from his carriage and bowed low to her. His suite, the high commanders of the Empire, were angered at this, and said, "Why didst thou humiliate thyself and bow to this despicable, soiled, and filthy one?"

He replied, "Fools! Indeed, in the future, all the nations of the world will bow to them."[89]

13 / A CUSTOM PRACTICED IN GOVAT-SHAMAI

Hebrew legend mentions a village by the name of Govat-Shamai. Presumably it was located in the northern part of the Jordan Valley, on the banks of the river, at the site of the Arab village of Ubeidiye.

It is told that a young student was once sitting in front of his master, Rabbi Yose, in the town Zippori.

Rabbi Yose discoursed, but the student did not understand.

Asked the Rabbi, "Why dost thou not understand?"

Said the pupil, "I am a stranger here."

Asked the Rabbi, "Whence comest thou?"

Said the pupil, "From Govat-Shamai."

Asked the Rabbi, "And wherein lies the difference?"

Said the pupil, "When a child is born, we crush cherries and we smear the scalp of his head with them so that the mosquitoes shall not bite him."

Said the Rabbi, "Blessed be the Almighty who graceth each place with its own characteristics!"[90]

VIII

NAZARETH AND TABOR

1 / THE ORIGIN OF THE NAME NAZARETH

Nazareth is first mentioned in the New Testament with the appearance of Jesus, who is known as "the Nazarene." This became the general name given to his followers, and to this day, "Christian" is *Nozri* in Hebrew and *Nasrani* in Arabic.

The origin and meaning of the name Nazareth are unknown. In Christian tradition, it derives from the Hebrew *nezer*, meaning "twig," as the word is used in Isaiah's prophecy: "And there shall come forth a shoot out of the stock of Jesse, "And a twig shall grow forth out of his roots."

The Christian interpretation of these verses is that Isaiah was referring to the advent of Jesus. According to the New Testament, Jesus was descended from the House of Jesse, the father of King David.

In Hebrew literature, Nazareth is spelled "Nazrat," and is first mentioned by Eliezer Hakalir, a Jewish poet who lived in Galilee about the seventh century C.E.[91]

FIG. 26. NAZARETH ABOUT THE YEAR 1660

2 / THE PRIESTLY FAMILY IN NAZARETH

The sons of the family of Happizzez were servants of the Lord in the Great Temple of Jerusalem. Their name is mentioned in First Chronicles: "According to their ordering in their service . . . the eighteenth [lot came forth] to Happizzez."

After the destruction of the Temple, many priestly families wandered to Galilee, and the Happizzez settled in Nazareth. Recently, their name was given to one of the mountains that surround the city.[92]

3 / THE SYNAGOGUE-CHURCH OF NAZARETH

In the heart of ancient Nazareth, close by a narrow market lane, stands a church of the Greek Catholics. On the side, a few steps lead down to an older building known as the Synagogue-Church, for, according to tradition, on this site a Jewish House of Prayer existed in Jesus' lifetime.

A Christian traveler of the year 570 C.E. described the Hebrew inhabitants of Nazareth and, telling of his pilgrimage to the holy places of the town, he added, "In the synagogue there is still the book from which the Lord [Jesus] was set to learn the alphabet. In the synagogue, too, is the bench upon which Jesus used to sit with the other children. Only Christians can lift it. Jews can not stir it by any means; nor does it permit itself to be carried out of doors. The traveler concluded his description of Nazareth with the words, "In this town, the charm of the Hebrew women is such that in the whole of the country one cannot find Hebrew women of greater beauty."

Legend tells of other cases where restraints are imposed on the followers of various faiths.

The German pilgrim, Ludolphus of Suchem, who came to the Holy Land in the year 1350 C.E., wrote: "Not far from Joppa there stands a fair city, once called Ruma but now called Bael, situated in a most beauteous, pleasant and delectable place, and inhabited by Christians alone. It is believed that no Jew or Saracen could dwell therein for more than a year." The implication is that any Jew or Moslem who would be so foolhardy as to settle in Bael would not survive the year.

The English traveler Edward Webbe, who visited Jerusalem about 1583, has a different tale with a similar sentiment. He writes: "In the land of Siria, there is a river wherein no Jew can get or catch any fish at all, and yet in the same river there is a great store of fish like unto salmon trouts; but let a Christian or a Turk come hither and fish for them, either of them shall catch them in great abundance; if they put their hand into the water with a little bread, a hundred will be about their hand."[93]

FIG. 27. SYNAGOGUE-CHURCH IN NAZARETH

4 / THE CHURCH THAT SAILED IN THE AIR

Most renowned among the churches of the Holy Land is the Church of the Annunciation, in Nazareth. According to

Christian tradition, on this spot the Virgin Mary received from the angel Gabriel this message: "Hail, thou that art highly favored, the Lord is with thee: blessed art thou among women. And, behold, thou shalt conceive in thy womb, and bring forth a son, and shalt call his name Jesus. He shall be called the Son of the Highest."

FIG. 28. CHURCH OF ANNUNCIATION IN NAZARETH
This eighteenth-century bas-relief, now in the Museum of Cluny, in Paris, shows the church being borne aloft on the wings of angels.

Today's magnificent church is built on the foundation of an ancient basilica, of which the following story is told: When the Moslems wrested Nazareth from the hands of the Crusaders, in 1263, they proposed to turn this church into a mosque. When their intention became clear, angels came down from the heavens, took hold of the church at its four corners, lifted it onto their wings, and carried it far away beyond the seas. The church was finally set down in Dalmatia, in the Balkans. Three years later, it was transported to the Italian side of the Adriatic Sea.

To this day, the church still stands in the small village of Loreto, near Ancona, where it is much revered by the population. The village is also known as Nazareth de Italia and the church as Santa Casa—the Holy House.[94]

5 / THE COLUMN OF ST. MARY

From the ceiling of St. Mary's Grotto, within the Church of the Annunciation, hangs the fragment of a granite pillar. Traditionally, it indicates the spot where the Virgin stood when she received the message of the angel Gabriel: "And the angel said unto her, Fear not, Mary: for thou hast found favor with God. And behold, thou shalt conceive in thy womb, and bring forth a son, and shalt call his name Jesus."

The story is told of a greedy Turkish pasha who broke this column in the hope of finding in it hidden treasure. To punish this desecration he was instantly struck blind.

Supernatural powers are attributed to the remnant. Christians rub their backs against it, trusting that this will cure them of all their aches and pains.[95]

6 / THE LEAP OF THE LORD—MOUNT OF THE PRECIPICE

A steep ridge hanging high over the fields of the Valley of Jezreel stands out among the mountains of Nazareth. The Christians call it *Mons Saltus Domini*—the Leap of the Lord.

According to the tale, Jesus leaped from the top of this peak to escape his pursuers, as told in the Gospel: "And he [Jesus] came to Nazareth, where he had been brought up: and, as his custom was, he went into the synagogue on the Sabbath day, and stood up for to read. . . . And all they in the synagogue, when they heard these things, were filled with wrath, and rose up, and thrust him out of the city, and led him unto the brow of the hill whereon their city was built, that they might cast him down headlong. But he passing through the midst of them went his way."

According to medieval pilgrims, here also was the stone on which he fell, and on which he left the imprint of his feet and hands.

A variation of the tale reads as follows: "The figure of Jesus may be seen to this day imprinted as though on soft wax upon the rock through which he passed."[96]

FIG. 29. CHURCH OF "MENSA CHRISTI"—TABLE OF CHRIST

7 / MENSA CHRISTI—TABLE OF CHRIST

In the old quarter of Nazareth, a tortuous narrow lane ascends to a small church hidden among the houses. It was built in 1860 by the Franciscan Order to cover and protect an enormous rock about twelve feet long, a foot wide, and three feet high, which almost fills the church. This rock is holy to Christians, for according to tradition Jesus ate here with his disciples after the Resurrection, wherefore it is called *Mensa Christi*—Table of Christ.

A spring, close by, which has given out only a thread of water since the earthquake of 1837, is called "the Fountain of the Apostles."

The Italian monk Franciscus Quaresmi, who spent several years in the Holy Land at the beginning of the seventeenth century, was the first to mention *Mensa Christi* and the nearby *Fons Aquae Vivae*—the Fount of Living Waters.[97]

8 / A MOSLEM TRAVELER IN NAZARETH

The Moslem traveler al-Masudi, who visited the Holy Land in the year 943 C.E., reported this about Nazareth: "I myself have seen in this village a church greatly venerated by the Christians. There are here sarcophagi of stone, in which are dead men's bones, and from these flow a thick oil, like syrup, with which the Christians anoint themselves for a blessing."[98]

9 / THE PRIESTLY FAMILY IN KEFAR-KANNA

Kefar-Kanna—Cana of Galilee of the Gospel—stands near Nazareth, on the highway to Tiberias. It is sacred to the Christians, for here Jesus performed his first miracle—the turning of water into wine, as related in the Gospels. The domes of two churches stand out among the small houses of the Arab villagers.

FIG. 30. KEFAR-KANNA—CANA OF GALILEE

Among the numerous pilgrims who set their faces to the holy places of Galilee was Antoninus Martyr, in 570

C.E., who mentioned Cana (Chana): ". . . where our Lord was at the wedding, and we reclined upon His very couch, upon which I, unworthy that I am, wrote the names of my parents."

After the destruction of Jerusalem, Kefar-Kanna became the refuge of the priestly family of Eliashib, whose sons had served in the Great Temple; from that time on they were known as the "Wardens of Kanna."⁹⁹

10 / THE CAVE OF MELCHIZEDEK ON MOUNT TABOR

After the patriarch Abraham smote his enemies he returned to his tents. "And," says the Bible, "Melchizedek king of Salem brought forth bread and wine; and he was priest of God the Most High. And he blessed him, and said: 'Blessed be Abram of God Most High, Maker of heaven and earth.' "

Melchizedek was king of Jerusalem, then called Salem (Peace), and although it is clearly stated that the meeting place of Abraham and Melchizedek was in the Valley of the King, whose location is unknown, a medieval legend holds that they met on Mount Tabor.

To this day, on the slope of Mount Tabor, there is to be found the cave where Melchizedek lived when Abraham came to him. The Russian pilgrim Abbot Daniel, who visited the Holy Land in the year 1106 C.E., recounted this tradition: "They show you upon Mount Tabor, at a level place, an extraordinary cave cut in the rock, like a cellar, which has a small window in the roof. At the bottom of the cave toward the east there is an altar. The door of the cave is very small, and you descend by steps from the west side. Small fig trees grow in front of the entrance, and around them are other kinds of trees; there was formerly a large forest there, but now there are only small shrubs. The holy Melchizedek dwelt in this small cave, and there Abraham visited him and called him three times, saying, 'Man of God!' There Melchizedek blessed Abraham who cut his hair and nails, for Melchizedek was hairy."

A Samaritan tradition has it that Melchizedek served as high-priest in their temple on Mount Gerizim; in that vicinity, according to their view, is the true location of Salem, on the site of the present Arab village Salim. Wherefore the Samaritans conclude that Abraham the Patriarch met Melchizedek on Mount Gerizim.

FIG. 31. MOUNT TABOR (1842)

A still different version of Abraham's meeting with Melchizedek appears on a Coptic charm. Thus it reads: "The prayer of the bread. The Lord God spoke to the Patriarch Abraham: 'Arise, take thee bread, wine, water, and an iron vessel, go up upon Mount Tabor and call three times: "Man of God!" When Melchizedek comes out to thee.' Then Abraham the Patriarch arose, took the bread, the wine, the water, and the vessel of iron, ascended Mount Tabor."[100]

IX
ZIPPORI AND ITS VICINITY

1 / THE TOWN OF ZIPPORI

After the destruction of Jerusalem, many Jews emigrated from Judah to Galilee and settled in its towns and villages. One of its main centres was Sepphoris—Zippori, in Hebrew—in Lower Galilee, in the vicinity of Nazareth. Today, a new settlement erected on its site has restored the ancient name.

"Why was this town called Zippori—the Bird?" asked the sages of Israel. "Because Zippori is perched like a bird on the top of the mountain."

It is told: "The people of Zippori have hard hearts; they fear the word of the Law, but they do not bow down before it."

The daughters of Zippori had a reputation for great piety. They used to go up to Jerusalem to keep the Sabbath in the Great Temple and then return home, and there was no one who got up earlier than they to gather fallen figs.[101]

FIG. 32. MEDIEVAL FORT ON RUINS OF ZIPPORI

2 / PROSPEROUS ZIPPORI

Zippori was an important town of Galilee, and its large markets served all the villages of the vicinity. Said Rabbi Yossi: "I saw Zippori at the peak of its prosperity, and it had one hundred and eighty thousand markets."

The surroundings of Zippori were very fruitful. Our forefathers stated: "Sixteen miles around Zippori, this is the land flowing with milk and honey."

It is told of Rabbi Yossi that, in Zippori, he asked his son to bring down dried figs fron the attic. When the boy went up, he found the attic flooded with honey oozing from the figs.

One of the notables of Zippori married his son to a girl from Acco. On the wedding day were put up "booths for distributing wine all the way from Zippori to Acco, and gold lamps on both sides. And the crowds did not disperse until all had been fed with lentils from the threshing floor, and wine from the press."[102]

3 / RABBI JUDAH HA-NASI IN ZIPPORI

Zippori was a great center of Hebrew culture and it attracted to its academies many great scholars of Israel.

The most famous among them was Rabbi Judah Ha-Nasi (the Prince), who lived in the second century. He compiled the Mishnah—the most important treatise of Jewish Law after the Bible.

Rabbi Judah dwelt in Zippori seventeen years, and he used to quote the following verse of the Bible, applying it to himself: "And Jacob lived in the land of Egypt seventeen years."

Of the seventeen years he lived in Zippori, Rabbi Judah spent thirteen of them suffering with his teeth. Why, pray, did he suffer so with his teeth? Because once, when he was passing by, he saw a calf being slaughtered. It lowed and said to him, "Rabbi, save me!"

He replied, "For this thou wast made."

And, at the end, how did Rabbi Judah become well? He saw a nest of mice being killed, and he said, "Let them alone! For it is written [in the Psalms]: 'His tender mercies are over all His works.'

A different version of this story tells: "And at the end of thirteen years, it happened that our holy Rabbi Judah Ha-Nasi was much angered at Rabbi Hiyya the Great. And the Prophet Elijah, may his memory be blessed, came to our holy Rabbi in the guise of Rabbi Hiyya, and laid his hand on his aching tooth. Forthwith, he was cured.

"The following day Rabbi Hiyya came to Rabbi Judah and

asked, 'Rabbi! That same tooth, how is it faring?'

"He answered, 'Since you set your hand on it yesterday it is cured.'

"Said Rabbi Hiyya, 'Not I put my hand on your tooth.'

"Whereupon our holy Rabbi knew that it had been the Prophet Elijah."

Rabbi Judah died at Zippori, and not one of his pupils had the heart to announce his demise to the anxious people of the town until the clever Bar Kappara broke the news in the form of a parable, saying: "The heavenly hosts and the earthborn men held the tables of the covenant; and the heavenly hosts were victorious and seized the tables!"

In medieval times, the tomb of Rabbi Judah was shown in Zippori. The twelfth-century traveler Petahiah wrote: "At Zippori, our holy Rabbi [Judah] is buried. A pleasing odor ascends from his grave. This odor is perceptible at the distance of a mile from his grave."[103]

4 / RABBI YOSSI IN ZIPPORI

Another scholar of Zippori whose fame spread far and wide was Rabbi Yossi in the third century.

"Justice, justice shalt thou follow," says Deuteronomy. To which the sages added, "Follow Rabbi Yossi to Zippori."

When Rabbi Yossi moved his House of Study to Zippori, the following verse of the Psalms was applied to him: "Yea, the sparrow has found a house."

It was reported: "When Rabbi Yossi gave up the ghost, blood poured forth from all the drainpipes of Zippori."[104]

5 / PRIESTLY FAMILIES IN ZIPPORI

After the destruction of the Great Temple of Jerusalem, the priestly families who had served in the holy sanctuary moved to Galilee and settled in its towns and villages.

The family of Jedaiah found refuge in Zippori and was known as *Kohanei Zippori*—the Priests of Zippori. The sages referred to them in the words of the Proverb: "As a bird [*zippor*] that wandereth from her nest, So is a man that wandereth from his place." An ancient poet mourned their plight, saying, "And they wandered like birds, the priests of Zippori."[105]

6 / THE VENDOR OF THE PHILTER OF LIFE IN ZIPPORI

*"Whoso keepeth his mouth and his tongue
Keepeth his soul from troubles."*

In ancient times, Zippori was surrounded by many Jewish villages.

The sages tell the story of a street vendor, who used to tramp through the villages around Zippori crying, "Whoever wishes to buy the philter of life, let him come to me!"

Once, while Rabbi Yannai was engrossed in study, he heard the street vendor's call; he hailed him, saying, "Come up here and sell me some!" The street vendor then produced the Book of Psalms and pointed out to the learned rabbi the following verse: "Who is the man that desireth life,/And loveth days, that he may see good therein?/Keep thy tongue from evil,/And thy lips from speaking guile."[106]

7 / THE FATE OF A TAILOR FROM ZIPPORI

Justa, the tailor of Zippori, went up to court and ingratiated himself with the king.

Said the king to him, "Ask a favor of me and I will grant it!" The tailor replied, "Give me the governorship of our region."

And the king conferred it on him.

When he came to Zippori, some of those who had known

him before said, "This is the same man." But others said, "This is not the same."

One of them suggested to the others, "Observe when he passes in the street. If he looks at the tailor's stool on which he used to sit and stitch, it is the same man, but if not, it is not the same." When the governor passed in the street, he began to look at the stool on which he used to sit and stitch, and they knew that he was the same man.

He said to them, "You are astonished at me, and I am astonished at myself more than you are."

8 / MAGICIANS IN ANCIENT ZIPPORI

Rabbi Yannai relates: "I was walking in a street of Zippori and I saw a heretic take a pebble and throw it into the air, and when it came down it became a calf."

Rabbi Hanina son of Rabbi Hananiah, tells: "I was walking on the riverside at Zippori and I saw a heretic take a skull and throw it into the air, and when it came down it became a calf. I came and told my father, and he said to me, 'If thou hast eaten of it, it was a fact; but if not, it was an illusion of the eyes.' "[108]

9 / RUMA—THE ABODE OF ANTONINUS CAESAR

In the neighborhood of Zippori, in the midst of the mountains of Lower Galilee, there is a ruin that the Arabs call Rumi. It is the site of ancient Ruma, a small townlet in talmudic times. Ruma was often called Romi—the Hebrew version of Rome, the capital of the Roman Empire in olden days.

According to legend, Antoninus Caesar lived in Romi of Galilee. The famous Rabbi Judah Ha-Nasi, the most outstanding sage of his period, was on friendly terms with Antoninus Caesar, of Rome.

The sages relate that Antoninus "went to study with Rabbi

Judah every day and every night," by a secret passage that led from the quarters of one to the other's.

Rabbi Moses Alsheikh, a famous rabbi of Zefat, who wrote a commentary on the Bible in the sixteenth century, held the conviction that Antoninus Caesar lived not in Rome of Italy but in the village of Ruma next to Zippori, and he expounded his view thus: "Is it possible to believe that a vaulted cavern extended from the capital Rome to Zippori, a walk of several months and the Great Sea is between them, and that he [Antoninus] went forth and back from one to the other every night?

"And here we have seen with our own eyes, even today, next to Zippori a town named Ruma. And there was the seat of Antoninus, and he changed its name to Romi, after his own capital.

"And of this Ruma [Elijah the Prophet] said that the Messiah sits at its gate."[109]

10 / RUMA—WHERE MESSIAH WILL APPEAR

"Moses cometh forth from the desert
and the Messiah goeth forth from Ruma."

Tradition depicts the Messiah sitting in the town of Ruma, waiting for the fateful hour when the Almighty will send him forth to proclaim the redemption of Israel. Usually this is taken to refer to Rome of Italy, the capital of the Roman Empire. But a belief, widespread among the Jewish pilgrims of the Middle Ages, held that it is none other than Ruma, the neighbor of Zippori of Galilee.

Rabbi Jacob the Messenger, who toured the Holy Land in about 1228 wrote: "From Zippori you go to Ruma, where is the cave of Benjamin, the son of the Patriarch Jacob . . . and it is a tradition among the inhabitants that the Messiah will come from there."

An anonymous disciple of Nahmanides (Ramban), of the fourteenth century, who followed the same route on his pilgrimage, repeated the tale in almost identical terms: "From Zippori we went to Rumi. There is a cavern there named after Benjamin the Righteous . . . it is accepted that therefrom the Messiah shall come forth, and I am convinced by ample proof that here stood Rome the Great."

A different version appears in the book *Merit of the Patriarchs and the Prophets,* written in 1537. Of Rumi in Galilee it says: "And here there is the cavern of Chizran, from which the Messiah is expected to appear."[110]

11 / THE REAPER IN THE VALLEY OF BEIT-NETOFA

The Valley of Beit-Netofa lies among the mountains of Upper Galilee, in the vicinity of Zippori and Jotapata, the famous stronghold held by the Jews during their rebellion against Rome in the first century C.E. In olden days, the rich fertile soil of this valley sustained many flourishing Jewish villages.

It once happened that a man was standing and digging in the valley of Beit-Netofa when he saw a certain herb, which he gathered and made into a garland for his head. A snake passed by and he struck it and killed it.

A certain snake-charmer came along and halted. He looked at the snake and remarked, "I am astonished at the person who slew this snake."

The man said, "I slew him." The charmer raised his eyes and saw the herb which the man had made into a garland about his head. "Of a truth," said he to the charmer, "I slew him." The charmer asked him, "Can you lift that herb off your head?" "Yes," he answered. When he had lifted it the charmer asked him, "Can you touch the snake with this stick?" "Yes," he replied. As soon as he touched the snake his limbs at once fell to pieces.[111]

12 / HOW RABBI JOSHUA DISSUADED THE REBELS

In the days of Rabbi Joshua son of Hananiah, the Roman state ordered the Temple to be rebuilt. Pappus and Julianus set tables from Acco as far as Antioch and provided those who came up from Exile with all their needs.

Thereupon Samaritans went and warned the emperor, "Be it known now unto the king that if this city be builded and the walls finished, they will not pay tribute."

"Yet what can I do," said the Emperor, "seeing that I have already given the order?"

"Send a command to them that they must change its site or add five cubits thereto or lessen it by five cubits, and then they will withdraw from it of their own accord," came the answer.

Now the community of Israel was assembled in the valley of Beit-Rimmon; when the royal dispatches arrived, they burst out weeping and wanted to revolt against the Roman power.

Thereupon the sages decided: Let a wise man go and pacify the congregation.

They let Rabbi Joshua son of Hananiah, go, as he was a master of Scripture. So he went and harangued them: "A wild beast killed an animal and a bone stuck in his throat. Thereupon he proclaimed: 'I will reward anyone who removes it.'

"An Egyptian heron, which has a long beak, came and pulled it out and demanded his reward.

" 'Go!' the beast replied. 'You will be able to boast that you entered the lion's mouth in peace and came out in peace.' Even so, let us be satisfied that we entered into dealings with this people in peace and have emerged in peace."[112]

13 / THE ROCK OF NAILS

The Vale of Rimmon is a smaller plain branching off the Valley of Beit-Netofa. It is named for its numerous pomegranate trees—*rimon* in Hebrew. In its vicinity stands the Arab village of Kefar-Kanna, Cana of Galilee of the Gospels, renowned to this day for its luscious pomegranates.

In the talmudic period, in the second and third centuries, this area was densely populated with flourishing Jewish villages. The sages tell: Seven elderly wise men gathered in the Vale of Rimmon to declare the current year a leap year, adding the month of second Adar to its calendar. When they had completed this solemn task, wishing to leave testimony of the weighty decision made on this spot, they decided to drive nails into a rock on the site. And lo and behold! a miracle was wrought in their behalf; the rock became yielding and soft, and the nails penetrated into it as if it were pulpy dough.

Thereafter this rock was designated in Aramaic by the name *Keifa-Masmera*—Rock of the Nails.[113]

X
LOWER GALILEE

1 / THE TWO GALILEES

There is no definite boundary line between Lower Galilee in the south and Upper Galilee in the north.

The border starts at about Lake Kinneret, in the plain of Ginnosar, and runs along the mountains through the Valley of Beit-Kerem till it reaches Acco, on the shore of the Mediterranean Sea.

The hills of Lower Galilee average about five hundred meters above sea level, and their topmost summit is only five hundred and fifty-eight meters high.

The mountains of Upper Galilee rise up to twice that height, and their highest, Mount Meiron, in the vicinity of Zefat, reaches twelve hundred and eight meters.

The ancients distinguished between Upper and Lower Galilee according to the distribution of the sycamore trees in the area. They said: "Where the sycamore tree does not grow, that is Upper Galilee."

"Where the sycamore tree does grow, that is Lower Galilee."

In our day, there is little left of the sycamore trees in

Lower Galilee. A few isolated specimens, of great age, grew until lately in the environs of Haifa.

The ancient town of Shikmona was named after the sycamore tree—*shikma,* in Hebrew. Today it is but a mound of ruins on the sea coast of Haifa.[114]

2 / USHA—THE SEAT OF THE DIVINE PROVIDENCE

Usha, a village on the lower reaches of the mountains of Galilee, perpetuates the name of ancient Usha, an important center of learning and the abode of great sages in the talmudic period.

During the second century, the Sanhedrin, the Supreme Court of Israel, held its sittings in Usha on several occasions. It is said: "The Sanhedrin wandered from Jerusalem to Yavneh [in Judah], and from Yavneh to Usha, and from Usha to Yavneh, and from Yavneh to Usha."

The disciples of Rabbi Haim ben Attar described their travels with their famous teacher in the holy places of Galilee, and they said: "And we went up to Usha and found her in ruins because of our many sins. And we were shown the place of the Great Sanhedrin when it sat here, and it was called the Place of the Divine Providence."[115]

3 / THE WONDROUS CAVERN OF CABUL

In medieval times, the tombs of the great commentator Abraham ibn Ezra and the famous poets Judah Halevi and Solomon ibn Gabirol were said to be in Cabul.

Several Jewish pilgrims mention Cabul and its extraordinary cavern.

Rabbi Yosef Sofer, who visited this site in 1762, wrote: "And I was there and I prayed on all the graves. Next to the town of Cabul there is a very deep cave. And on the night of Tisha be-Av [the ninth of the month of Av—the day of the destruction of the Temple], a great wailing comes out of this place, and no one knows what its nature is."

Rabbi Haim Horowitz, a traveler of about the year 1830, told: "I shall sing to the Lord, blessed be He, who has granted me the privilege of being in the said village [Cabul]. When I visited all the holy tombs of the famous sages, and while I prayed there at eventide on the graves of Rabbi ibn Ezra and Rabbi Solomon ibn Gabirol, may their memory be blessed, an old Arab told me in good faith the following story:

"The cave that is near the grave of ibn Gabirol reaches to Jerusalem. He said that it was customary to kindle a lamp of oil every evening at the mouth of this cave, in honor of these holy men. Every year, however, on the eve of Tishah be-Av, the memorial day of the destruction of the Temple, it is impossible to kindle the lamp, for it goes out the moment it is lit, and if you put your ear to the mouth of the cave, you can hear a dreadful noise, which makes the hair of the listeners rise. This Gentile swears on his oath that his father told him this in the name of his father, and all people agree that it is true.

"May the Lord restore the ruins and turn our grief into joy and bring relief to our sorrow soon in our days, Amen."[116]

4 / WHY WAS CABUL DESTROYED?

*"And the fifth lot came out for the tribe of the
children of Asher according to their families . . .
and reached to Zebulun . . . and it went out to
Cabul on the left hand."*

On the mountains of Lower Galilee, which overlook the plain of Zebulun, is to be found the Arab village of Cabul. In former days, Cabul was in the territory of Asher, whose sons inherited all this region known in the Bible as the land of Cabul.

Cabul was among the cities given by King Solomon to King Hiram of Tyre, in recompense for his help in building the Temple: "Then King Solomon gave Hiram twenty cities in the land of Galilee. And Hiram came out from Tyre to see the cities which Solomon had given him: and they pleased him not. And he said: 'What cities are these which thou hast given me, my brother?' And they were called the land of Cabul, unto this day."

The talmudic scholars were perplexed by the name Cabul and explained it in various ways. Some related it to the Hebrew *cabel*—tied all round. Others derived it from *cabla*—ankle.

"Why is it called the land of Cabul?" Said Rabbi Huna: "Because its inhabitants were wrapped [*mekubal*, in Hebrew] in silver and gold and therefore they found no favor in the eyes of Hiram, King of Tyre, for they were wealthy and were not used to work."

Rabbi Nahman son of Isaac, said of the land of Cabul: "It is a sandy and salty land, and one's foot is entangled in the sandy soil up to the ankleband, wherefore its name."

Rashi, the famous commentarian, added: "Land of Cabul —land of bonds—a land of mud in which the foot sinks and becomes bound."

The town of Cabul was well known in the time of the Mishnah and the Talmud. It had a large Jewish population, and was the home of several famous scholars. The priestly family of Shecaniah, servants of the Temple, moved to Cabul after the destruction of Jerusalem.

According to legend, Cabul was one of the three villages in Galilee whose books registering the contributions to the Great Temple were so huge that special carts had to draw them to Jerusalem.

And why was it destroyed? "Because of quarrels and dissensions."[117]

5 / THE FERTILITY OF ANCIENT SIKHNIN

The Arab village of Sikhnin, in Lower Galilee, has preserved the memory of the Jewish townlet of the same name, whose site it occupies.

In olden days, Sikhnin was an important Jewish center, renowned for the fertility of its surroundings.

About Moses' words: "And He made him to suck honey out of the crag," the sages expound: "As in Sikhnin and its neighboring settlements."

"Once, Rabbi Judah said to his son in Sikhnin, 'Go up and bring us dried figs from the barrel.'

"He went up to the attic, stretched his hand to the barrel and found it full of honey. He called out, 'Father, it is [full] of honey!'

"Said the father, 'Dip your hand deeper and bring up the figs!' "

"Once, Rabbi Eliezer went to Sikhnin and found a goat crouching under a fig tree, and the milk pouring out of the goat and the honey dripping from the tree mixed together. 'This,' he exclaimed, 'is truly the land flowing with milk and honey!' "[118]

6 / WHY WAS SIKHIN DESTROYED?

In the vicinity of Zippori, in Lower Galilee, there was a townlet called Sikhin. It probably owed its name to the numerous pits—*sikhin*, in Hebrew—which dotted the ground around it.

Apparently Sikhin stood in the fruitful valley of Beit-Netofa, on the mound named, in Arabic, *Tel Bedawiye.* To this day, ruins of the ancient town are strewn on the top of the hillock.

After the destruction of Jerusalem, following a general movement of population, the priestly families which had ministered in the Temple wandered north and settled in Galilee. One of these, the well-known Jeshebeab, mentioned in Chronicles as the fourteenth watch, took up its abode in Sikhin. It is said that though they formed the smallest watch of priests, they contributed eighty-five thousand young men to the service of the Temple.

To illustrate the fertility of the area, the story was told of a three-boughed mustard plant that grew in Sikhin. One branch broke down and was used to build the roof of a booth where pottery was made. And from that one piece, it was said, three measures of seeds of mustard were taken out.

Legend adds that at the time when the Holy Temple stood in Jerusalem: "There were eighty carts made of iron in Sikhin." Said Rabbi Yannai, in the third century, "In our days there is not one."

It is also told that in Sikhin there was kept a list of all the donations to the Great Temple made by the inhabitants, and when the volume was completed, it was ceremoniously conveyed to Jerusalem in a metal cart.

And why was Sikhin destroyed? Because of the witchcraft that prevailed in its midst.[119]

7 / THE STONE OF HANINAH

Amid the mountains of Galilee, by the village of Arabah, which is in the Valley of Zebulun, the shepherd Haninah, the son of Dosa, used to pasture his flock. He was famed far and wide for his great piety.

Once, as he sat on a stone, his sheep scattered around, he thought to himself, All the men of the village take offerings up to the Temple of God save me, poor shepherd that I am! And he rose, and said, "I dedicate to the house of our Lord this stone on which I sat and thought, and I myself shall take it thither!"

So he hewed out the stone, shaped and polished it, and

then cried out joyfully, "Here is my gift! Now I must take it up to the city of my fathers." But the stone was far too heavy for him to carry alone, so he sought to hire laborers to aid him.

Five men chanced to pass by, and he said to them, "Will ye carry this stone up to Jerusalem?" They answered, "Aye, for fifty dinars." But as he had no money with which to pay them the men went their way.

Then the Holy One, blessed be He, sent five angels in the likeness of men to Haninah. And he said to them, "Will ye take this stone up to Jerusalem?" They answered, "For five dinars, if you but set your hand to aid us." He lent a hand and found himself standing in Jerusalem with them, but when he went to pay them they had disappeared.

The stone of Haninah used to stand in the forecourt of the Temple, but when one of the later Hasmonean monarchs wished to build a new wall to protect the Holy City, he used the stone as a foundation.

When you go forth from the Damascus Gate of Jerusalem, you will see by the wayside a well-cut stone from the third wall. This is probably the stone of Haninah, son of Dosa, the Galilean shepherd.[120]

8 / THE PIOUS WOMEN OF TIRAN

Between Tiberias and Nazareth, in the mountains of Lower Galilee, lies the Arab village named Turan. This is undoubtedly the site of the ancient Jewish settlement of Tiran, whose women were famed for their piety.

When the lover of the Song of Songs exclaimed: "Thou art beautiful, O my beloved, as Tirzah," it was said that this referred to the women of Tiran. The women of Tiran were virtuous, and made up their minds not to give their rings to "the [cult of the golden] calf" that the sinful Israelites put up in Sinai during the wanderings.

At least, it was said, this would have been their determination if they had belonged to the "generation of the desert" who roamed through the wilderness on the way from Egypt to the Promised Land.[121]

9 / FROM YAMA TO TIGNI (TIGNA)

In ancient times, in Lower Galilee, at the site of today's Yavneel, there prospered a village named Yama. Yama was a large Jewish townlet, the birthplace of several renowned scholars who were named after their hometown: Rabbi Shimon of Yama, Rabbi Joshua of Yama, and others.

In the vicinity of Yama stood a hamlet named Tigni, or Tigna. Because of this proximity, a saying was born. When a Galilean wished to indicate a short distance, he would say "from Yama to Tigni." This expression appears several times in talmudic literature.

At the end of the tenth century, Rabbi Hananel expounded: "From Yama to Tigna—these are two places set near each other."[122]

10 / WHY IS BEIT-KESHET SO NAMED?

Kibbutz Beit-Keshet—House of the Bow—in Lower Galilee, lies at the foot of Mount Tabor. It was the first settlement established by the Palmah units that played such a decisive part in the War of Liberation of Israel, in 1948. The name Palmah is a contraction of the Hebrew *Pelugot Mahatz*— Striking Forces.

The settlers called their village after the bow, for this weapon already symbolized the defense of Israel in olden days. When King Saul and his son Jonathan were killed on Mount Gilboa, David, lamenting their death, said, "to teach the sons of Judah the bow."

Beit-Keshet was established in 1944 at the time of the

British Mandate in Palestine. It was the base of the Palmah at which young men were trained in the art of war. The authorities kept a wary eye on these young fighters and scrutinized all their activities.

Once, the English governor of Galilee was received at Beit-Keshet. His suspicions were aroused by the large number of sturdy youths strolling about the settlement. He turned to the secretary of the kibbutz and asked pointedly: "Why was the name 'House of the Bow' chosen for this place?"

The young man answered composedly, "Lift up your eyes to Mount Tabor. Does not its beautiful rounded shape standing out against the clear horizon remind one of the arch of some giant bow?"

"But why are they called 'Palmah'?" pressed the governor.

" 'Palmah' stands for the initials of the Hebrew Pelugot Le'ezrat Meshakim Haklaiyim—Contingents for the Help of Agricultural Villages," was the immediate reply.[123]

XI

THE SEA OF GALILEE (KINNERET)

1 / WHY IS IT CALLED KINNERET?

The Sea of Galilee—*Kinneret,* in Hebrew—lies amidst the softly rounded mountains of Galilee and Golan. It is the most beautiful and the most blessed of all the seas of the Holy Land.

And why is it called "Kinneret"? Because its shape is like that of the harp—in Hebrew, *kinnor.* Some say that the music of its waves is as sweet to the ear as the song of the harp.

The ancients gave another explanation: "Kinneret," they said, "stems from the Hebrew *kinnara*—a species of sweet fruit, today unknown, which grew in plenty on the shores of the lake."

According to legend, the Sea of Galilee is favored by the Lord God above all others. "Said the Almighty: I have created seven seas and of them all I have chosen for myself only the Sea of Galilee."

Similarly, the Ancients stated: "Seven lands did the Almighty, blessed be He, create, and of them all, he chose only the Land of Israel for his own, as it is said, 'For the land, whither thou goest in to possess it . . . the eyes of the Lord thy God are always upon it, from the beginning of the year even unto the end of the year.' "[124]

2 / HOW THE SEA OF GALILEE WAS CREATED

Before the world was created, a tiny little lake hovered in space. It was the lake which is now called the Sea of Galilee, or the Lake of Tiberias, after the town which is on its shores.

FIG. 33. SEA OF GALILEE AND SNOW-CAPPED HERMON

And the day came when God Almighty passed over this lake and He saw the great bird Satanel swimming in its blue waters. And God said to him, "Who are thou?" "I am God," Satanel answered proudly. "And if thou art God, who am I?" asked the Lord of the Universe. "Thou art God of the gods and Lord of the lords," said Satanel. And the Lord of the Universe said to Satanel, "Dive down into the waters and bring up earth and flint." And he did so. And God strewed the earth round Kinneret, and thus dry land was created; and He took the flint and struck upon it with all His might so that sparks flew from it. From these sparks were created angels, who are the servants of the Almighty.

And when Satanel saw the omnipotence of the Almighty, he wished to imitate His deeds. But the Lord was so angered that He took away from his name the end letters, *el*—God—and called him "Satan," the source of all the evil in the world.[125]

3 / THE TASTE OF THE FISH OF KINNERET

In the Sea of Galilee—Kinneret—live many kinds of fish, some of which are very tasty. It is said that the Leviathan, the gigantic whale which is to be prepared in Paradise for the repast of the righteous, will taste like the fish in the Sea of Galilee, or the Sea of Tiberias, as the ancients called it.

In the time to come, "The Almighty, blessed be He, will remove the skin of the Leviathan and make therefrom a tabernacle to shelter those who serve Him.

"And," continues the legend, "those who have faithfully fullfilled My laws and commandments shall come and eat of its head, which tastes like the head of the fish in the Sea of Tiberias."*[126]

* See *Legends of Jerusalem,* p. 137.

4 / WHO HAD FISHING RIGHTS IN LAKE KINNERET?

Lake Kinneret was in the inheritance of the Tribe of Naphtali, and its sons settled around its shores.

Moses blessed Naphtali, saying, "O Naphtali, satisfied with favor,/And full with the blessing of the Lord:/Possess thou the sea and the south."

The sages explained: "Satisfied with favor"—that is with seas, fish, and boats. "The Sea"—that is the Sea of Somhi (Hula).* "And the South"—that is (the sea) of Tiberias.

Fishing rights over the whole surface of the Sea of Tiberias were reserved for the children of Naphtali. The other tribes were "permitted to fish with an angle . . . provided that no sail is spread, as this would detain boats. It is, however, permitted to fish by means of nets and traps." Our rabbis taught that the tribes stipulated at the outset that nobody should spread a sail and thus detain boats. It was, however, permitted to fish by means of nets and traps. The Sea of Tiberias was included in the portion of Naphtali. In addition, he received a rope's length of dry land on the southern side to keep nets on, in fulfillment of the verse: "Possess thou the sea and the south."[127]

5 / THE WELL OF MIRIAM IN THE KINNERET

It is written: "The people strove with Moses, and said: 'Give us water that we may drink!' . . . And the people thirsted there for water; and the people murmured against Moses, and said: 'Wherefore hast thou brought us up out of Egypt, to kill us and our children and our cattle with thirst?' And Moses cried unto the Lord, saying: 'What shall I do unto this people? they are almost ready to stone me.' And the Lord said unto Moses: 'Pass on before the people, and take with thee of the elders of Israel; and thy rod. . . . Behold, I

* See legend XIX:7.

will stand before thee there upon the rock in Horeb [the mountains of Sinai]; and thou shalt smite the rock, and there shall come water out of it, that the people may drink.' And Moses did so in the sight of the elders of Israel."

While wandering on their way to Canaan, the tribes of Israel stationed in a place called Beer—in Hebrew, well. And the Bible tells: "That is the well whereof the Lord said unto Moses: 'Gather the people together, and I will give them water.' Then sang Israel this song: Spring up, O well—sing ye unto it—/The well, which the princes digged,/Which the nobles of the people delved,/With the scepter, and with their staves."

FIG. 34. WELL OF MIRIAM (1859)
In the center, Miriam's Well with water pouring out of it. The translation of the Hebrew legend surrounding it reads: "This is the shape of the Well of Miriam within the Sea of Tiberias. It appears in the morning before sunrise."

This well was named after Miriam, the sister of Moses. It is said that it was already brought into being on the sixth day of Creation—one of the ten things created by the Almighty on the eve of the Sabbath, in the twilight—but it only appeared to the Children of Israel during the Vicissitudes of

Exodus. It journeyed in front of the tribes as they wandered in the wilderness. It climbed the mountains with them, and with them went down into the valleys. Where Israel rested, there rested the well, opposite the entrance of the Tent of Meeting.

When the people needed water, the leaders of Israel came round it with their staves and sang the song of the well. The water then bubbled and rose like a pillar, and each chieftain of a tribe held his staff, made a channel to his camp, and the water flowed like mighty rivers.

When the children of Israel came to the land of Canaan— "A good land, a land of streams of water, of founts and deeps coming forth in cleft and mount"—they paid no further attention to Miriam's Well, and it disappeared into the Sea of Kinneret.

"If you wish to see it," say the sages, "climb the mountain Yeshimon (which rises above Tiberias), and look down upon the blue waters of the Sea. On the coast, you will see a sort of sieve; there Miriam's Well sank."

In bygone years, Jews showed the tomb of Miriam next to Tiberias, and pilgrims used to come and prostrate themselves upon it.[128]

6 / THE MERITS OF MIRIAM'S WELL

Many curing powers were attributed to the waters of Miriam's well, which sank in Lake Kinneret.

Sages of Israel tell of a man afflicted with boils who bathed in the lake. It so happened that the hour was propitious; he encountered the Well of Miriam and came out cured of his affliction.

The Cabalists, the mystics of Israel, also attributed special significance to the water of Miriam's Well. Rabbi Haim Vital, the foremost disciple of Ha-Ari, the holy leader of the Cabalists of Zefat (Safed) in the sixteenth century, related: "When

I, Haim, came as a youth to my master, blessed be his memory, to learn from him the hidden mysteries [Cabala], he brought me to Tiberias, and into a small boat on the sea; he gave me from its water to drink. Then he told me: 'Behold, now you are prepared to grasp the secrets of the Cabala; you drank from the Well of Miriam the prophetess.' "[129]

7 / MIRIAM'S WELL WANDERS IN THE DIASPORA

Rabbi Yitzhak Taub, who died in the year 1821, was a famous rabbi in the town of Galup, in Hungary; he was outstanding among the leaders of the Hasidim and famous for his contribution to Hasidic melodies, which play such an important part in Hasidic ritual and ceremonials.

A Hasidic story relates that Rabbi Yitzhak was deemed worthy to dip himself in the Well of Miriam, which was revealed to him in a vision while he was at his prayers in his hometown.

Once, toward evening, as the congregation was assembling in the synagogue just before the recitation of Kol Nidre, the opening prayer for the Day of Atonement, the suppliants, attired for the occasion, were in the traditional prayer shawls and white robes weeping bitterly when Rabbi Yitzhak suddenly arose, and above the din of the worshipers, called Rabbi Yaakov Fish and said to him, "Rabbi Yaakov, go at once, harness your horse, as I wish to go for a ride." Rabbi Yaakov was startled, but said nothing, as he knew his rabbi well. He went at once, fetched his horse and wagon, and the two men proceeded to the outskirts of the town, toward the fields of Rabbi Yaakov, where they found a small pool of water. Immediately, the holy man removed his garments and dipped himself several times.

Rabbi Yaakov stood gazing as if transfixed, not knowing what to do. In the meantime, the holy man hurriedly dressed, and in no time at all, the two were on their way back to the synagogue, where they inconspicuously began their prayers as if nothing had happened.

But Rabbi Yaakov could not stop wondering, because he knew there was not even so much as the tiniest water hole in his fields.

On the night of Atonement Day, after the breaking of the fast, Rabbi Yaakov went to his field to find the pool that his own eyes had seen the day before but, search as he would, he found nothing.

Rabbi Yaakov went directly to Rabbi Yitzhak and said to him: "Rabbi, as you know, despite our long friendship I never mix into your affairs, but I beg you to enlighten me about the pool of water that appeared and disappeared so mysteriously in my fields."

The holy man replied, smiling, "If Rabbi Yaakov had the sense, he would have dipped himself the same as I did, for at that moment, Miriam's Well passed by."[130]

8 / THE BUCKET OF MIRIAM

The anonymous disciple of Nahmanides, one of the outstanding rabbis of the thirteenth century, related his visit to Tiberias and its surroundings. He wrote: "We went to Kefar-Hittim. There is the grave of Jethro, Moses' father-in-law, and on it stands a handsome building, and near the place there is a spring whose waters fall from the top of the mount within the crevices of a large rock, and one does not see them. And the water makes a noise as if it were dropping into a copper basin. It is told that this is Miriam's bucket. But that is unlikely, for Miriam never entered the Land of Israel during her lifetime."

The spring described here is probably the same one that emerges to this day near the tomb of a-Nabi Shueib, the Arab name for Jethro.

An ancient legend places the well of Miriam within the Sea

of Galilee, and her tomb near the shore of the lake, on the ascent of a hill over which the path leading to Kefar-Hittim winds its way.[131]

9 / FROM THE HOLY OF HOLIES TO THE SEA OF GALILEE

Describing Jerusalem redeemed at the end of time, the prophet Zechariah exclaims: "And it shall come to pass in that day,/That living waters shall go out from Jerusalem." Legend adds: "[These waters] shall flow to the Sea of Tiberias to heal its waters." The Sea of Tiberias is the talmudic name of Lake Kinneret.

The prophet Ezekiel says of the same waters: "These waters issue forth toward the eastern region, and shall go down into the Arabah; and when they shall enter into the sea, into the sea of the putrid waters, the waters shall be healed." Legend expounds: "This is the Sea of Tiberias."[132]

10 / THE ARCH OF THE COVENANT IN LAKE KINNERET

An Arab legend of medieval times describes the Arch of the Covenant, known in Arabian tradition as "the Arch of the Divine Providence," as hidden at the bottom of Lake Kinneret, deep within the earth. The Moslems hold that the tomb of King Solomon is also concealed there and, some add, the tomb of King David as well.

At the end of time, the Messiah, who in Arab lore is called *el-Mahdi*, meaning "the Led One," because He will be guided by Almighty God Himself, will appear. Forthwith He will bring again to light the "Arch of the Divine Providence," make Jerusalem the capital of the world, and, in the Temple built anew in all its splendor, he will set up again the Arch of the Lord.[133]

11 / THE ROCK OF THE ANTS

Close by the shore of Lake Kinneret, between Tiberias and Migdal (ancient Magdala), a solitary rock rises out of the water.

In former times, when the strand was broader than it is now, this rock was part of the mainland, and a nest of ants thrived upon it. These ants lived their peaceful lives and knew naught of evil.

But one day misfortune fell on them. A great storm began to rage; the waves of the lake lashed the shore, tore away the earth around the rock, and it became a tiny island. The endangered ants left on the rock scurried and turned in all directions, looking for a way to reach the shore. Moreover, they had no food, and they longed desperately for the main-

FIG. 35. ROCK OF THE ANTS IN SEA OF GALILEE

land that beckoned to them nearby. So they turned in prayer to the Lord of the Universe, begging Him to heed their distress and put them on dry land.

By the shore grew long reeds which, on hearing the ants' prayers, felt pity and agreed among themselves to deliver their diligent neighbors from their peril. And the tall reeds bowed down till their heads reached the rock, and they became bridges whereon the ants passed with great joy to the safety of the mainland.

And since then the rock has been called the Rock of the Ants.

The ancients told of a rock named *Shen Shel Teveriya*—the Tooth of Tiberias—which, according to them, was similar to the stone put up by the Patriarch Jacob: "And Jacob took a stone, and set it up for a pillar."

Possibly the Tooth of Tiberias is none other than the Rock of the Ants.[134]

12 / WHEN WILL LAKE KINNERET BE DRIED UP?

When the time of the Messiah draws near, tells the Hebrew legend, this is when Gog and Magog will appear: "And they will besiege Jerusalem seven days and one-half day and they will conquer Jerusalem."

Following Gog and Magog, many and various nations will proceed to Jerusalem to wage war. On their way, they will be divided into three groups. To quench their thirst, the first group will drink up all the waters of Kinneret. The third group will tread on the dry bottom of the sea and wonder, Was there ever water here?

And under the heavy march of the multitudes and the hoofs of their horses the rocks of the mountains will crumble into dust.

Arab legend, too, lengthily describes the wars of Gog and Magog—*Yajuj wa-Majuj*. Their multitudes will camp on the shores of Lake Kinneret and drink all its waters, and from there they will proceed to Jerusalem. After many cruel wars, they will be killed there with all their hordes.[135]

13 / THE MIRACULOUS STREAM OF THE JORDAN

The River Jordan falls into Lake Kinneret at its northern end.

Since it comes down with force through a steep, rocky gorge, its path can be discerned a long way within the lake. Our forefathers believed that the waters of the Jordan, flowing incessantly day and night, never mingled with those of Lake Kinneret.

During a scholarly debate, Rabbi Yonah, head of a study house in Tiberias, exclaimed, "Do not wonder thereat, for lo! the Jordan passes through the Lake of Tiberias yet does not mingle with it. The thing is indeed miraculous!"

Naphtali Imber, the well-known composer of *Hatikvah*, the Israel national anthem, compares the Jordan to the people of Israel, who wander among the nations and yet do not mingle with them, as the Jordan passes through Lake Kinneret without mingling its waters with those of the lake, and thus he writes: "To Lake Kinneret, with a roar, / The Jordan enters lonely, / Its waters do not mingle, / And proudly it steers its way through. / So my wandering people Israel, / Who settles in all countries, / But yet remains solitary, / Among the nations unaccounted."[136]

14 / THE BLUE HEARTS OF GALILEE

Whoever climbs the mountains of Galilee enjoys a beautiful view of Mount Hermon, its high summit lost in clouds, and at its foot small Lake Hula next to a fertile valley flowing with copious springs.

Southward, serene Lake Kinneret (Sea of Galilee) lies in

quiet repose amid the softly undulating mountains. From the snows of Hermon, the Jordan runs down into Lake Hula, then streams turbulently through a steep rocky gorge to Lake Kinneret.

On a clear day, it is possible to see in the distance the blue ribbon of the Jordan trickling between the two lakes. Lake Hula and Lake Kinneret are both heart-shaped, and the Jordan joins them together.

"O God!" exclaimed a poet, "you have joined Kinneret and Hula by a rope—Your River Jordan—but to link the hearts of men You have not found among all Your treasures even a thread."*[137]

* Today, Lake Hula has been almost entirely drained of its waters and green fields and luxuriant orchards grow on its site.

XII

THE SHORES OF LAKE KINNERET

1 / THE REDEMPTION OF ISRAEL IS
LIKE THE MORNING STAR

The Valley of Arbel stretches among the mountains of
Lower Galilee overlooking Lake Kinneret. In the early
morning, it offers a beautiful view of the sun rising above the
mountains of Golan, which mark the horizon eastward, beyond the lake. Before dawn, the morning star sparkles
brightly through the last mists of the night.

Rabbi Hiyya and Rabbi Simon son of Halafta, were once
together in the valley of Arbel and saw before them the
glistening morning star, whose light shines forth and
breaks into myriads of bright rays in the darkness of the
night.

Rabbi Hiyya said to his friend, "Do you see the dawn of the
morning star? Thus shall be the redemption of Israel; in the
beginning it will rise slowly, but as it proceeds it will go from
strength to strength with ever increasing speed and
vigor!"[138]

FIG. 36. VALLEY OF ARBEL
This picture shows the northern end of the Sea of Galilee.

2 / THE VALLEY OF ARBEL IN OLDEN DAYS

In olden days, the Valley of Arbel was the site of the ancient city of Arbel, and the ruins of its synagogue can be seen to this day.

The Valley of Arbel was very rich in fields of corn and in flocks. It is said that a measure of corn sown in this soil would yield one full measure of good flour, one measure of medium flour and one measure of ordinary flour.

After the destruction of the Temple, the Valley of Arbel lost all its excellence; it became sterile and desolate, and one measure of corn planted in its soil did not yield even one measure of flour. It was as if the valley were consumed by an inner fire. The story is told of a man who was ploughing and sowing in Arbel. As he pressed his plough into the ground, a mound of burning soil was thrown up and burned the seed.[139]

3 / THE MESSIAH IN THE VALLEY OF ARBEL

A Jewish farmer was ploughing his field in the Valley of Arbel when suddenly his ox gave out with a long bellow. A passing Arab heard its voice and said to the farmer, "O son of a Jew! O son of a Jew! Loosen thy ox, loosen thy plough, for the Holy Temple has been destroyed."

The Jew asked, "How do you know this?" and the Arab answered, "I know it from the bellowing of the ox."

In the meantime, the ox bellowed a second time, whereupon the Arab said, "O son of a Jew! O son of a Jew! Bind the oxen, bind thy plough, for behold, the King Messiah has been born and the redeemer of Israel has come."

And the Jew asked him, "What is his name? And the Arab answered, "Menahem, the Consoler."

Menahem son of Amiel, the Messiah of Israel, will come suddenly in the month of Nisan, on the fourteenth day of the month. He will stand in the Valley of Arbel, and all the righteous of that time will gather around him. The prophet Elijah will be with him, and together they will all proceed to Jerusalem.

Eliezer ha-Kalir, the Galilean poet of the seventh century, sang: "The Messiah, Menahem son of Amiel,/Will arise in the Valley of Arbel,/He will come in the month of Spring,/In

Nisan, when the birds do sing,/Clad in Retribution's somber dress/Mankind in goodness to bless."[140]

4 / WHY WAS IT CALLED GINNOSAR?

Around the western shore of Lake Kinneret, near Tiberias, stretches a valley known as the Valley of Ginnosar. In days of old, many beautiful gardens flourished here. They were destroyed by subsequent wars, and only the modern villages Migdal and Ginnosar have brought back the blessing of fertility and the beautiful sight of flourishing gardens.

"Why was it called the Valley of Ginnosar?" asked the sages of Israel.

Because Ginnosar is a contraction of the two Hebrew words *gannei sarim*—the gardens of the nobles.[141]

5 / THE FRUIT OF GINNOSAR AND JERUSALEM

Why do not the rich fruits of Ginnosar grow at Jerusalem? In order that the children of Israel who come up to Jerusalem at the annual festivals should not be able to say, "If we came up only that we might eat the fruits of Ginnosar at Jerusalem, it would be sufficient for all our trouble and expense." For this would show that they came up not for divine worship but for pleasure.[142]

6 / GINOSSAR WAS IN THE LAND OF NAPHTALI

The Valley of Ginossar belonged to the tribe of Naphtali, which inherited the whole of eastern Galilee.

The ancients said, "And it [the Land of Israel] was divided among the tribes only by virtue of *Urim VeTumim*"—the ceremonial breastplate worn by the High Priest, on which every tribe was represented by a precious stone.

"And how was this done?"

"Eleazar [the High Priest] was wearing the *Urim* and *Tumim,* while Joshua and all Israel stood before him. An urn [containing the names] of the tribes and an urn [containing] descriptions of the boundaries were placed before him. Animated by the Holy Spirit, he gave directions, exclaiming, 'Naphtali is coming up and the boundary lines of Ginnosar are coming up with it.' [Thereupon] he shook well the urn of the tribes and Naphtali came up in his hand. He likewise shook well the box of the boundaries and the boundary lines of Ginnosar came up in his hand."[143]

7 / NAPHTALI, SATISFIED WITH FAVOR

When Moses blessed the children of Israel, he said to Naphtali, "O Naphtali, satisfied with favor,/And full with the blessing of the Lord:/Possess thou the sea and the south."

The sages of Israel explained: "Naphtali satisfied with favor"—that is, satisfied with lakes, fish, and ships. "And full with the blessing of the Lord"—that is because the valley of Ginnosar was in his portion.

Others say: "The great house of study, which was in Tiberias in Naphtali's portion, that was the favor and the blessing of the Lord."

And about Moses' words: "Possess thou the sea and the south"—"the sea" is the Sea of Sumchus, that is, Mei Merom. "The south" is the Sea of Tiberias.[144]

8 / NAPHTALI, A HIND LET LOOSE

Because the Valley of Ginnosar lies about two hundred meters below the Mediterranean sea level its climate is hot, even in winter, and its fruits ripen before all other fruits in Galilee.

The patriarch Jacob blessed his children before his death

and said: "Naphtali is a hind let loose:/He giveth goodly words."

Why should it be Naphtali who resembles a hind, and not another tribe? Because Naphtali had in his inheritance the Valley of Ginnosar, which is the swiftest to ripen its fruits, just as the hind is the swiftest of animals.

Another variation: The fruit of the Valley of Ginnosar ripened early; it was luscious and quickly digested, as is the meat of the hind.

And why is it said, "He giveth goodly words"? Because his fruits were offered to kings, who praised them with goodly words.

A different commentary connects the words "let loose" (Hebrew, *sheluha*) to *bet ha-shalhin*—Hebrew for a land of irrigation, and says: "Naphtali is a hind let loose"—this refers to his territory, all of which was dependent on irrigation.[145]

9 / EIN-KAHAL—THE HIDING-PLACE OF THE TREASURES

In the mountains of Galilee, there flows a spring in a gorge called Wadi al-Amud—Ravine of the Pillar. It descends from the heights of Zefat through the Valley of Ginnosar to Lake Kinneret. The spring is called Ein-Kahal.

Legend tells that in this place were hidden the treasures of the Temple after its destruction—the numerous precious vessels and utensils used in the worship of the Lord. On the authority of five sages, it is related: "And these are the measures of silver which were hidden in Ein Kahal by Baruch, the disciple of the prophet Jeremiah, and by Zedekiah, the last king of Jerusalem: Pieces of silver, one million two hundred thousand, and of good silver, one million six hundred thousand. Of copper utensils and of good copper vessels, two million, and of iron, one million one hundred thousand. And cherubin, basins of copper, pans of fine gold, three thousand,

and golden tables, which stood under the tree of life in the holy garden and on which the holy bread was presented, seventy; sycamore trees made of gold and hanging with sweet offerings made of pure gold refined by David, King of Israel. All these did Zedekiah hide, and no one knew where they were hidden till David (King of Israel) will arise, and all the silver, gold, and precious stones will be delivered into his hands, when all Israel from the four corners of the world will come in strength to the Land of Israel."

In the year 1835, a rabbi on his way from Tiberias to Safed told about Ein-Kahal: "Toward the east rises a very steep, high mountain. On its top is carved the semblance of a blocked gate. People say that here are hidden the treasures of the Holy Temple."[146]

10 / NAPOLEON AND THE TREASURES IN EIN-KAHAL

Napoleon Bonaparte, at the head of the French army, came to the Holy Land in 1799. While the bulk of his forces laid siege to the city of Acco, then the capital of Palestine, some of his troops went up and conquered Zefat, and its surroundings as far as the upper Jordan.

In 1850, Rabbi Reisher related: "The Emperor of France, Napoleon, was in Palestine about fifty years ago. And from ancient chronicles he learned that in the mountain of Ein-Kahal are hidden the precious vessels of the Temple. And he and his men went to the mount of Ein-Kahal, excavated almost half the hillside, but all in vain. For he did not know that only with the advent of the Messiah, the son of David— may he come soon and in our days—will these treasures be revealed unto the children of Israel."[147]

11 / JOB ON THE SHORES OF LAKE KINNERET

"Job," says the legend, "came from exile; he was an Israelite and his house of study stood in Tiberias."

On the shores of Lake Kinneret, north of Tiberias, a small cave is hewn out of the rock at the foot of a hill. The Arabs call it *Mugharat Ayub*—the Cave of Job. Here, it is told, the holy man lived, suffering from leprosy. In a spring nearby, he bathed his afflicted body and was cured. So the spring bears his name, *Hammam Ayub*—the Bath of Job.

The Arabs in the surrounding territory attribute miraculous qualities to the spring, and they come thither to dip themselves in its blessed waters. Jews, too, used to bathe there, confident that they would thus be cured of their ills, thanks to the merit of the righteous Job.

Another small source of the vicinity is known as *Tannur Ayub*—the Oven of Job.

A medieval tradition sets the tomb of Job and that of his wife in the mountains of Golan rising to the east, beyond Lake Kinneret.

The nineteenth-century English explorer C.R. Conder wrote: "At the so-called Oven of Job, near Tabgha springs, on the borders of the Sea of Galilee, I found blue beads and shells strung on thread and hung on a stick between the joints of the masonry; pieces of barley bread had been thrown into the stream flowing from the well, and there can be no doubt that these were propitiatory offerings to the local deity, who is now called Job."[148]

12 / THE MIRACLE OF THE LOAVES AND FISHES

At Tabgha, on the side of the Tiberias–Safed highway, is the Christian holy place *Mensa Christi*—Christ's Table.

Here, according to tradition, Jesus miraculously fed the multitude of his followers. As the Gospel tells: "And when it was evening, his disciples came to him, saying, this is a desert place, and the time is now past; send the multitude away, that they may go into the villages and buy themselves victuals. But Jesus said unto them, They need not depart, give ye them to eat. And they say unto him, We have here but five loaves, and two fishes. He said, Bring them hither to me. And he commanded the multitude to sit down on the grass, and took the five loaves, and the two fishes, and looking up to heaven, he blessed, and brake, and gave the loaves to his disciples, and the disciples to the multitudes. And they did all eat, and were filled; and they took up of the fragments that remained twelve baskets full. And they that had eaten were about five thousand men, besides women and children."

Excavations conducted on the site of Mensa Christi have

FIG. 37. ROCKS OF THE FIVE LOAVES (1838)
The Arabic name for the rocks is *Hamsa Khubzat*. Behind them are the Mountains and the Sea of Galilee.

brought to light the remains of an ancient church. Next to the remnant of an altar, a mosaic floor depicts a large basket filled with loaves of bread with a fish on each side, a pictorial allusion to the miracle performed here.*[149]

13 / CAPERNAUM ON THE SHORE OF LAKE KINNERET

" 'The sinners'—these are the people of Capernaum."

Capernaum—in Hebrew, *Kefar-Nahum* (Village of Nahum)—an important Galilean city in days gone by, stood on the northern shore of Lake Kinneret. It is not known who was the Nahum for whom the town was named. In the Middle Ages, it was believed that the reference was to the prophet Nahum and some even tell that his tomb is to be found in the place. Today, Capernaum is but a heap of ruins and the remains of its ancient synagogue are some of the most interesting Jewish relics in Israel.

Jesus preached in Capernaum and performed many of his miracles there. But the people of the town heeded him not and he cursed it, saying: "And thou, Capernaum, which art exalted unto heaven, shalt be brought down to hell: for if the mighty works, which have been done in thee, had been done in Sodom, it would have remained until this day. But I say unto you, That it shall be more tolerable for the land of Sodom in the day of judgment, than for thee."

Because Capernaum became renowned in the Gospels for the confusion Jesus created among its people, its name has become a synonym, in French, for a disorderly house.[150]

---

* At a later period, this site was shown on the mountain towering above Tiberias, where a group of basaltic rocks is called by the Arabs, *Hadjar en-Nasara*—the Stones of the Christians, or *Hamsa Khubzat*—the Five Loaves (Cinque Panni). See fig. 37.

14 / THE SPRING IN CAPERNAUM

In the first century C.E., Josephus Flavius describing Capernaum, wrote: "The country is watered by a highly irrigating spring. Some have imagined it to be a branch of the Nile, since it produces a fish resembling the coracin that is found in the lake of Alexandria."

The fish mentioned is the catfish named mustache fish—in Hebrew, *sefamnun*—for the long filaments around its mouth.

Today, there is no spring next to Capernaum. The nearest is one at Tabgha, enclosed within an artificial pool, and emerging by the side of the highway leading from Tiberias to Capernaum.[151]

15 / CHORAZIM NEAR CAPERNAUM

Chorazim, in the vicinity of Capernaum, was another important Jewish town in Jesus' time. Only ruins of the synagogue, built of the large black basalt stones typical of this region, testify to the importance of its population in the talmudic period.

Jesus preached in Chorazim with as little success as he had in Capernaum, and he cursed the town with the same violence: "Woe unto thee, Chorazim! . . . for if the mighty works, which were done in you, had been done in Tyre and Sidon, they would have repented long ago in sackcloth and ashes. But I say unto you, It shall be more tolerable for Tyre and Sidon at the day of judgment, than for you."

A Christian pilgrim who visited the Holy Land in 1137 tells the following tale: "Once when Jesus came here, he found the inhabitants building the synagogue. He asked, "What are you doing?"

They answered, "Nothing."

He said, "If indeed you are doing nothing, it will remain nothing for ever."

And however much they endeavored to build it, whatever they put up in the daytime was destroyed at night."[152]

FIG. 38. RUINS OF SYNAGOGUE OF CHORAZIM

16 / CHORAZIM—BETHSAIDA—CAPERNAUM

Sir John Mandeville wrote, in 1322, "Chorazim is where the Antichrist will be born, as people tell, and this archenemy will live in Bethsaida and rule in Capernaum; therefore it is written in the New Testament: 'Woe unto thee, Chorazim, woe unto thee, Bethsaida. . . . And thou, Capernaum!' "

Bethsaida, or Zeidan, stood on the banks of the Upper Jordan, near its outlet into Lake Kinneret.

From Bethsaida came important disciples of Jesus: "Now Philip was of Bethsaida, the city of Andrew and Peter." The most famous disciple was Peter, whose name means "rock," in Greek. Once Jesus addressed him thus: "Thou art Peter, and upon this rock I shall build my church."[153]

17 / BETHSAIDA'S GIFT TO EMPEROR HADRIAN

Bethsaida, or Zeidan, was an important Galilean townlet near the northern shore of Lake Kinneret. As its name testifies, its inhabitants lived mainly on fishing; Bethsaida, in Hebrew, means "House of Fishing."

A second-century scholar wrote: "I went to Zeidan and more than three hundred different kinds of fish were brought to me."

To this day, this section of the Sea of Galilee is the richest in fish and offers the greatest variety.

Bethsaida was also renowned for its plump pheasants, whose flesh was much relished by the inhabitants. It was said that the manna collected by the Israelites in the desert had the taste of pheasant flesh.

The Talmud uses the pheasant as a symbol of good living; a talmudic proverb says: "Some feed their fathers pheasant flesh but nevertheless shorten their days."

The reputation of the Bethsaida pheasants spread far and wide. Once the accursed Hadrian asked Rabbi Joshua son of Hananiah: "'it is written in the Torah: "a land wherein . . . thou shalt not lack any thing in it." Are you able to bring me pheasants?' He brought him pheasants from Zeidan."

Some say that Rabbi Joshua brought the pheasants from Ahbarim, or Ahbara, a village south of Safed in the mountains of Upper Galilee.[154]

18 / WHEREFORE THE NAME KURSI?

On the eastern shore of the Sea of Galilee, in the vicinity of Kibbutz Ein-Gev, there is a ruin named Kursi, a word meaning "seat" or "chair" in Arabic (in Hebrew, *kursa*).

Yakut, the Moslem geographer of the Middle Ages, mentioned this site about 1260, and explained the origin of the name: "It is told that once Jesus came to this place, and here he sat down."[155]

19 / GOG AT THE SHORES OF LAKE KINNERET

Ezekiel prophesied the destiny of Gog at the end of time: "And it shall come to pass in that day, that I will give unto Gog a place fit for burial in Israel, the valley of them that pass through on the east of the sea; and it shall stop them that pass through; and there shall they bury Gog and all his multitude; and they shall call it The valley of Hamon-Gog [that is, the Multitude of Gog]. And Hamonah [Multitude] shall also be the name of a city."

The old Aramaic translation of the Holy Scriptures adds to the above mentioned "east of the sea" the name Gennesareth—that is, Kinneret.

Hebrew tradition tells that when the Divine Presence appears on the Mount of Olives in Jerusalem at the time of Resurrection, the tombs of Gog and Magog will open up from the Valley of Kidron to a place called Gargashta to the east of Lake Kinneret.

The name Gargashta is Aramaic and means "soft, damp earth"; this description fits the soil of the Valley of Beteiha, which stretches along the eastern shore of Lake Kinneret.[156]

XIII
TIBERIAS–ANCIENT RAKKATH

1 / THE NAME TIBERIAS

Tiberias was founded in the beginning of the first century, on the ruins of an ancient city. Its founder, Herod Antipas, son of Herod the Great, named it in honor of Tiberius, the renowned Roman Emperor.

Jews in subsequent centuries could not reconcile themselves to the fact that such an important cultural center and the scene of such important literary creativity should be named after a Roman emperor, and consequently propounded alternative derivations.

Rabbi Jeremiah, an inhabitant of Tiberias in about the third century, attributed the name Tiberias to the Hebrew *tabur*—navel—for Tiberias was, in his time, the center of Jewish life in the country: "And why was it named Tiberias? Because it is situated in the center [*tabur*] of Eretz-Israel."

In a letter written from Tiberias in 1742 by its famous Rabbi, Haim Abulafia, leader of the newly reestablished Jewish community in the town, he praised its sanctity in these words: "And it is exceedingly holy, and it is situated in the center of Eretz-Israel, and therefore named Tiberias—the center of the Lord." (*Tabur*—center; *Yah*—the Lord.)

One of the country's most glorious landscapes can be seen from Tiberias. Legend, therefore, credits the aforementioned Rabbi Jeremiah with considering the word Tiberias a form of the Hebrew *tov*—good—and *reiyyah*—sight—that is to say, a beautiful landscape. "And why was it named Tiberias? Because its surrounding landscape is beautiful."

FIG. 39. TIBERIAS SURROUNDED BY MOUNTAINS OF GALILEE (1839)

The ancient rabbis applied the following verses of Psalms to the naming of Tiberias after a Roman emperor: "Of them that trust in their wealth, / And boast themselves in the multitude of their riches . . ./Their inward thought is, that their houses shall continue for ever. . . ./They call their lands after their own names." "Like Tiberias for Tiberius/," the rabbis said.[157]

2 / WHEREFORE THE NAME RAKKATH?

In biblical times, the site of present-day Tiberias was occupied by the town of Rakkath, in the territory of Naphtali, as told in the book of Joshua: "And the fortified [city] Rakkath." The name Rakkath may possibly stem from *rakkata*—shore —for the town lies on the shores of Lake Kinneret.

Legend, however, derives the name from *reika*—worthless and uncultured person. "And why was it called Rakkath? Because even the worthless among its inhabitants—*reikanim* —are as full of good deeds as the pomegranate is of seeds."[158]

3 / THE INHABITANTS OF RAKKATH—LOVERS OF REMAINS

In the olden days it was customary to bring the dead from neighboring countries for burial in Tiberias, for many advantages were attributed to the city. It was said: "At the end of days, Resurrection will take place in Tiberias forty years ahead of time. May the one who can forsee the future be blessed."

Maimonides wrote: "It is a tradition that Return [to life] will first occur in Tiberias and from there [the resurrected] will be conducted to the Holy City."

Once, while some scholars were walking round Tiberias, they looked up and saw a coffin that had been brought from abroad for burial in the Land of Israel. Said one of the scholars to his friend, "What is the purpose of bringing the body to be buried in the Land of Israel when the soul departed from it outside the Land of Israel?" And the other replied in the words of the prophet Jeremiah, " 'Ye defiled my land [during life] and made mine heritage an abomination [in death]'; but when the dead are buried in the Holy Land, God forgives them!"

From Babylon too the bodies of great rabbis were brought for burial in Tiberias. Babylon is known as "the Valley," for it lies in low lands between the beds of two great rivers—the Tigris and the Euphrates. On the occasion of such a funeral, it was the custom to say: "O lovers of remains, you dwellers of Rakkath,/Come and accept the dead of the valley."

Many holy tombs are to be found in Tiberias to this day.[159]

4 / HOW TIBERIAS WAS PURIFIED

"He purified the city of Tiberias,
made it clean; praise him from the Heavens,
our master Bar Yohai."

According to an ancient Hebrew tradition, Tiberias was built on the site of an old cemetery. Priests were therefore forbidden to dwell there, for it was considered ritually impure.

When Rabbi Simon bar Yohai left the cave in which he had been hidden for thirteen years, his body was covered with boils and eruptions. He went down to Tiberias and washed himself in its hot springs—"the Flame of Tiberias," in the idiom of the ancients. Cured, he approached the inhabitants of Tiberias and asked them if there were ills in the town which he could remedy, "for a man must be thankful to the place which benefits him." They replied, "Yes, there are areas in our city suspected of impurity which must be cleansed."

Rabbi Simon then planted seeds of the lupin plant* in all suspected areas.

---

* In Botany, *Lupinus Termis;* in Hebrew and Arabic, *turmus.*

The lupin seeds did not grow in hard ground, but wherever the soil was loose and moldy because of the corpses buried under it, the seeds flourished. In this manner, he determined which were impure places, and from them he removed the bones of the dead and buried them far from the city. Tiberias was thus purified, to the great joy of its inhabitants.

A Samaritan then living in Tiberias wished to discredit Rabbi Simon. He secretly placed a corpse in a spot which had been cleansed. He then summoned the population and said: "See how Rabbi Simon has purified Tiberias!" But Rabbi Simon, with the aid of divine inspiration, perceived the spot in which the Samaritan had concealed the corpse. He approached it, and said, "I command him who is above to descend, and him who is below to rise."

The Samaritan was immediately disentombed and the corpse rose to the surface and was removed.

Soon after these events, Rabbi Simon left Tiberias and passed through the nearby town of Migdala. There he overheard the voice of a school teacher from the synagogue, saying, "Rabbi Simon claims that he purified Tiberias, yet a corpse was discovered there!" Rabbi Simon came up to him and declared, "I have proofs as numerous as the hairs on my head that Tiberias is pure!" The school teacher was forthwith transformed into a heap of bones.

The lupin was thus instrumental in cleansing the areas suspected of impurity, enabling priests to live in the town and to increase the Jewish areas, much to the discomfiture of Israel's enemies. Therefore the Aramaic saying: "The lupin plant cuts the grass under the feet of Israel's enemies."[160]

5 / THE REDEMPTION WILL BEGIN IN TIBERIAS

"Tiberias has intimations of grandeur."

Tiberias is the lowest city in northern Israel, situated about two hundred meters below sea level. It is entirely surrounded by mountains and set in a bowl-shaped valley. With reference to the words of Zephaniah, the prophet, "Wail, ye inhabitants of Maktesh [the mortar]," the sages commented: "That is Tiberias, set low as if at the bottom of a mortar."

Hebrew legend has it that the redemption of Israel will begin in Tiberias, and the people will proceed from there to Jerusalem: "And Tiberias is deepest of all [the cities of Galilee] and from there Israel will be redeemed, for it is written [in the book of Isaiah]: "Shake thyself from the dust . . . O captive daughter of Zion!"

The ancients said, "Tiberias is ideal for the coming of the Messiah."

Maimonides, the famous rabbi and philosopher of the twelfth century, wrote: "According to tradition, Israel is destined to return first to Tiberias and proceed thence to the Temple."*[161]

6 / THE MESSIAH'S ROD IS CONCEALED IN TIBERIAS

"The rod of thy strength the Lord will send out of Zion:
Rule thou in the midst of thine enemies."

Legend has it that the rod which the Messiah is to wield on the day of eternal redemption is concealed in Tiberias, the biblical "Rakkath." The rod, made of almond wood, was given to Hephzibah, mother of the Messiah, Menahem son of Amiel.

* See legend XII:3.

An old messianic composition adds: "And the rod which the Lord shall give to Hephzibah, mother of Menahem, is of almond wood. It was hidden in Rakkath, city of Naphtali. And it is the rod of Aaron, as also of Moses and of David, King of Israel. It is the same rod which blossomed in the Holy Ark and bore ripe almonds; the rod which Eliyahu ben Eliezer concealed in Rakkath, that is, Tiberias."[162]

7 / THE PEOPLE OF TIBERIAS GIVE GOOD WORDS

In the Middle Ages, Tiberias was an important Jewish cultural center. Its inhabitants were famous for their fine language. A renowned Hebrew grammarian tells of "the people of Tiberias, whose language is purer than that of all the Hebrews."

Tiberias was within the territory of the tribes of Naphtali, of whom the patriarch Jacob said, "Naphtali . . . giveth goodly words." Therefore, this blessing was applied to the inhabitants of Tiberias, who are meticulous in the use of the language, punctilious in the choice of words, and fastidious in the exact pronunciation of the punctuated consonants.[163]

8 / THE TWELVE MONTHS IN TIBERIAS

During the summer months, Tiberias is extremely hot and infested with fleas. Scorners maintain that the King of the Fleas dwells in Tiberias, with many armies at his command. During the winter months, the rainwater forms soft, thick mud in its unpaved streets. A wild bush, known in Arabic as *sidra* and in Hebrew as *shezaf,* grows on the slopes of the surrounding mountains. Its sweet fruit, *dom,* is greatly prized by the population. In the Middle Ages, the fruit was known as *nubak.** The inhabitants of Tiberias also enjoy

* *Nubak* is the Arabic name of the bush whose botanical name is *Zizyphus Spina-Christi.*

the sugarcane, and suck its sweet juice with great relish. An Arab geographer of the Middle Ages, Al-Mukaddasi, the Jerusalemite, writing in about 985, mockingly described the occupations of the inhabitants of Tiberias throughout the year: "For two months in the year they dance, for is not Tiberias the Kingdom of the Fleas? For two months of the year they gorge themselves with the fruit of the *nubak* [jujube], for it grows wild and costs them naught. For two months in the year they beat the air with fly flaps, for they must chase the wasps from the meat and the fruit. For two months in the year they walk abroad naked, for the heat of the sun is great in Tiberias. For two months in the year they make music upon the reed, for they love to suck sugarcane, which is like unto a reed. For two months in the year they wallow in mud, for the earth is soft with the rain, and the streets are muddy."[164]

9 / THE BLACK STONES OF TIBERIAS

Many Tiberian houses are black, having been built of the basalt stone quarried in the area.

Rabbi Moses Bassola, who visited Tiberias in 1522, wrote: "And I have already mentioned that all the stones of Tiberias are black. It is said that the town was thoroughly consumed by flames when captured by the Roman emperor who executed the Ten Martyrs of Israel."[165]

10 / PURIM OF TIBERIAS

A bedouin sheikh, Daher el-Amer, rose to prominence in Galilee in the eighteenth century. He rebelled against the Turkish Government and declared himself ruler of Galilee.

In those days, Tiberias was waste and desolate. The sheikh restored its ruins and invited the Jews to settle there. He wrote to Rabbi Haim Abulafia: "Come take possession of Tiberias, the land of your fathers."

A great Jewish community was formed in Tiberias. "The people flourished and became prosperous," wrote one of its inhabitants, "rejoicing in their well-being, for the land was free from all evil and fear was unknown. Peace reigned as in the days of Solomon."

But this peace did not last long: in 1742, the Turkish ruler of Damascus gathered a great army against the rebellious sheikh and besieged Tiberias.

For a long time the city was shut fast, none entered and none left, and its Arab and Jewish inhabitants stood constant guard. The enemy, despite its superior numbers, was unable to breach its walls. The following account is given by one of the defenders of Tiberias: "It is well known that the greater conquers the lesser, but in this case a miracle came to pass. The men of Tiberias were few and their roads were closed, while the ruler of Damascus commanded a great army of men skilled in war and experienced in strategy. Nevertheless, he was not successful. This proved to the eyes of all mankind that a miracle had come from the Lord."

At the end of eighty-five days, on the Sabbath, December 1, 1742, the siege was suddenly lifted, and joy reigned in Tiberias: "The Jews went into their synagogues, glad of heart and rejoicing, and they sang as on the days of holiday and festival. On this day, a feast was proclaimed to the people of Tiberias for all future generations, a day of rejoicing, similar to Purim, for the wonders and miracles which the Lord, blessed be He, had performed in preserving their lives."[166]

11 / THE HOLY ARI IN TIBERIAS

There was an old synagogue in ancient Tiberias which the great flood of 1934 destroyed. On its entrance was written: "How lovely and how pleasant art thou, synagogue of the Rabbi of Tiberias. And may your praises be sung at the gates, at the gates of the daughter of Zion."

In a corner of the synagogue was a reserved place at which the Holy Ari, chief of the mystics of Zefat (Safed) in the sixteenth century, was wont to pray. It bore the following inscription: "This place is holy. In this corner prayed our master, the Holy Ari, may he be remembered for life everlasting and may his virtues intercede for us, Amen."

The mystics relate that once the Holy Ari passed in front of Rabbi Yohanan's great house of study in Tiberias, which exists to this day, and pointed out a stone in the wall to his disciples, saying, "A soul is enclosed in this stone which cries out that I pray for it."

And to this the prophet Habakkuk referred when he said: "For the stone shall cry out of the wall."[167]

12 / WHEN THE WALL OF TIBERIAS IS REBUILT

For many generations, during the Middle Ages, Tiberias lay waste and in ruins, its wall broken down and open to all the winds, and not one soul dwelt within its area.

After the conquest of the country by the Turks, Sultan Suleiman the Magnificent gave Tiberias to the Jews. They promptly restored its ruins and erected a new wall around it, which was completed and consecrated in December, 1564.

Before Tiberias was rebuilt, a business transaction took place in Zefat (Safed) between two Jews. Since the transaction was to be effected in two payments, and only the first payment was made at the time, the purchaser promised to remit the remainder when the wall of Tiberias was built again, trusting that this would never happen. When the wall was completed, the seller demanded his due.

The famous rabbi of Zefat, Rabbi Moses ben Joseph Taranni, was requested to settle the dispute: "Reuben sold Simon an object worth two for eight, with the provision that payment be made when the wall of Tiberias is rebuilt (may it be rebuilt and reestablished speedily in our own days) at the command of His Majesty. And now the wall is completed, and Reuben demands his payment as was contracted. Simon claims that the condition was made in jest, since he did not believe that the wall would be rebuilt before the coming of the Messiah." And the questioner concludes by asking, "Kindly instruct us, our Rabbi, whether or not he must pay the entire debt."

Rabbi Taranni replied at length, and concluded, "And accordingly he must pay the worth of the object received from Reuben, for if the wall had not been built, he would have profited. Now that it has been built, he must suffer the loss and pay double the value."[168]

13 / THE EMPEROR AND RABBI JUDAH THE PRINCE

Antoninus, the Roman Emperor, once said to Rabbi Judah the Holy, Prince of the Jews: "I am anxious that my son Severus should be my successor, and that the town of Tiberias should be a free colony for ever. The Roman Senate will, no doubt, sanction one of the proposals, but not both. I therefore ask your advice. What am I to do to secure both?"

Instead of replying verbally, the Rabbi ordered two men to appear before the Emperor, one riding upon the shoulders of the other. He gave a pigeon to the rider and said to the other, "Tell the man whom you carry to let the pigeon fly." The Emperor said, "I comprehend your meaning. First, I am to get the Senate to declare my son my successor, and then get my son to proclaim Tiberias a free colony."[169]

14 / THE OLD PLANTER AND THE EMPEROR

Hadrian was once walking along the road of Tiberias when he saw an old man standing and cutting down shrubs to set plants. He said to him, "Old man, old man, what is your age today?"

The old man answered, "I am a hundred."

The king said to him, "You, a hundred years old, and you stand cutting shrubs to set plants! Do you think you will eat of their fruit?"

The old man replied, "If I am worthy, I shall eat; if not, just as my forefathers toiled for me, so I toil for my children."

Hadrian told him, "By your life, if you are fortunate enough to eat of this fruit, let me know."

In due course the plants produced figs, and the old man said to himself, "Now is the time to inform the king."

What did he do? He filled a basket with figs, and went up and stood at the palace-gate. There he was asked, "What do you want?"

He replied, "Go and tell the king: An old Jew whom you once met wishes to greet you."

The guards went and told the king, "An old Jew wishes to greet you."

He said, "Bring him in!"

When the old man entered, the king asked, "What do you want?"

The planter replied, "I am the old man whom you met when I was cutting shrubs to set plants, and you said to me that if I was fortunate enough to eat of the fruits I should inform you. Behold, I have been worthy to eat of them, and these figs are the fruits they produced."

Hadrian thereupon said, "I order that his basket be emptied of the figs and filled with denarii."

His attendants asked him, "You display all this honor to this old Jew?"

And Hadrian answered, "His Creator has honored him, so shall not I?"[170]

15 / THE MIRACULOUS HERB OF TIBERIAS

In spring, the slopes of the mountains around Tiberias are covered with a rich carpet of wild flowers of a great variety of kinds and colors.

Legend tells of a special sort of herb, endowed with unusual powers, that appears then among all the plants. And this is how the story is related:

"It once happened that two men were walking along the paths of Tiberias, one of them blind and the other possessed of sight.

The man with the eyesight supported the one who was blind. They sat down to rest on the road, and it so happened that they ate a certain herb. The one who had been blind regained his sight, while the one who had possessed his eyesight turned blind, so when they left that place, the one who had been blind was supporting the one who had possessed his eyesight."[171]

16 / WHAT DID DANIEL DO IN TIBERIAS?

Daniel the Just was a scion of the royal family of Judah, which was exiled to Babylonia after Nebuchadnezzar's conquest of the Land of Israel. As it is written in the book of Daniel: "And the king spoke unto . . . his chief officer, that he should bring in certain of the children of Israel, and of the seed royal . . . youths in whom was no blemish, but fair to look on, and skillful in all wisdom . . . that he should teach them the learning and the tongue of the Chaldeans. . . . Now among these were, of the children of Judah, Daniel, Hananiah, Mishael and Azariah."

After Daniel had been saved from the den of the lions and his friends from the fire of the kiln, they came back to the Land of Israel, as says the Midrash: "Daniel and his friends all went up [to the Land of Israel] at the same time. They said, 'Better that we partake of sustenance in the Land of Israel and that we make the blessing in the Land of Israel.'

"And wither had Daniel gone? Said Rabbi, 'To dig a great spring at Tiberias.' "

Rashi expounds: "To dig and bring out a spring in Tiberias and produce the seed of a grass that is fodder for the cattle."[172]

17 / EARLY TIBERIAS AND LATE ZIPPORI

The large Arab village of Saphuria, Jewish Zippori, a town well known in talmudic times, is situated near the Tiberias–Nazareth road.

Tiberias is more than seven hundred feet below sea level while Zippori is some eight hundred feet above, the difference between the two towns being about fifteen hundred feet. Night falls later and day lasts longer in Zippori than in Tiberias, which is low and surrounded by mountains.

Rabbi Yossi therefore said, "May it fall to my lot to welcome the Sabbath in Tiberias," for there night falls earlier and the residents are privileged to be the first to welcome the Sabbath Queen. "May it fall to my lot to end the Sabbath in Zippori," Rabbi Yossi also said, for there daylight lasts longer and the residents are privileged to enjoy the lingering Sabbath more fully.[173]

18 / FROM TIBERIAS TO SUSSITA

Tiberias lies on the shore of Lake Tiberias, facing the village of Ein-Gev on the eastern shore. Ein-Gev is at the foot of one of the Golan hills, the very one which was the site of ancient Sussita—Roman Hippos—a town which gained its renown during the Jewish revolt against Rome. At a later period, the number of non-Jews in Sussita increased, and they bore enmity to neighboring Jewish Tiberias.

In interpreting a passage from the Book of Lamentations: "The Lord hath commanded concerning Jacob, that they that are round about him should be his adversaries," the rabbis commented: "Such as Sussita is to Tiberias."

The distance from Tiberias to Sussita, about six miles as the crow flies, is occasionally mentioned in Hebrew legend: "Noah's ark floated on the water as if supported by two beams, like the distance from Tiberias to Sussita."

Rabbi Judah said, "The wild ox did not enter the ark with Noah; only its young entered with him."

Rabbi Nehemiah said, "Neither the ox nor its young entered the ark. Noah bound the wild ox to the rear of the ark and he made furrows [in Lake Tiberias] as wide as the distance from Tiberias to Sussita. And to this [the Book of Job] refers in saying: 'Canst thou bind the wild-ox with his band in the furrow?' "[174]

19 / TIBERIAS AND ZEFAT BENEFIT FROM EACH OTHER

"Zefat has what Tiberias lacks
Tiberias has what Zefat lacks."

Tiberias, the capital of Lower Galilee, lies on the shores of Lake Kinneret, about two hundred meters below sea level. In summer, the heat waves are frequent and the sun blazes unmercifully. However, in winter, the weather is mild and pleasant, and many are the visitors who come to dip their aching bodies in the city's healing springs.

A short distance away from Tiberias, but a thousand meters above it, stands Zefat (Safed), the capital of Upper Galilee. There the winter is severe and stormy, while summer is cool and breezy.

When anyone asks a resident of Zefat or Tiberias how he makes his living, he is told that in winter the weather in Tiberias is excellent, and there is pleasant bathing in the hot springs, but neighboring Zefat is cold, and from time to time even visited by snow. So what do the people of Zefat do? They go down to Tiberias, tarry a while, and provide the inhabitants with a chance to earn their living by catering to their needs.

In summer, the weather in Zefat is excellent, and the cool breezes a pleasure, while neighboring Tiberias is hot, and from time to time even visited by burning winds. So what do the people of Tiberias do? They go up to Zefat, tarry a while, and provide the inhabitants with a chance to earn *their* living.

Thus it is that the residents of Tiberias and Zefat benefit from each other.[175]

XIV
THE HOT SPRINGS OF TIBERIAS

1 / THE HOT SPRINGS STREAM PAST HELL

Near Tiberias, on the shore of the Sea of Galilee (Lake Kinneret), emerge thermal hot springs whose fame has been widespread since ancient times.

In the biblical period, a town was built around the hot springs and was named Hammath, from the Hebrew *ham*—hot.

Later, Hammath and Tiberias merged into one city and it was said: "Hammath is Tiberias. And why was it called Hammath? Because of the hot springs of Tiberias."

The sages of Israel relate that the springs of Tiberias stream past the entrance of Hell and are thus constantly kept hot.

Because of their unabating heat they were also known as *Moked de Tevereya*—the Flame of Tiberias.

The hot springs are said to be remnants of those "fountains of the deep" that gushed forth in the days of Noah and flooded the world: "On the same day were all the fountains of the great deep broken up."

Rambam (Maimonides), the most outstanding Hebrew

scholar of the Middle Ages, pondered on the source of the heat of these springs, and this the explanation he offered: "It is known that thermal waters flow in Tiberias, and it is said that these waters are hot because they pass through layers of sulphur and such like matter."[176]

2 / WHY ARE THERE NO HOT SPRINGS IN JERUSALEM?

The sages asked, "Why are there no hot springs in Jerusalem like those in Tiberias?" And they answered, "That the pilgrims to the holy city should not say, 'If we had come to Jerusalem only to bathe in its hot springs, we should find it enough.' "

That is to say, the pilgrimage to Jerusalem would not be solely a holy duty, but would be tainted with wordly pleasure.[177]

FIG. 40. HOT SPRINGS OF TIBERIAS (1850)

3 / A MIRACLE AT THE HOT SPRINGS OF TIBERIAS

Rabbi Eliezer, Rabbi Joshua, and Rabbi Akiba went in to bathe in the public baths of Tiberias. A heretic saw them. He uttered some magic word and the vault (of the bath) held them spellbound.

Rabbi Eliezer said to Rabbi Joshua: "Joshua son of Hanina, see what thou canst do!"

When the heretic was going out, Rabbi Joshua uttered a magic word and the gate pinned him, and everyone who entered the gate gave him a blow, and everyone who went out gave him a squeeze.

He said to the holy men, "Undo what ye have done."

They said to him, "Release us and we will release thee!"

They released one another.

When they were going out, Rabbi Joshua said to the heretic, "Look here, what canst thou do?"

He said, "Let us go down to the sea."

When they came down to the sea, the heretic spoke a magic word and the sea divided; and he said, "Did not Moses, your Rabbi, do so with the sea?"

They said to him, "Dost thou not admit to us that Moses, our Rabbi, walked in the midst of the sea?"

He said to them, "Yes!"

They said, "Walk thou in the midst of it!" And he did so.

And Rabbi Joshua adjured the Prince of the Sea; and he swallowed him up.[178]

4 / STEAM BATHS IN TIBERIAS ON THE SABBATH

The sages deliberated whether bathing in the hot springs of Tiberias was allowed on the Sabbath. They decided to permit hot baths but ruled out steam baths, for these weaken the body, which is in need of rest on the Sabbath. And thus it is written: "So they forbade the hot springs of Tiberias, but permitted cold water. But when they saw that this [restriction] could not stand, they permitted the hot springs of Tiberias, while sweating remained forbidden."

In the fourteenth century, a rabbi from the Land of Israel addressed himself to the famous Spanish scholar, Rabbi Nissim ben Reuben Gerondi, with the question: "Is sweating in the hot springs of Tiberias permitted on the Sabbath?" Relying on accepted precedents, he answered: "Sweating is altogether forbidden, even in the baths of Tiberias."

An opposing opinion was expressed by an eighteenth-century rabbi, who reports that he and his fellow rabbis authorized steam baths in the town of Teplitz, in Bohemia, and thus he wrote: "If it is allowed to sweat in the hot baths of Tiberias on Sabbath and holy days, we here in the baths of Teplitz have ruled to permit."

In rabbinic literature of the Middle Ages, the name "Hot Baths of Tiberias" was applied to any source of hot water or washroom. In the seventeenth century, a rabbi from Germany told of a man who purchased a house in which there was a washroom, and he said: "One man bought a house from a Gentile and within the house there are *Hamei Tevereya*— Hebrew for "Hot Baths of Tiberias."[*179]

5 / THE CURE SEEKERS AT THE HOT SPRINGS

Since olden times people have flocked to the hot springs of Tiberias to bathe in their salubrious waters. In the Middle Ages, Jews thronged to the springs from neighboring countries, including Egypt, in which a large Jewish community flourished.

A collection of Hebrew manuscripts discovered in the synagogue of the old city of Cairo contains many letters composed by the ailing who sought a cure in the Tiberias springs

---

* Similarly, the name "Spa," a city in Belgium reputed for its mineral springs has come to designate all water-cure resorts.

—"the dwellers on the coast of Rakkath," as they metaphorically called themselves.

A letter written from Tiberias in the tenth century enumerates the ailments of the cure seekers: "Our fingers fall off, our limbs waste away, our hands are maimed, our feet mutilated, our knees totter, our eyes are dimmed." The letter is signed by "Your tortured brethren, the dwellers on the coast of Rakkath."

Another letter of the same period describes "the pitiful, tortured youths, afflicted with boils on their bodies, reduced by skin eruptions, so weakened that they must stay indoors, imprisoned, some of them deaf, some crippled, some lame, prey to all manner of infections, and nonetheless we say, 'Blessed be the most Sublime of the Sublime who revives all creatures, both the sweet [natured] and the bitter.'" It is signed: "Your young brethren, the dwellers of Rakkath."

These wretched creatures found cure and deliverance in the blessed hot springs of Tiberias.[180]

6 / WHO HEATS THE SPRINGS OF TIBERIAS?

The Arabs relate: A number of ailing men came to King Solomon and said to him, "O King Solomon, May thou live forever! Wiser art thou than all men and thou hast adorned Jerusalem and builded the Temple; yet of what avail are these if thou canst find no cure for our ills, our aching limbs, our boils, or the leprosy that mars us? We beseech thee to aid and heal the poor!"

Then King Solomon commanded a troop of demons, saying, "Hearken now, ye demons! In Galilee, by the city of Tiberias, there is a fountain which like all fountains flows with but cold water. Go ye down to the depths of the earth and heat the waters of this fountain!"

The demons, fearing Solomon, hastened to the fount. They dug down to its very source and heated the water. And the hot waters sprang out of the deep, and these are the famed hot springs of Tiberias, which cure all ills, including rheumatism, boils, and leprosy.

When the demons began their work, Solomon made them deaf. For he well knew that should news of his death reach them they would no longer fear him, and would cease to heat the founts.

Solomon is dead, but the deaf demons, not having heard of his death and thinking that he still reigns in his palace in Jerusalem, continue to heat the fountains to this day.

The Arabs, therefore, call the hot springs of Tiberias, *Hammam Malikna Suleiman*—the Baths of our King Solomon—thus repeating an assertion already made by a Syrian historian of the twelfth century.

A reference to the demons who heat the baths is also made in the Midrash, the homiletical commentary on Scripture. In the Book of Ecclesiastes, attributed to King Solomon, it is written: "And the delights of the sons of men—she-demon and she-demons." The ancients interpreted this in the following manner: "The delights of the sons of men"—these are the hot baths. "She-demon and she-demons"—these are the demons who heat these baths."

In the original Hebrew version of the Bible, after "the delights of the sons of men," come two Hebrew words, *shidah veshidot,* which are translated as "legendary she-demon and she-demons"; actually, the exact meaning of these words is unknown. They may be derived from the Aramaic *shadeh,* meaning "to pour."

The Jewish Publication Society Bible reads instead, "Women very many"; the King James Bible reads, "As musical instruments, and that of all sorts"; the Aramaic translation paraphrases, "The delights of men are the public baths and the private baths, and there are taps which pour cold water and pour hot water."[181]

XV
𝒥𝒩 𝒥𝐻𝐸
𝒮𝒰𝑅𝑅𝒪𝒰𝒩𝒟𝒥𝒩𝒢𝒮 𝒪𝐹 𝒥𝐼𝐵𝐸𝑅𝒥𝒜𝒮

1 / THE PALACE OF BERENICE, DAUGHTER OF THE KING

The mountain that rises above Tiberias is named after Berenice, sister of Agrippa the Second, following a tradition widespread among the Jews of Tiberias that her palace was set on the mountaintop. The summit affords a beautiful view of Tiberias, the lake, and the surrounding ranges. A ruin, located on the height of the mountain, is known in Arabic as *Kaser Bint el-Malek*—the Palace of the King's Daughter.

Berenice was the daughter of Agrippa the First, of whom it was said: "Even Agrippa, the King, bears a basket of first fruit on his shoulders [during the Pentecost] and enters the Temple."

Berenice lived during the Jewish revolt against Rome. When in Tiberias, she stayed in the King's palace, apparently the same palace that was built by Herod Antipas, founder of the town.

The walls of the rooms were plated with gold, and some were decorated with animal figures. This violation of Jewish custom angered the residents and, during the revolt, the fishermen of Tiberias stoned the palace and razed it to the ground.[182]

2 / THE PALACE OF THE EMPEROR'S DAUGHTER

"He who has visions of Ishmael son of Elisha
in his dreams should beware of punishment."

Rabbi Moses Bassola, who visited Tiberias in 1522, mentions in his description of its holy places, "And on the summit of the highest mountain, an ancient building may be seen. It is said that here was the palace of the emperor's daughter, who was charmed by the beauty of Rabbi Ishmael."

Rabbi Ishmael son of Elisha the High Priest, was one of the "Ten Martyrs of Israel." His Roman captors are said to have removed the skin from his face and preserved it. This is referred to in the Talmud as the *karkiflo* (scalp) of Rabbi Ishamel. Rashi, the great Biblical commentator, summarizes the tradition: "He was a High Priest and one of the 'Martyrs.' His beauty pierced the heart of the emperor's daughter and they removed the skin from his face and embalmed it in balsam, to preserve its features. And to this very day it is guarded in the treasuries of Rome."

Legend narrates: "It is said of Rabbi Ishmael, High Priest, that he was one of the seven handsomest men on earth. And his face was like unto the face of an angel of the Lord of Hosts. His friend was first to be executed before the eyes of the emperor. Then they seized Rabbi Ishmael; he was still wailing and mourning when the Emperor's daughter happened to look out of her window. Perceiving the beauty of Rabbi Ishmael, High Priest, compassion rose in her breast. And she sent to her father to beg for one favor. The Emperor replied, 'My daughter, anything that you wish shall be granted except the release of Rabbi Ishmael and his friends.' She said to him, 'I beg of you to spare his life.' He replied, 'I have already taken an oath.' She said, 'If so, order that the skin of his face be removed.' "[183]

3 / THE BLESSING OF THE RAIN IN MIGDAL

The townlet of Migdal (Magdala) stood on the shore of Lake Kinneret, at the foot of the mountains of Galilee, near the site of today's village of Migdal.

It is told: "Rabbi Jose son of Jacob, went up to visit Rabbi Judah of Magdala. While he was there, rain came down and he heard his voice saying, 'A thousand thousands and a myriad of myriads ought to give thanks to Thy name, O, our King, for every single drop which thou art causing to fall upon us; for thou art rewarding good to the guilty.' "[184]

4 / THE PRIESTLY FAMILY OF MIGDAL-NUNIA

The sons of the priestly family of Jehezkel served in the Great Temple of Jerusalem. As written in Chronicles: "The twentieth [lot came forth] to Jehezkel."

After the destruction of Jerusalem the priestly families wandered to Galilee, and the sons of Jehezkel settled in Migdal-Nunia. Ancient Galilean poets bewailed the fate of these exiles who had been servants of God the most high and were now stranded in faraway small villages, and they prayed for their speedy return to the ministry of the Almighty in His Holy City: "O God, fill up the streets of Jerusalem/With children of Israel;/O Thou Sublime God of Israel,/Have mercy upon us,/Bring speedily the Redeemer to Zion;/Ransom Thy nation from captivity,/Strengthen our brethren, /And bring back to the Temple/The priestly guardians of Jehezkel."[185]

5 / HANDICRAFTS IN ANCIENT MIGDAL-ZOVIM

In Migdal-Zovim—Tower of the Dyers—there was woven a garment called *pelinin*—a cloak similar to the cape worn by Roman horsemen.

It is said: "[There were] three hundred stalls of sellers of *pelinin* in Migdal-Zovim." It is also said: "There were three hundred stalls of sellers of birds for ritual purification in Magdala [Aramaic: Tower] of the Dyers."[186]

6 / FROM MIGDAL-ZOVIM TO JERUSALEM

"Nikai was beadle in Magdala of the Dyers [Migdal Zovim]. Every Friday evening after he had prepared his candles, he used to go up to the Temple [in Jerusalem] to observe the Sabbath, and then he came down and kindled the candles.

Some say he was a Scribe, and that every Friday evening he used to go up and expound his chapters in the Temple, and then he came down to keep the Sabbath in his home."[187]

7 / THE ACACIA TREES IN MIGDAL-ZOVIM

The Sages relate: "There were acacia trees growing in Migdal-Zovim"; and the inhabitants thereof had special regard for them, for the wood of the acacia tree was used by the Israelites in the desert of wanderings for building the tabernacle and its sacred furniture. As God commanded Moses: "And thou shalt make the boards for the tabernacle of acacia-wood." "And . . . an ark of acacia-wood." "And . . . the altar of acacia-wood." "And . . . a table of acacia-wood. And thou shalt set upon the table showbread before Me alway."

Rabbi Hanina was asked whether it was permitted to cut down for use the acacia trees of Migdal-Zovim. He answered, "Since your forefathers forbid their use, do not alter the practice of your forefathers, whose souls rest in peace."[188]

8 / MAZKA—THE PLEASANT HAMLET

In the mountains of Lower Galilee, in the vicinity of Tiberias, there stands a ruin known by the Arabic name of Mazka. This is the site of Mazga—a townlet in talmudic times.

The story is told of Rabbi Resh Lakish, a famous scholar in Tiberias, who once, while concentrating on his studies, was disturbed by two women passing by on their way to their village in the vicinity. He heard one say to the other, "Thank God, who is taking us out of this stench-filled air."

He called out, "Where are you from?"

They said, "From Mazga."

Said he, "I know Mazga, it is but a hamlet with no more than two dwellings." And he added, "Blessed be the Lord who makes each place pleasing in the eyes of its inhabitants."[189]

XVI
ZEFAT–THE MYSTIC CITY

1 / THE NAME "ZEFAT"

Zefat (Safed), the capital of Galilee, is situated on a protruding summit in the heart of the highest mountains of Israel. It commands a magnificent view of its surroundings, whence its name, from the Hebrew *zafo*—to look over.

Because Zefat is lovely and is set in beautiful countryside, legend holds that its name is composed of the initials of three Hebrew words: *zevi*—deer, symbol of beauty in Hebrew literature; *pe'er*—glory; *tiferet*—splendor. Indeed, enchanting Zefat well deserves these three accolades.

The rabbis, on the other hand, claim that the initials stand for the words *zizit, peah, tefillin.*

Zizit are the fringes which are fastened to the corners of the praying shawl *(talith),* in conformity with the words of the Torah: "And it shall be unto you for a fringe that ye may look upon it and remember all the commandments of the Lord and do them."

Peah means "earlock." Pious Jews do not cut the hair between the ear and the temple but leave an earlock, in accordance with the Law: "Ye shall not round the corners of your heads; neither shalt mar the corners of the beard."

Tefillin are the phylacteries—two small square black leather boxes containing, on pieces of parchment, the passages of Exodus and Deuteronomy in which it is enjoined: "Ye shall bind them for a sign upon your head, and they shall be for frontlets between your eyes." One of the boxes is placed on the left arm, at a point nearest the heart; the other on the center of the forehead. Except on Sabbath and festivals, the *tefillin* are fastened at morning prayers as a reminder that the Torah must be studied and obeyed every day. The pious residents of Zefat are indeed very observant of these three commandments.

Zefat attracts not only scholars and pious men who spend their lives in her houses of study but also artists, who come to paint her picturesque nooks and crannies, and poets, drawn by the lingering memories of her ancient splendor and mystic beauty.

In recent years, in fact, a large artists' colony has developed on the western slope of Mount Zefat; whence the newest interpretation of the name Zefat: *ziyur*—painting; *piut*—poetry; *Torah*—learning.[190]

2 / FIRE SIGNALS ON THE MOUNT OF ZEFAT

Since Mount Zefat commands a wide range of the neighboring contryside, the ancients lit fire signals on its summit to inform Jewish settlements in the area of the advent of holidays and the first day of a new month.

The first signal was lit on the Mount of Olives in Jerusalem. It was then relayed from summit to summit until it reached Mount Tabor, which is clearly observable from the mountains of Zefat.

The sages of Israel relate: "After what fashion did they kindle the fire signals? They would bring long cedar beams and reeds and oleaster wood and flax tow and bind them with a rope; then kindle them atop the mountain, wave them to and fro, up and down, until a similar signal was displayed on the summit of the second mountain, and then, too, on the summit of the third mountain."[191]

FIG. 41. ZEFAT (C. 1914)
From a paper sheet covered with colored pictures of sacred cities and sites of the Holy Land which was used for the decoration of booths at the Feast of Tabernacles.

3 / THE PRAISE OF HOLY ZEFAT

Zefat, principal city of Upper Galilee, served as the center of the Jewish Cabalists in the sixteenth century. They caused it to become one of the four holy cities of the country.

The Cabalists attributed many virtues to Zefat, the Pearl of Galilee. Rabbi Abraham Azulai, who lived in Palestine in the beginning of the seventeenth century, praised it in the following words: "Zefat has intimations of eternity. It is a most suitable place in which to penetrate the secrets and profundities of the Torah, for its air is the purest in the Holy Land. He who resides in Zefat enjoys an advantage over the residents of all other cities in the Land of Israel, for if he dies and is buried in Zefat, his soul flies swiftly to the Cave of Machpelah, in Hebron, in order to pass directly to the Lower Garden of Eden."

The Holy Ari, chief of the Zefat Cabalists in the sixteenth century, said, "The number of righteous men, martyrs, and geniuses buried in Zefat is manyfold the number of Israelites who came out of Egypt!"[192]

4 / ZEFAT DESTROYED BY AN EARTHQUAKE

Zefat has suffered many earthquakes which destroyed the city and accounted for the lives of many of its inhabitants. One such quake occurred on October 31, 1759.

Rabbi Yosef Sofer, who visited the city two years later, described the following incident that preceded the catastrophe: "A man came to me and told me [this story]. Several nights before the earthquake, his [dead] father appeared in his dreams, crying loudly and bitterly, tearing out his hair and trembling violently. He was seized by deep anguish and addressed his father, 'My father, my father, why do you grieve so?'

"And he answered, 'My son! Know that a terrible judgment has been passed on this congregation. See to it that they atone for their sins, fast communally and pray tearfully. And perhaps the terrible judgment will be annulled.'

"And so he rose early in the morning and, rushing to the synagogue, he mounted the pulpit and related his dream. The people heard it with great fear, and decreed a day of fasting. They prayed all day with intense fervor and weeping, and observed it as the Day of Atonement. But because of their sins God forgave them not, and the earthquake came upon them."[193]

5 / ZEFAT SHALL BE SUDDENLY REBUILT

The powerful earthquake that shook Zefat in January 1837 practically destroyed the entire town and buried four thousand souls beneath the debris of the fallen houses. Many scholars were found dead with their faces lying on the holy books. It was then said: "There has been no greater ruin than that of Zefat since the day the Temple was destroyed."

Rabbi Israel of Sheklov, an important figure in the Jewish community of the Holy Land in the nineteenth century, intoned the following lament in the Yohanan ben Zakkai synagogue, in Jerusalem, in memory of the victims of the quake. (Each line contains three words, the initials of which form the name Zefat).

"*Zefat pitom teharevi*—Zefat, suddenly thou shalt be destroyed.
Zefat pitom tamuti—Zefat, suddenly thou shalt die.
Zefat pitom tizaki—Zefat, suddenly thou shalt wail.
Zefat pitom tibbalei—Zefat, suddenly thou shalt be engulfed.
Zefat pitom tibaneh—Zefat, suddenly thou shalt be rebuilt.
Zefat pitom tikonen—Zefat, suddenly thou shalt be restored.

Zefat peduta tekadem—Zefat, suddenly thou shalt be delivered.

Zidkat peulata tagen—Thy righteous deeds shall protect thee![194]

6 / THE HOLY ARI—LEADER OF THE ZEFAT CABALISTS

Rabbi Izhak Luria, better known by his title of Ha-Ari Hakadosh—the Holy Ari (lion)—was the head of the Zefat Cabalists. The title Ha-Ari is formed from the initials of his name Ha-eloki Adonenu Rabbi Izhak—Our Master the Divine Rabbi Isaac. He was born in Jerusalem, in 1534, lived in Egypt for some time, and finally settled in Zefat, in 1569. Two years later, he died there at the age of thirty-eight.

The Cabalists believed that he would reappear to redeem Israel and to "retrieve the Land of Israel from Ishmael."

The Ari claimed to have constant interviews with the prophet Elijah, who communicated to him sublime doctrines. He visited the sepulchers of ancient teachers and there, by prostration and prayer, obtained from their spirits all manner of revelations. He saw how the souls were set free from the body at death; how they hovered in the air or rose out of the grave.

Pupils and disciples flocked to the Ari from the whole Jewish world. They were called *"Gurei Ha-Ari"*—"the young lions," or, "his whelps."

The Holy Ari expounded his doctrines orally. They were handed down in writing to posterity by his disciple, Rabbi Haim Vital.

Once the sages of Spain asked him: "Master, Light of Israel, the Lord Almighty, blessed be His Name, has revealed so much wisdom to Your Highness. Why not inscribe this science so that it perishes not from Israel?"

He replied in the following words: "Were all the seas ink,

all the reeds pens, and all the heavens scrolls, they would not suffice for the writing down of all my wisdom. And whenever I begin to reveal to you one of the Torah's secrets, I am swamped as if by a mighty river, and must seek various expedients to open a small narrow conduit through which one mystery of the Torah may reach you so that you hear it without being overcome. Otherwise you would lose everything, like the suckling who chokes on an overabundance of milk. Therefore, I counsel you to write down what you hear from my lips and it shall thus be preserved for the coming generations."[195]

7 / THE SEPHARDIC SYNAGOGUE OF THE ARI

The synagogue of the Sephardim named after the Ari is situated at the end of a tortuous alley in the lower part of the old quarter of Zefat. The Ari engaged in the study of the Torah's mysteries in a small dark cave set in one of its walls.

Legend relates the following: "Once, on the holy Sabbath, the Ari said to his disciples, 'If you will undertake not to speak in the synagogue during the early morning service until after the "blessing of the moon," nor to laugh at what you behold, then I shall conduct the service myself and summon the Seven Holy Shepherds of Israel to the reading of the Law.'

"And the disciples answered, 'We joyfully undertake to fulfill all your commands.'

"And he summoned Aaron, the High Priest, who appeared and read the first portion, intoning the blessing at the beginning and at the end.

"Next followed Moses, who read the second portion and, after intoning the blessing, disappeared.

"Then followed the patriarchs Abraham, Isaac, and Jacob. Joseph was summoned for the sixth portion. The Ari then summoned David son of Jesse, King of Israel, for the seventh portion. David danced and cavorted joyfully, leaping and whirling with vigor in front of the Ark of the Lord, clad in a white robe of linen and wearing priestly garments."[196]

8 / THE SYNAGOGUE OF ELIJAH THE PROPHET

Formerly, the Sephardic synagogue named after the Ari had been dedicated to the prophet Elijah, for it was believed that the holy man had sought solitude and communion with the Lord of the Universe in the cavern opening on the side of the prayer hall.

Rabbi Moses Bassola, who visited Zefat in 1522, describes the three synagogues which existed at the time: "And one is of the North Africans and it is called the synagogue of Elijah, blessed be his memory, for it is exceedingly old and tradition has it [among the Jews of Zefat] that Elijah, of blessed memory, prayed there."

The Cabalists believed that Elijah revealed himself frequently to the Holy Ari and unveiled to him the deepest mysteries of the Torah. A disciple of the Ari relates that his revered master learned "from the mouth of Elijah of blessed memory, who always revealed himself to him, to disclose profound secrets, and this," he adds, "I hold in truth from his own lips."[197]

9 / THE ARI'S SEAT IN THE SYNAGOGUE

Rabbi Benjamin, beadle of the Ari's synagogue in Zefat, once fell ill and was bedridden for twelve weeks. He was finally cured through the merit of the Holy Ari, who appeared to him in a dream. And this is how the story is told:

While on his sickbed, Rabbi Benjamin dreamed that he had gone forth to the synagogue to kindle the "perpetual

FIG. 42. CABALISTS IN ZEFAT
Painting in the museum of Heichal-Shelomo, Jerusalem.

light." He found the Ari sitting in his accustomed place, covered with a prayer shawl and of good countenance. Rabbi Benjamin asked him, "Who art thou?" And he answered, "I am Rabbi Izhak Luria."

The beadle then implored his favor in overcoming his ailments. The Ari said, "Why dost thou not repair the leaks in the building? Rain drips into the synagogue!"

The beadle repeated that he was ill. The Ari said, "Beware that no one ever occupies the place that was mine when I was of this world!"

The beadle repeated for the third time that he was ill. The Ari said, "Give me thy hand!"

Rabbi Benjamin gave it to him and immediately woke up. Then he arose from his illness; he ordered that a big stone be rolled onto the Holy Ari's place so that no one could ever sit or stand there, and he repaired the cracks and crevices of the Holy House."[198]

10 / THE ASHKENAZIC SYNAGOGUE OF THE ARI

The Ashkenazic synagogue named after the Ari is to be found at the end of a narrow alley in the old quarter of Zefat. The inscription on the lintel reads, "How awe-inspiring is this place, the holy synagogue of our master, the Ari, may his memory be blessed for ever and ever!" In the days of the Holy Ari, the site of the synagogue was at some distance from the town and was known as *Sadeh Tapuhim*—the Field of Apples.

On Sabbath eve, the Holy Ari was wont to go out there with his friends and disciples to welcome the Sabbath—the Bride—amidst prayers and rejoicings. It was his custom to wear four white garments for the ceremony, one for each of the four letters of the "Ineffable Name"—YaHaVaH.

In welcoming the Sabbath, the Cabalists sang a hymn, composed at the time in Zefat, "Come My Beloved to Meet the

Bride," which expresses Israel's passionate desire for redemption: "Rise, o my folk, from the dust of the earth,/Garb thee in raiment beseeming thy worth./Wake and bestir thee, for come is thy light!/Up! With thy shining the world shall be bright./Sing! For thy Lord is revealed in His might./Fear not and doubt not. The people oppressed,/Zion, My city, in thee shall find rest,/Thee, that anew on thy ruins I raise."

Once, on Sabbath eve, the Holy Ari and his disciples, all clad in white, went forth to the Field of Apples to welcome the Sabbath Queen.

Legend relates: "And in the midst of their song and prayer, the Holy Ari asked his disciples: 'Brethren, is it your wish that we repair to Jerusalem ere the Sabbath comes and abide there the whole day?'

"Some of the disciples answered, 'Yes, such is our wish!'

"And others answered, 'Let us first tell our womenfolk.'

"And because they said 'Let us first return to our homes,' the Rabbi trembled violently, struck one palm against the other and said, 'Woe unto us that we were found unworthy of redemption! For had you all answered "yes, with great joy," Israel would have been delivered of its bondage, for the hour was ripe for redemption. But since you were reluctant, exile has returned upon us in full strength to chastise us for our many sins!.' "[199]

11 / THE FIELD OF APPLES

Near the Ashkenazic synagogue of the Ari stands a house of study known by its Aramaic name, *Hakel Tapuhim*—the Field of Apples. The site was thus designated by the Cabalists even before the synagogue and house of study were built.

The sages likened Israel unto an apple tree. Recalling the words of the Song of Songs, "As an apple-tree among the trees of the wood," they said, "Verily, Israel is like unto an apple tree. The apple tree blossoms before it shoots forth its leaves. So did Israel, who awoke to good deeds before we were enjoined to do them. As says the Torah: All that the Lord hath spoken will we do, and obey."

And enlarging upon the comparison, the sages add, "That same apple tree, how long does it take for its fruit to ripen from the moment it first appears? Fifty days. In the same way, from the moment Israel left Egypt to the time it received the Torah, there passed fifty days."

Legend further likens the apple tree to Mount Sinai and to the Torah which was given from its height, by saying, "When the psalmist sings, 'Under the apple tree I awakened thee,' he refers to Mount Sinai. And why is Mount Sinai compared to an apple tree? Because as the apple tree ripens its fruit in the month of Sivan, so was the Torah given in Sivan."

The Zohar bestows the title of "The Field of the Holy Apples" to the Garden of Eden. The Cabalists quote the Ari's saying, "To welcome the Sabbath, go forth to the fields of holy apples."

And the popular song, which is sung in the annual pilgrimage to Meiron in memory of Rabbi Shimon bar Yohai, praises him thus: "And to the field of the apples thou went to collect their sweet juices/The secrets of the Torah, blossoms and flowers."[200]

12 / THE ABODE OF THE HOLY ARI IN ZEFAT

In the neighborhood of the Sephardic synagogue of the Ari, there was shown in days gone by the house where the Ari lived. In our time, not even the smallest remnant of this building has remained.

Legend narrates: It happened that a rich Jew once built a big house on this spot. A venerable old man who happened to pass there warned him, saying, "Let it be known to thee that the ground thou art treading upon is holy; it is the site of the Ari's house, may his memory be blessed. Mind, a place that has been consecrated may not be profaned, for one should sustain holiness and not diminish it."

But the rich man would not pay heed. And when he had completed the building and desired to dedicate it, a flame burst forth consuming several persons among those who were present. And it caused the stones to crumble, devoured the wood, and charred the soil until a mound of ashes remained, "which shall never be rebuilt until the Spirit from above descends and envelops us."[201]

13 / OSTRICH EGGS IN THE SYNAGOGUES OF ZEFAT

In past generations, it was customary to suspend ostrich eggs in the synagogues. Rabbi Menahem Mendel, a resident of Zefat about the year 1835, mentions this custom in his description of the town's synagogues: "And there are synagogues in which the Ari, of blessed memory, was wont to pray. And they also observe the custom of suspending the shell of an ostrich egg in every synagogue."

Today, ostrich eggs can be seen over tombs holy both to Jews and to Arabs, such as that of the Patriarch Jacob, which is in the mosque built over the Cave of Machpelah, in Hebron.

Rabbi Jacob Emden, writing in the eighteenth century, explained the custom in the following manner: "I have heard that the Jews in Turkish lands suspend ostrich eggs in their synagogues so as to intensify their devotion and to avoid being distracted. For the ostrich hatches its young by staring intently at the egg. This demonstrates how powerful sustained observation and concentration are. And indeed they befit prayer."[202]

14 / THE RITUAL BATH OF THE HOLY ARI

A ritual bath—*mikveh*—built over a small spring is to be found in the lower part of the old quarter of Zefat, at the end of the cemetery.

This *mikveh* was already in existence in the days of the Ari. The people would flock to it on Friday afternoon to purify themselves, preparatory to welcoming the Sabbath Queen. The Cabalists quote the Ari as having said, "One must make two ablutions every Sabbath eve: the first to remove all profane acquirements of the week; the second to garb oneself in the sanctity of the Sabbath." It is also told of the Ari that "he would not dry himself after having completed his ablutions. For he maintained that these were 'Sabbath waters' and the body would benefit by absorbing them."

After the Ari's death, on the fifth day of the month of Av, in the year 5432 after the creation of the world (1572 C.E.), his body was dipped in this *mikveh,* and it has since borne his name.

His disciple, Rabbi Haim Vital, is the author of the following narrative: "My master, may the righteous be remembered for life everlasting, ordained that he be immersed in the *mikveh* after his death. And when we immersed the body of the holy one, may the righteous be remembered for life everlasting, we said, 'O pardon us our sins, our master!' At that very moment, he lowered his body, head first, in order to immerse himself. And that was a miracle indeed."

Many Jewish pilgrims describe the *mikveh* of the Holy Ari, and praise its waters. One of them, in the year 1835, stated: "And when I was in Zefat it happened that a woman washed there [in the *mikveh*] soiled linen, and she drowned in the waters. May God save us from a similar fate! And the access is free at all times. May it be God's wish that in our day the words of Ezekiel the prophet shall be quickly fulfilled: 'And I will sprinkle clean water upon you.' "[203]

15 / THE SYNAGOGUE OF ABUAB IN ZEFAT

In a narrow, crooked lane of Zefat stands the venerated synagogue of Abuab. In its Holy Ark, set in the southern wall, which faces Jerusalem, is preserved an old Scroll of the Law —the Torah of Abuab. This scroll is said to have been the work of the sage Rabbi Isaac Abuab, author of the renowned book, *Menorat Hamaor*—The Chandelier of Light—who lived in Spain during the fourteenth century.

It is said that the Torah of Abuab was brought to Zefat by the exiles from Spain, and to this day it is the most ancient and revered of all the scrolls in the town.

Legend has it that the inhabitants of Zefat once wanted to transfer this sacred scroll to another synagogue. Before doing so "ten men dipped themselves in the ritual bath, purified themselves, and then made the transfer. The ten men died before the year was out."

Later, a scribe "patched the worn parchment, and he did not last through the year. May God preserve us from a similar fate!"

It thus became apparent to everyone that the Holy One, blessed be He, did not wish this Torah to be repaired or removed from its place.

In the great earthquake that destroyed Zefat in 1759, only a few persons escaped death. When they returned to the town, they found only one wall standing whole—the southern wall of the Abuab synagogue. The Ark and the scroll were intact. The synagogue was rebuilt, and its fame spread throughout the land, attracting to it multitudes of worshipers.

The Torah of Abuab is taken out of the Ark only three times a year—on the New Year, on the Day of Atonement, and on the Feast of Pentecost.

The rabbis of Zefat chose the word *kasher* to help remind the people that the Torah of Abuab may be taken out only

on these three holidays. The three Hebrew letters making up
the word represent the three initials of the Hebrew names
of the holidays—*K*ippur, *Sh*evuot and *R*osh Hashanah. Only
on these three days is the congregation of Israel *kasher*—
Hebrew for ritually pure—and worthy to behold this holy
Scroll of the Law.[204]

16 / THE CITADEL ON MOUNT ZEFAT

On the heights of Mount Zefat lie the remains of a powerful fortress of the Middle Ages, which was built on the foundations of a more ancient stronghold dating back to the Jewish rebellion against Rome. The Galilean rebels, lead by Yosef
ben Matityahu—Josephus Flavius—fortified the mount,
which controls its surroundings and all the roads of the vicinity. Yosef ben (son of) Matityahu is designated in Hebrew
legend as Yosef ben Gurion, and the Zefat citadel is often
referred to as the stronghold, or castle, of Yosef ben Gurion.

Rabbi Simha ben Yehoshua, writing in the year 1765, stated
that the inhabitants of Zefat collected stones from the debris
of the fortress with which to build their homes. He added,
"Formerly this tower was an impregnable fortress, and the
following inscription was discovered there: 'Know ye that
there is fresh water in this tower in such and such a place, so
many cubits from such and such a place to the east. But when
we were besieged and unable to withstand the enemy, we
sealed up the water, lest it come to their knowledge.' "[205]

17 / RABBI ABRAHAM HALEVY IN THE STREETS OF ZEFAT

"Those whom the Lord favors
He suppresseth with suffering."

Abraham Halevy Brouchim, born in Morocco, was a disciple of the Ari and one of the famous mystics of Zefat in the

sixteenth century. He was author of "The Rules of Sabbath" —*Tikkunei Shabbat,* in Hebrew—a booklet which was widespread among the people. "And the Rabbi, the Ari, of blessed memory, highly praised his piety and said of him that he was the reincarnation of the prophet Jeremiah."

"Abraham Halevy," so the story goes, "whose home was in Zefat, may it be built and restored speedily in our day, arose every midnight, made the rounds of the Jewish Quarter, and raised his voice, saying, 'Brethren, house of Israel, verily it is known to you that because of our many sins the Divine Presence is exiled, our Temple burned down to ashes, and Israel dispersed in the bitter Diaspora, suffering anguish and frightful torments; and many pious men and women, youths and maidens, aged and young, have been slain and hanged and slaughtered and been put to weird and painful deaths! And you, my brethren, you repose in your beds, peaceful and secure? Arise, and we shall cry to the Almighty, the Merciful and the Compassionate, who may hearken unto our voices and have pity on the remnant of Israel!'

"And the pious man would continue to clamor, giving the townsmen no rest until they arose, one hour after midnight, and repaired to the house of worship to recite night prayers for the restoration of Israel. Then each would meditate following his own inclination: some delved in the doctrines of mysticism [Cabala] and the book of Zohar; some applied themselves to the Talmud; and some studied the Holy Scriptures. Then they sang hymns and supplications until the day dawned."

Rabbi Abraham often practiced repentance and influenced others to return to God: "We encountered a pious man by the name of Rabbi Abraham, the pupil of the Ari, of blessed memory. He would gather groups of notables, lead them to the Ashkenazic synagogue and say to them, 'Do as you see me do; come and suffer the four forms of capital punishment—stoning, burning, beheading, and strangulation.'

"Then he would crawl into a cloth sack, ordering them to drag it on the floor to the length and breadth of the synagogue, in order to mortify his flesh and humiliate his spirit. Then he commanded that stones, each weighing a pound and a half, be thrown at him, and only when they had complied would he come out of the sack.

"A bed, covered with nettles, would be readied in the courtyard and he would undress, fling himself upon the thorns and roll on the bed until his entire body was blistered. Then they would flog him thirty-nine lashes, signifying death by beheading. Then he would plunge into the *mikveh* [public bath], signifying death by strangulation. Then he would turn to those assembled, saying, 'My brethren! Whosoever wishes to save his soul from Hell should follow my example!'

"And immediately they all rushed together and submitted themselves to the same torments with love and devotion, raising their voices in great lamentation, confessing their sins; nor would they move from the place until they had completed penitence, and they remained repentant for the rest of their lives."[206]

18 / A DESCENDANT OF KING DAVID IN ZEFAT

Rabbi Simha ben Yehoshua, who was in Zefat in 1765, wrote: "I met in Zefat a man named Hakham Rabbi Ephraim Dayan, from Syria, who trades in silk threads from that country. And he is of the seed of King David, may he rest in peace. And he has two wives but no son. And he is a modest, honest, and very handsome man and he has an unusually high forehead. And I asked him, 'Sir, how many generations removed are you from King David, may he rest in peace?'

"He answered, 'Eighty-four generations separate me from him, may he rest in peace.'

"And I was told that he sits as as a judge [*dayan*, in Hebrew] at the religious court; and when his name is signed to a verdict even the Sultan of Turkey himself would not revoke it, out of reverence for King David, peace be upon him."[207]

19 / "TASHLICH DAY" IN ZEFAT

On the afternoon of the New Year holiday, it is customary among pious Jews to shake out their garments on the shores of the sea or the banks of a river, thus signifying that with the inauguration of the new year all old sins have been cast in the water. This rite is known as *Tashlich*—Thou shalt cast.

Zefat, set on the mountaintop, is far from the sea, and from any source of water. How, then, do its pious Jews observe "Tashlich Day"? They climb to the top of the citadel and pray in the direction of Lake Tiberias, which can be seen from afar, set amidst the mountains. They empty their pockets, shake them out and thus "throw" all sins and offenses into the lake, all the while reciting the verses of Micah the prophet: "Who is a God like unto Thee, that pardoneth the iniquity . . ./of the remnant of His heritage?/He will again have compassion upon us;/He will subdue our iniquities;/And Thou wilt cast all their sins into the depths of the sea."[208]

20 / THE CAVERN OF THE DAUGHTERS OF JACOB

A cavern, known among the Arabs as *Magharat Benat Yaacub*—the Cavern of the Daughters of Jacob—is situated in the Arab quarter of Zefat. The Jews also call it, "The House of Study of Shem and Ever."

Arab legend has it that the cave contains the tomb of the messenger who brought Jacob, the patriarch, word of the death of Joseph, his favorite son, torn to pieces by a wild beast.

An inscription carved in stone at the entrance to the cavern, which dates back to 1412, reads: "In the name of Allah the Merciful and the Compassionate was ordered the construction of this blessed place of pilgrimage over the cenotaph of the messenger who brought the shirt of Joseph to his father Jacob, peace be upon both of them."

Beit Alkhazan—The House of Lamentation—is another Arabic name bestowed upon the cave, because Jacob is said to have sat in it mourning and bewailing the death of his son.

A famous Turkish traveler who visited Zefat in the seventeenth century mentioned the House of Lamentation and its importance in the lives of both Arabs and Jews: "Here Jacob, our patriarch, sat in mourning. The air is pervaded with perfume, like the scent of precious balsam, and its sanctity intoxicates the pilgrims, who are mostly Jews. The holes in the rock walls of the cave were carved by the many tears that Jacob shed, which also account for the many springs and streams in Zefat and its surroundings."

A long crevice slices one of the walls. It is recounted that the Archangel Gabriel entered through the crack and consoled Jacob in his great sorrow.

Rabbi Simha ben Yehoshua, who came to Zefat in 1765, wrote, "This is the cave that Jacob built after he lost Joseph, and no Jew is permitted to enter it."

When Sir Moses Montefiore, together with his wife, visited Zefat in 1839, the Arabs honored him with a visit to the cave of Jacob. Judith Montefiore described this visit: "The House of Study of Shem and Ever, designated by the Arabs as 'The House of Lamentation' . . . and to this day they do not permit any but their coreligionists to approach it. On our way we were offered a splinter of wood in memory of this holy place.[209]

21 / THE STUDY HOUSE OF SHEM AND EVER

The cave which the Arabs have named after the daughters of Jacob is called by the Jews "The Study House of Shem and Ever," after Shem, the son of Noah, and Ever, the grandson of Shem. Jewish pilgrims of the nineteenth century made mention of this name. Menahem Mendel, writing in 1835, said: "A walled building, which is said to have been the house of study of Shem and Ever." Sir Moses Montefiore too reported this name in the diary of his Palestine voyages.

It is written of Rebecca that when she was with child she went "to inquire of the Lord." Concerning this phrase, the sages remarked: "There were no synagogues or houses of learning in those days. She could have gone only to the study house of Shem and Ever."

"Jacob," it is written, "was a quiet man, dwelling in tents." Legend interprets this to mean that "he used to learn in the study house of Ever and the study house of Shem."

Legend also claims that the laws that Jacob received from Shem and Ever he passed on to his son, Joseph, in the cave of Shem and Ever.

Whosoever engages in the study of the Torah in this world will not be put to sleep in the next but will be led to the study house of Shem and Ever.[210]

22 / ZEFAT—THE BIRTHPLACE OF QUEEN ESTHER

Christian pilgrims of the sixteenth and seventeenth centuries believed that Queen Esther was born in Zefat.

The first one to mention this tale, apparently, was a Polish traveler of the year 1583; he described Zefat as "sitting on the top of the mountain, the birthplace of Esther, and inhabited by a great number of Jews."

A French monk, about 1630, depicted the fortified town of Zefat "and the fortress, of which the foundations prove that it is of great antiquity, and that was the palace of Queen Esther."

Jewish tradition placed the tomb of Queen Esther in the vicinity of Zefat, in Kefar-Biram, where impressive ruins of an ancient synagogue can be seen to this day.[211]

23 / HOW FIREFLIES HELPED THE JEWS OF ZEFAT

In the summertime, there hover and flutter over Zefat multitudes of fireflies whose tiny sparks flicker in the grass and among the shrubs in the darkness of night. The Jews of Zefat show great respect for them and would do them no harm, for well they remember that in olden times the fireflies once rescued them from a cruel edict.

Under Moslem rule, there once reigned in Zefat a wicked tyrant. He decreed that Jews might not light up their homes at night, but must remain in the dark, and he ordered them to relinquish into his hands every single lamp they owned. The Jews were especially pained because this prevented their studying the Torah in the evening. With heavy hearts, they came to their rabbi and asked him sadly what would become of them, since life has no meaning without the study of the Holy Scriptures.

The Rabbi said to them, "Go out, all of you, and gather up the fireflies into the house of study."

So all the people of Zefat, little children and old men as well, went out into the fields and collected the fireflies in their multitudes.

When the people brought them all into the dark study house, they shone so brightly that every corner of the large room was ablaze with light, and the scholars settled happily to the study of the Holy Torah amidst this joyful illumination.[212]

24 / THE SULTAN'S PRAYER

The Arabs of Zefat—Safed, in Arabic—had the reputation among their brethren of being quarrelsome people, troublemakers who incited the populace against the Turkish government and its representatives in Palestine. The common saying was: *"Safediye, fasediye*—that is, Safedites, mischiefmakers."

On Fridays, when the Turkish Sultan went for prayers to his beautiful mosque in Constantinople, he would beseech the Lord of the Universe, Allah the Merciful and the Compassionate, to give peace and serenity to his numerous subjects all through his vast empire spreading over many and various lands. At the end, he never failed to make special mention of the inhabitants of Safed, and particularly asked the Merciful to provide then with a good livelihood in their own hometown.

One of his puzzled retinue once asked, "O Sublime Sultan, Great Prince of the Believers! Why does Safed deserve to be specially mentioned in the prayers of His Majesty? Are there not in His Majesty's empire thousands of greater and more important cities?"

Replied the Sultan, "Honorable Emir, you do not know the people of Safed. If they find blessing in their deeds they will stay in their hometown. If not, Allah forbid! They will wander through our lands, plant discord wherever they go, incite the population against my governors, and then woe to my empire and to my rule!"[213]

25 / THE RIVALRY BETWEEN JERUSALEM AND ZEFAT

In the beginning of the nineteenth century, Zefat attracted a large number of newcomers and, in consequence, the town grew considerably while few came to Jerusalem, which remained forsaken on the barren hills of Judah.

When the earthquake left Zefat in ruins, it was said that this had been caused by Jerusalem's displeasure and frustration.

The famous Hungarian Rabbi Moshe Sofer, better known by the title of his important work *Hatam Sofer*, delivered a eulogy on the holy victims of Zefat, and attributed the tragedy to Jerusalem's jealousy. He said, "And Jerusalem, the holy city, is devastated and deserted, and no one takes it to heart; wherefore the earth quaked. It quaked because of Jerusalem's displeasure and Jerusalem's envy is the cause of it, for the Gate of Heaven is there, a town "builded as a city that is compact together." Mount Moriah is there—the Mount of the Lord—and now for about one hundred years people have set forth to Zefat, and Jerusalem has been utterly forgotten—the city named for God. And even now (when it lies in ruins) it is God's commandment to ascend to the holy city, but no one set his heart to it, and everyone went up to Zefat." And Rabbi Sofer concluded his discourse by telling about Rabbi Israel Bak, one of the survivors of the earthquake who went up to Jerusalem to restore the city: "[And he] the pride of our power, our Master and Teacher has collected the remnant of Zefat and brought it up to Jerusalem."

The survivors of Zefat who settled in Jerusalem established themselves in the Jewish Quarter of the Old City, in a special courtyard where they erected a synagogue that they named *Sukkat Shalom*—Tent of Peace.

Jewish Jerusalem gained new strength with their coming, and it was said: "Jerusalem has increased because of Zefat's disaster."

The names of the victims who had met their death in Zefat's earthquake were inscribed on the walls of the synagogue, and in their memory a memorial candle used to be lit on the anniversary of that tragic day, the 24th of the month of Tevet.

Unfortunately the Tent of Peace was destroyed during the War of Liberation of 1948. Lately, new dwellings have been put up on that site, and are bringing it to life again.[214]

XVII
MEIRON AND PEKIIN

1 / ON THE WAY TO EIN-ZEITIM

From the heights of Zefat a road running downhill to Meiron passes by the village of Ein-Zeitim and the grave of Judah son of Ilai, a venerated sage of the second century.

This tomb was the goal of pilgrims from time past, and the Holy Ari did not fail to visit it. His disciples, the Cabalists of Zefat, attributed to their master many extraordinary powers and, among other virtues, "He was versed," they said, "in the science of physiognomy and the knowledge of souls and their transmigration. And he knew and told of the transformation of the wicked, whose souls entered trees and stones, animals or fowls, and he could understand the twittering of birds. And from their way of flying he made wonderful deductions."

This marvelous knowledge revealed itself on the occasion of the Ari's pilgrimage to Ein-Zeitim. As the story is told: "At the very beginning of the Ari's coming to Zefat, the memory of the righteous be blessed, he went to prostrate himself on the grave of Judah son of Ilai. As he approached the olive and fig trees that surround the grave, he saw, perched on a branch, a raven, which croaked continuously. Said the Ari to his friend Moses Galante who accompanied him, 'In this raven can be seen the features of a man called Shabbatai, who was a tax-collector in Zefat.' And Rabbi Moses answered, 'I know him to be a cruel and wicked man.'

"The Ari replied, 'His soul has passed into this raven because he treated the poor with great cruelty when he collected the taxes; he took away the clothing from their bodies and the bedding from under them. For that reason, God has punished him and his soul now dwells in the body of this raven. Now he is asking me to pray for him.'

"The Ari turned to the raven and said, 'Wicked one, go away. Do you think I would pray for you?'

"And the raven flew away."[215]

2 / WHERE DO THE WATERS OF EIN-ZEITIM FLOW FROM?

Ein-Zeitim, by the side of the Zefat–Meiron highway, was a prosperous village in the Middle Ages. It was called after the source, *ein,* which flows in its midst and after the numerous olive trees—*zeitim*—which grow all round. The waters of Ein-Zeitim are reputed for their sweetness and purity.

About the year 1607, a pupil of the Holy Ari related how Rabbi Abraham Galante, the famous religious leader of Zefat, passing through Ein-Zeitim on his way to Meiron, once "bought a new pitcher and filled it with the live waters from the well of Ein-Zeitim, which are most goodly waters."

Popular belief connects the source of Ein-Zeitim with the springs of Jerusalem, wherefrom it acquires its excellence and freshness. And, in 1765, a Jewish traveler, referring to the fountain of Ein-Zeitim, wrote: "A big spring comes out of Jerusalem; its waters filter through subterranean channels and gush forth from under the ground inside this village."[216]

3 / THE COCKEREL SAINT

In the village of Ein-Zeitim is the grave of Rabbi Joseph Saragossi, a great and pious saint who lived at Zefat in the beginning of the sixteenth century. Rabbi Saragossi gained the love not only of his own people but also that of the Arabs of Zefat, toward whom he displayed a spirit of conciliation and great tolerance.

At one time, Saragossi was on the point of leaving Zefat when he was prevailed on, by the inhabitants to remain. They promised him an annual salary of fifty ducats—two-thirds of which was furnished by the Arab governor of the city.

Once, Rabbi Saragossi went to visit the tomb of Rabbi Judah bar Ilai. When he reached the place, Elijah the Prophet appeared to him. Rabbi Saragossi bought the spot and asked his pupils to bury him there.

The ruler of Zefat once suddenly ordered the Jews to bring him five hundred white cockerels on pain of severe penalty. The Jews gathered all the cocks needed but they were not all white. The sorrowful leaders of the congregation did not know what to do. The people went to pray at the holy graves, but without avail, until they went to Ein-Zeitim—to the grave of Rabbi Joseph Saragossi. There too they prayed and wept bitterly. When they returned to the city they found that all the cockerels had turned pure white.

Ever since then Rabbi Joseph Saragossi is spoken of as *ha-Zaddik ha-Lavan*—the White Saint—or *Zaddik ha-Tarnegolim*—the Cockerel Saint.[217]

4 / THE SPRING IN NAHAL HATAHANOT

At the foot of Mount Zefat, toward Meiron, there runs a deep, narrow gorge named Nahal Hatahanot—River of the

Mills—after the flour mills which, in the past, were kept in motion by its waters. In the Middle Ages, the Arabs called it Wadi Daliba, from the Arabic *dalib*—maple trees, which grow to this day on its sides.

The marriage contracts drawn up in Zefat in past generations usually described the town in the following terms: "Here in the town of Zefat, which is situated in Upper Galilee, on the River Daliba, and is provided with water from cisterns and fountains."

Several sources emerge in the bed of Nahal Hatahanot; one of them, Ein Atina—the Fig Spring—supplies water to Zefat through a pipeline.

Another fountain became famous in the Middle Ages among the inhabitants of the region. It is, in all likelihood, the same spring known today to the Arabs as Ein ed-Djinn—the Spring of the Demon.

In 1310, the Moslem governor of Zefat noted: "Between Meiron and Zefat there is a gorge which is called Wadi Daliba. From its rocky depths a spring bubbles forth. People come to bathe in it and to drink from its waters. From time to time, the spring stops flowing as if it had never carried any water. Then the people call out, "O, thou old man who bestows happiness"—in Arabic, *ya sheikh mas'oud*—"we are thirsty!" Forthwith, the waters appear in the bed of the river and flow to the flour mills. And when the spring dries up again, the people repeat their incantations, and the waters stream anew. And thus this chant is intoned again and again along the years and at all times."[218]

5 / "LIKE THE PEOPLE OF MEIRON"

In olden days, a steep and winding path led up to the village of Meiron. When a group of men climbed up this way, the narrowness of the path obliged them to walk one behind the other in a long file; whence the Hebrew expression, *ke-*

bnei Meiron—like the people of Meiron—for men walking in single file.

The sages of the Mishnah said: On New Year's Day, all that come into the world pass before Him like the people of Meiron. What does "like the people of Meiron" mean? It means "as [they walk] on the ascent to Beit-Meiron." The commentator adds, "The way is narrow, and two cannot walk abreast because there are precipices on both sides."

According to another version, the word *meiron* means "sheep." *Bnei Meiron*—the sons of Meiron—is similar to the Aramaic *bnei amira*—the sons of the sheep.

Sustaining this interpretation, Rabbi Ovadia of Bartenora expounded: "They pass in front of me like the sons of Meiron —that is, like the sheep that jump one after the other through a narrow gate while the shepherd checks and counts them."

In a different rendition of the Mishnah, instead of *bnei Meiron* there is written *bnei noumerin*. This writing gives rise to a third explanation, which relates *numerin* to the Latin *numeri*—soldiers. This last spelling brings to mind the words of the prophet Isaiah: "He that bringeth out their host by number."[219]

6 / THE LINTEL AND THE MESSIAH

In Meiron are found the ruins of an ancient synagogue, of about the end of the third century, said to be that of Rabbi Shimon bar Yohai. The plan of the building can yet be discerned and its main entrance still stands. The gateway is built of huge single stones and the upper lintel is made of one large slab. This lintel is cracked, and a section of it seems to be about to fall. It is said that when the fragment falls, it will be a sure sign of the coming of the Messiah.

A Jewish traveler of the year 1495 related: "I saw the synagogue of Rabbi Shimon bar Yohai, the memory of the righteous be blessed; it is a large building made of great stones, but now it lies in ruins, only one wall standing. The men of Zefat say there is a tradition that when this wall falls, the Messiah will come, may it be speedily in our days, Amen. I was told that in the year of the expulsion from Spain, 1492, part of the wall fell and the people of Zefat held a festival."*

Similarly in the book *Nistaroth* [Mysteries of] *Rabbi*

FIG. 43. CENTRAL GATE OF THE ANCIENT SYNAGOGUE OF MEIRON

* In several other tales, the collapse of a gate is an indication of the coming of the Messiah. See legend XIX:16.

Shimon bar Yohai, the fall of a gate of the Great Mosque of Damascus will also signify the approach of Redemption. And thus it is written: "And that will be for thee a sign, when thou shalt see that the *guiron* which is on the western side of the Mosque of the sons of Ishmael in Damascus has fallen, their kingdom has fallen, and then redemption shall flourish for Israel and the Messiah, son of David, shall come and [all Israel] will go up to Jerusalem and rejoice in it."

Guiron—Arabic, *Djirun*—is the name of a gate of the Great Mosque of Damascus. The Moslem traveler al-Masudi describes, in 943, a beautiful palatial building standing in Damascus and called Djirun. The gate of the Mosque nearby is named after it—Bab [Gate of] Djirun. He adds that the building is named after Djirun, a descendant of Noah the Just, who made Damascus his capital.[220]

7 / THE TOMB OF RABBI SHIMON BAR YOHAI

Meiron, a small village situated opposite Zefat on the slope of the highest peak of Upper Galilee, is renowned for the shrine of Rabbi Shimon bar Yohai.

Rabbi Shimon bar Yohai—Rashbi—was one of the most famous scholars of the second century. He was renowned for his love of the nation and its land, and always referred to them in terms of praise: "The Holy One," he said "appraised all nations and found none deserving of the Torah but Israel. The Holy One appraised all mountains and found none more suitable for the handing down of the Torah than Mount Sinai. The Holy One appraised all cities and found none for the site of the Temple but Jerusalem. The Holy One appraised all countries and found none deserving of Israel but Eretz-Israel.

"Israel was the recipient of three select gifts, which are coveted by all nations of the world, and these were given to them only after great ordeals, and one of them is the Land of Israel.

"Israel is seasoned with all qualities, but not so other countries; one country is endowed with a quality the other is lacking, while the other possesses a quality lacking to the first, but Eretz-Israel lacks nothing."

He is also quoted as having said, "Anyone who leaves Eretz-Israel in time of prosperity and goes to a foreign country is regarded as an idol worshiper."

The story is told of one of the pupils of Rashbi who traveled abroad and returned a wealthy man. The other pupils envied his good fortune and begged that they also might go abroad. Rabbi Shimon, hearing this, led his pupils to a ravine near Meiron and said, "O ravine! O ravine! Fill thyself with pieces of gold." And lo and behold! There came from heaven a shower of golden coins, which spread out before their eyes. Turning to the pupils, Rabbi Shimon said, "If it is gold you seek, here it is in the ravine at your feet, but remember that he who takes this gold now yields his share of the world to come, for there is no reward in the Torah save in the world to come."

Not one piece of gold was taken from the ravine.[221]

8 / THE REBELLIOUS RABBI SHIMON

In the days of Rabbi Shimon, the yoke of the Romans rested heavily upon the shoulders of Israel; they decreed many restrictions and robbed the Jews of the limited religious freedom they still enjoyed. Rabbi Shimon hated the Romans and spoke of them unsparingly.

At one time, during a rabbinical discourse, one of those assembled praised the Roman administration in the land: "How gratifying are the deeds of this people; they have provided for marketplaces, built bridges, and constructed bathhouses." Rabbi Shimon answered him and said: "Everything they instituted, for themselves have they done it—provided for marketplaces to purchase slaves, bathhouses for their pleasures, and bridges to levy tolls."

When this became known to the authorities, the Roman governor sentenced Rabbi Shimon to death. Shimon and his son, Eleazar, fled and took refuge in a cave in the vicinity of the village Peki'in.*

There, according to tradition, they wrote the book of Zohar—Brightness—the standard work of the mystics of Israel.[222]

9 / THE GRAVE OF RABBI ELEAZAR

Rabbi Eleazar, the son and faithful follower of Rabbi Shimon bar Yohai, is buried in Meiron, next to his father, under the same roof. This was not always so, for at first, Rabbi Eleazar was interred at the village of Gush-Halav, which is in the vicinity.

The explanation is as follows: After Rabbi Eleazar's death, Rabbi Shimon would appear in dreams to the men of Meiron and say, "I have only one right eye. Why do you not bring it to me?" The men of Meiron understood this to refer to his only son, Rabbi Eleazar. So they went to Gush-Halav to take him thence and bury him anew near his father's tomb. However, the men of Gush-Halav drove them out, for they wished the saint to rest in their city. But then, on the eve of the Day of Atonement, when the people of Gush-Halav were busy with preparations for the holy day, the Meironites succeeded in stealing the body of Rabbi Eleazar, and they buried him next to his father.

Ever since, it is said, Rabbi Shimon has not disturbed the sleep of the men of Meiron.[223]

---

* See legend XVII:19.

10 / THE HOLY ARI AND HIS FRIENDS AT MEIRON

"And most of the mysteries he [the Ari]
solved in the fields and in the wilderness."

The Holy Ari and his friends often left Zefat and went to Meiron to prostrate themselves on the tombs of Rabbi Shimon and his son Eleazar. There they learned the book of Zohar and delved into the mysteries of the Torah.

"And," say the Cabalists, "sometimes he went with his followers to the village of Meiron, and he sat there in the place where Rabbi Shimon son of Yohai, peace be upon him, revealed to them *Idra Rabba.* And he [the Ari] used to say: 'Here sat Rabbi Eleazar, and here Rabbi Abba; here sat Rabbi Yehudah, and so forth the rest.' And he sat them each in the place that he deserved, according to the merits of his soul. He himself sat in the place of Rabbi Shimon, and Rabbi Haim in the place of Rabbi Eleazar, and Rabbi Yonathan in the place of Rabbi Abba, and Rabbi Gedaliah in the place of Rabbi Yehudah, and Rabbi Yoseph Maarani in the place of Rabbi Yossi, and Rabbi Izhak Cohen Ashkenazi in the place of Rabbi Izhak, and so the rest of them.

"And he used to say that he saw a fire blazing around his companions, but their eyes were not keen enough to see it, only his alone."[224]

11 / THE PILGRIMAGE TO MEIRON

According to ancient tradition, Rabbi Shimon bar Yohai died and was buried in the village of Meiron. The Cabalists recount: Before his death, he sat and completed the Zohar in the presence of his students, and, upon reaching the passage in Psalms, "For the Lord commanded the blessing, even the life for evermore," before uttering the word "life," his soul departed him. That day, the flame burning in the room where he sat did not die out but brightly shone upon him.

When the flame was extinguished, the Holy Light—*but-zina kadisha,* in Aramaic, a title of honor given to saintly rabbis—was seen departing from this world with a smiling countenance, lying on his side and enveloped in a prayer shawl. A voice was then heard calling: "Ascend, come and assemble to lament Rabbi Shimon bar Yohai."

Rabbi Shimon died on the eighteenth of the month of Iyar, twenty-six days after Passover, when the festival of Lag be-'Omer is celebrated. On the eve of that day, many tens of thousands of Jewish pilgrims, obeying the ancient injunction, gather in Meiron to celebrate the festival known as *Hillula de Rashbi*—the Praise of Rabbi Shimon bar Yohai.

The celebrants first assemble in Zefat. In the afternoon, they carry in solemn procession the flag-bedecked Scroll of the Law. They then proceed to Meiron, where before night-fall they gather in their multitudes inside the shrine. They dance in the courtyard and sing hymns and songs to the praise of the holy master Shimon bar Yohai. Thousands of candles are lit over the tombs of Rabbi Shimon and his son Eleazar, while men and women stand around praying fervently.

After darkness, two bonfires dedicated to the two holy men are lit on the roof, in large basins filled with clothes soaked in oil. The conflagration lasts all night. Ecstatic visitors have even been known to throw their garments into the fire.

On the next day, small children gather in the shrine and are given their first haircut; the hair is thrown into the fire as an offering. This rite is called *halaka,* an Arabic word meaning "shaving." The custom of "shaving" is a variation of the ancient Israelite practice of offering the first fleece to the priest, as prescribed in the Torah: "And this shall be the priest's due from the people, from them that offer a sacrifice. The first of the fleece of thy sheep shalt thou give him."

And thus, love and reverence to the great Rabbi Shimon

bar Yohai, one of the luminaries of Judaism, is rekindled every year in the hearts of all Israel.[225]

12 / THE PRIESTLY FAMILY IN MEIRON

In the Great Temple of Jerusalem, twenty-four watches of priests ministered to the ritual. The first watch fell to the Jehoiarib family, the ancestors of the Hasmoneans: "Now the first lot came forth to Jehoiarib. These were the orderings of them in their service, to come into the house of the Lord, according to the ordinance given unto them."

Legend relates that on the day of the destruction of the Temple the priests of Jehoiarib's watch were on duty.

The sages said: "When the Holy House was laid waste the first time, on the 9th of the month of Av, that very day was the eve of a Sabbath in the last year of a sabbatical cycle [shevi'it]; the watch of Jehoiarib was serving, and the priests and levites were standing at their pulpits chanting the following psalm: 'But the Lord hath been my high tower,/And my God the rock of my refuge./And He hath brought upon them their own iniquity,/And will cut them off in their own evil;/The Lord our God will cut them off.'

"And before they could utter the last verse, 'The Lord our God will cut them off,' the enemy came and overpowered them."

Among the priests of Jehoiarib's watch were the sons of the Messarbei family. "And," comments legend, "these two names, Messarbei and Jehoiarib, were a portent of the ill-omened role these two families were to play. For Jehoiarib means "God quarelled [with the sons who rebelled and disobeyed Him]" and Messarbei is a contraction of the Aramaic MaSSaR Beit—those who handed over the House [of God].

When Jerusalem was destroyed, the priestly companies wandered into Galilee and settled in its towns and villages. The Jehoiarib group and the Messarbei family in its midst established themselves in Meiron and, after that time, they were known as Messarbei of Meiron.[226]

13 / THE CAVERN OF THE PRIESTS NEAR MEIRON

On the heights of the mountain rising south of Meiron there is a grotto known as *Mearat Hakohanim*—the Cavern of the Priests. In all likelihood, this is the last resting place of the priests who resided in Meiron in times past.

The disciple of the famous Rabbi Haim ben Attar mentioned his visit to Meiron together with his master in 1742. And thus he wrote: "Next to it [Meiron] there is a large grotto named the Cavern of the Priests. It is told that once a woman came here bringing her son. And he entered by himself into the cave. And when they went looking for him and found him within the cavern he said to them, 'There are here several men clad in white, and they kissed me and blessed me.' "[227]

14 / THE THRONE OF ELIJAH THE PROPHET

On the height rising above Meiron, among thick bushes, stands a large rock over sixteen feet high. It is called *Kisei Eliyahu*—the Throne of Elijah, or *Kisei ha-Mashiah*—the Throne of the Messiah. This, it is said, is the very rock on which the forerunner of the Messiah, the Prophet Elijah, will first appear, as prophesied by Malachi: "Behold, I will send you Elijah the prophet before the coming of the great and terrible day of the Lord."

Here, on this stone seat, Elijah will sit, and here he will sound the big trumpet of Redemption that will proclaim the coming of the Messiah and the deliverance of all Israel, as prophesied by Isaiah: "And it shall come to pass in that day, that a great horn shall be blown."

In 1769, the Jewish pilgrim Moshe Yerushalmi—the Jeru-

FIG. 44. "THRONE OF ELIJAH THE PROPHET"

salemite—already mentions "the throne of the Prophet Elijah, his memory be blessed, which is made of one large block of marble."

Zefat faces this site and its people will be the first to hear the sound of the trumpet of Redemption. This, according to the Holy Ari, is proved by the numerical identity of the name Zefat and the Hebrew word *teka*, meaning "to blow [the horn]." Indeed, the numerical equivalents of the three Hebrew letters that comprise the word "Zefat" amount to 570 ($z=90$, $f=80$, $t=400$); likewise, the word *teka* ($t=400$, $k=100$, a [ayin]$=70$). And this is the hidden meaning of the following verse of the

morning prayer: *"Teka beshofar gadol leherutenu"*—
Sound the great horn of our freedom.*[228]

15 / THE BATH OF THE PROPHETESS DEBORAH

In the depths of the ravine running along the southern side
of Meiron, there bubbles forth a spring. It spreads into a small
pool called "The Ritual Bath of the Prophetess Deborah," for
it is believed that the holy woman dipped herself into these
waters.

The height rising above the nearby village and called
Mount Meiron after it has been confused in tradition with
Mount Tabor, where the prophetess gathered the tribes of
Israel to repulse the Canaanite invasion. The battle was con-
tinued along the banks of the Waters of Megiddo, and the
same faulty tradition holds this stream to be none other then
the source mentioned above, which courses along the side of
Meiron.

The same mistake was repeated by an anonymous disciple
of Rabbi Haim ben Attar, who followed his famous master to
this vicinity in 1748. He wrote: "And in the valley between
the mountains a large river streams, named the Waters of
Megiddo."

And again, in the poem entitled "Pilgrimage to the Land
of Israel," written in about 1839, the Waters of Megiddo and
Mount Tabor are mentioned in the vicinity of Meiron: "The
shadow of the Almighty hovers over them and the Waters of
Megiddo stream between them. High cliffs are on the
mounts and in the valley there is Mount Tabor.**[229]

* See legend XVIII:1.
** Indeed, Mount Tabor stands on the margin of the Valley of Jezreel, at the
southern end of Lower Galilee; Megiddo is on the southwestern limit of the
same valley.

16 / TEKOA IS FIRST FOR OIL

In olden days there was a townlet named Tekoa, in Galilee. Its site is unknown today, but it probably stood facing Meiron, where ruins of an ancient settlement called, in Arabic, *Shama* and its synagogue have been brought to light.

Tekoa sat on the top of a hill, and around it spread luxuriant olive groves. It was famous for its oil production, and thus came the saying "Tekoa ranks first for oil." Wherefore the talmudic expression was born: *atir Tekoa*—rich man from Tekoa—to indicate a person whose wealth is founded on the yield of the earth.

Another Tekoa existed in the Land of Judah, in the surroundings of Jerusalem, on the border of the Wilderness. It was the home of the prophet Amos. Today, although but a heap of ruins, it has retained its ancient name. Nearby, a recently established Tekoa perpetuates the biblical appellation.

The well-known commentator Rabbi David Kimhi was of the opinion that Amos came from the Galilean Tekoa, and thus he wrote: "And Tekoa is a big city in the inheritance of the sons of Asher. Amos was of the people of [King Jeroboam's] kingdom, for Tekoa is a town of Asher."

Similarly, the wise woman who appeared before Joab, the captain of King David's armies, came from Tekoa of Judah, as it is written: "And Joab sent to Tekoa, and fetched thence a wise woman." The belief is held here that she must certainly have originated not from the Judean Tekoa but from the Galilean one. Why? "Because they [the people of Tekoa] were accustomed to olive oil, wisdom could be found among them."

Possibly the name Tekoa derives from the Hebrew *takoa* meaning "to blow [the trumpet]," for here the ancient Hebrews used to blow the call to arms for their men at the approach of an enemy.[230]

17 / HOW WAS TEKOA BUILT?

The townlet of Tekoa was built from the top of a steep hill all the way down to its base, which dropped into a narrow vale where a spring flows—the main source of water of the vicinity.

The houses were built in grades down the hill, and one could reach the bottom by jumping from roof to roof and by way of the courtyards and small vegetable gardens grown by the inhabitants.

Rabbi Judah Ha-Nasi was a disciple of Rabbi Shimon bar Yohai. Said Rabbi Judah, "When we were studying Torah at Rabbi Shimon's [school] in Tekoa, we used to carry oil and a towel to him on the Sabbath—from the courtyard to the roof, and from the roof to an enclosure, and from one enclosure to another until we came to the fountain where we bathed."

Why did the disciples choose that strenuous way of going down the hill instead of simply walking around it? Because they thus kept within the Sabbath boundary of the town; for roofs or courtyards, or enclosures, constitute one single domain, and one may carry from one to the other articles that were kept in either of them when the Sabbath began.*231

18 / WHY DOES HANUKKAH LAST EIGHT DAYS?

When the Hasmoneans conquered the Temple of Jerusalem in 165 B.C.E., they found only "one jar of consecrated oil marked with the seal of the High Priest, and just enough to burn one day. A miracle was wrought and it burned for eight days."

The rabbis tell that the oil for the use of the Temple of Jerusalem was brought from Tekoa of Galilee in the territory

* The Sabbath boundary is the marked-off area around a town or place within which it is permitted to move on the Sabbath.

of the tribe of Asher, at a walking distance of eight days there
and back from Jerusalem.

"Why do we celebrate Hanukkah for eight days? Because
the oil came from the inheritance of Asher, and there was a
place named Tekoa from where the oil was brought. And
from there to Jerusalem is a walk of eight days between going
and coming back; therefore they waited for them until they
brought back from there pure oil. And that is why the miracle was made to last eight days."[232]

19 / THE CAVE OF SHIMON BAR YOHAI

In the village of Pekiin, one can dimly discern a narrow
cave, almost completely lost among a thick growth of trees.
In this cave dwelt Rabbi Shimon bar Yohai and his son Rabbi
Eleazar after their escape from Roman persecution.*
Miraculously, there appeared in that place a carob tree and
a spring of fresh water, so they cast off their clothing, buried
themselves in sand up to their necks, and studied the Torah
all day long.**

In this manner, they lived in the cave for twelve years.
One day, seeing that a bird had repeatedly escaped the net
set for it by a hunter, Rabbi Shimon and his son were embold-
ened to leave the cave, considering the escape of the bird to
be an omen that God would not forsake them. When they
stood outside the cavern, the Prophet Elijah came to them
and said, "Who can inform Shimon bar Yohai that Caesar is
dead; that his decree is nullified and that they are free?"

In the great pilgrimage to the tomb of Rabbi Shimon, the
crowds sing: "The story will never die/Of Rabbi Shimon bar
Yohai./From the day of his birth/Blessed is his name on
Earth,/The bright shining star of Galilee./In a cave he lay
hidden,/By Roman Law forbidden,/Our Rabbi bar Yohai./In

* See legend XVII:8.
** See *Legends of Judea and Samaria,* "The Cave of Lod," p. 161.

the Torah he found his guide,/With spring and carob tree by his side,/Our Rabbi bar Yohai."[233]

FIG. 45. VILLAGE OF PEKIIN
In the background can be seen the mountains of Upper Galilee.

20 / THE PRAYER IN THE CAVE OF RABBI SHIMON BAR YOHAI

Legend holds that from time to time the souls of righteous men gather in the Cave of Rabbi Shimon bar Yohai to pray to the Almighty. And to confirm this belief the following story is told: There was a Jew living in Pekiin who used to grind corn in a water mill some distance away from the village. Every day he would bring on his ass a sack of flour, which he sold to the people of the village, and in this way he maintained himself and his family.

One day, at the time of the evening prayer, he passed by the cave of Rabbi Shimon bar Yohai, which is in Pekiin, driving in front of him his ass, laden with the sack of flour. Suddenly, an old man appeared from amongst the trees and said, "Come with me to this cave and pray with me, for we have already nine men and only require one to complete the *minyah.*" The miller answered, "How can I leave the ass by himself? He may be stolen from me." And the old man said to him, "Fear not, I will guard your ass for you and will be answerable for him to you."

The miller went with the stranger and saw nine old men with beards as white as the brightest silver. They prayed together and then said to the miller, "Take heed that you do not speak of this to any man, for then you will surely die." The miller took his ass, which was waiting for him, and returned to his home in Pekiin. As he emptied his sack of flour, behold, the blessing of the Lord was upon it and the flour filled the whole room.

This happened every day, and the miller grew exceedingly rich in a short time. When his neighbors saw this, they asked, "Is Saul also amongst the prophets?," and they demanded to know how he came by his wealth. He answered, "I have taken an oath on my life not to speak of this matter; and if I break that oath I shall surely die." But they said to him, "You fool, nothing can injure you." Finally, they prevailed on him, but, before he began to tell them all that had happened in the cave of Shimon bar Yohai, he made his will, leaving all his possessions to his children. When the story was ended, he passed out of this life to enter the world to come.[234]

21 / ELIJAH AT THE CAVE OF RABBI SHIMON

Rabbi Joshua son of Levi met Elijah standing by the entrance of the cave of Rabbi Shimon son of Yohai.

Rabbi Joshua asked him, "Have I a portion in the world to come?"

The reply came, "If His Master desires it."

Rabbi Joshua son of Levi said, "I saw two but heard the voice of a third" (the voice of the Shechinah—the Divine Providence). He then asked, "When will the Messiah come?"

"Go and ask him himself," came the reply.

"Where is he sitting?"

"At the entrance" (of the town).

"And by what sign may I recognize him?"

"He is sitting among the poor lepers."

So Rabbi Joshua went and greeted Him, saying, "Peace upon Thee, Master and Teacher!"

"Peace be upon thee, O son of Levi," He replied.

"When wilt Thou come, Master?" asked he.

"Today," was the answer.

On his returning to Elijah, the latter enquired, "What did He say to thee?"

"He spoke falsely to me," Rabbi Joshua rejoined, "stating that he would come today, but has not."

Elijah answered him, "This is what He said to thee, 'Today,' if ye would but hearken to His voice!"[235]

22 / HOW THE ZOHAR WAS FOUND

The Zohar is the Holy Book of the Cabalists. The famous Cabalist Rabbi Abraham Azulai, who was a resident in Hebron in the seventeenth century, wrote: "It is rumored that the Book of Zohar was hidden in a cave in Meiron, where an Ishmaelite chanced to find it and then sold it to peddlers in Upper Galilee. Some of its pages chanced to come into the possession of a savant who had come from the west. Spurred on by this discovery, he made a round of all the peddlers in the neighborhood, in order to collect the missing pages of the book. He even went as far as to search the garbage dumps, where he discovered that the peddlers had used pages of the book in which to wrap the spices they sold."[236]

23 / THE SAINT OF THE MILLS

Years ago, there lived in Pekiin a poor unfortunate whose only asset was a very large family. None of his ventures prospered, and he and his children lived very hungry lives.

Once an old man passed through Pekiin, and the Jew told him his troubles and asked his counsel. The old man laughed and said, "You have the grave of Rabbi Yossi here. Why don't you reap benefit from his great merits? Go and start some work near his grave and you will find your labors blessed."

Acting on the old man's advice, the Jew began to build a mill near the grave and to direct the water from the village spring toward his mill. That night, Rabbi Yossi appeared to him in a dream and asked him to stop building, so that he should not disturb his rest. The old man rose in the morning much disturbed, but went on working, for he put his many children above the saint.

The saint appeared to him again the second night and spoke to him anew. The poor man could not restrain himself and answered, "My family are perishing from starvation and I have no hope other than your merit; that is why I wish to build a mill near your grave."

The next day, he rose to continue his work as usual, but he found that all he had built was smashed down to its foundation. On one of the heaps, however, there was a sack of good white flour.

Then he understood that Rabbi Yossi had heard his plea and wished to repay him by the sack of flour for the loss of the mill. After that, he found a sack of flour at the same place every day and ere long he became very wealthy.

Now when you come to Pekiin, the villagers will show you Rabbi Yossi's grave, at the side of which is a heap of stones. This is the destroyed mill.

And since that time, Rabbi Yossi has been called, in Arabic, *Zaddik al-Tawahin*—the Saint of the Mills.[237]

XVIII
ON THE HEIGHTS
OF UPPER GALILEE

1 / THE MESSIAH WILL APPEAR IN UPPER GALILEE

An ancient tradition prophesies the advent of the Messiah in Upper Galilee. And thence, it is said, He will lead the multitudes of Israel to Jerusalem. This belief was mainly current among the Cabalists of Zefat, the city of the mystics in Israel.

The Zohar, the standard work of the Cabala, which is attributed to Rabbi Shimon bar Yohai, mentions this tale several times.

Said Rabbi Shimon: "At the same time that the dead of the world shall stand up in the Holy Land, they will all rise, hosts by hosts, on the soil of Galilee. For there the King Messiah will first manifest himself."

Legend adds: "We are taught that Israel will be all gathered in Upper Galilee and there the Messiah, son of Joseph, shall behold them. And all Israel will ascend with him to Jerusalem, and He [the Messiah] will go up and build the Temple and offer sacrifices and the fire will come down from heaven."

When Rabbi Hai Gaon, a well-known scholar of the eighth

century, was asked by a suffering Jewish community for signs of approaching redemption, he answered, "When we shall see the evil rule of Edom in the Land of Israel, we shall be confident that salvation has set in. At that time a man shall stand up from among the sons of Joseph and he will be called the Messiah of God. And many people will gather around him in Upper Galilee and he will be their king, and then the Messiah, son of Joseph, with the people assembled with Him, shall go up from Galilee to Jerusalem."[238]

2 / THE PRAISE OF GALILEE IN THE OLDEN DAYS

In ancient times, Galilee was a very fertile and prosperous region. It was praised for its vineyards and for its numerous olive groves. The sages of Israel said, "It is easier to raise a legion of olives in Galilee than one child in Eretz-Israel." The land produced rich wines and excellent oil, and it is said that the inhabitants drank more wine than water.

The people of Galilee, in the northern part of the Holy Land, were wealthier than those of Judea, in the south. The south, on the other hand, was renowned for its great scholars and its centers of learning: Yavneh, Lod, Benei-Berak, etc. Therefore, the sages used to say:/"For wealth to the north you must go;/But wisdom in the south you find;/Choose south, for wisdom, you know,/Will bring wealth, and so peace of mind."

Legend draws a parallel between the distinctive qualities of the inhabitants of Galilee and Judea, and the disposition of the holy vessels within the Tabernacle.

God ordered Moses, saying: "And thou shalt set the candlestick on the side of the tabernacle toward the south; and thou shalt put the table on the north side."

The table with the shewbread, the symbol of wealth and materialism, faced north, while the candlestick and its light, the symbol of wisdom and spirituality, was placed toward the south.

The Galileans were renowned for their strong spirit and fearlessness; they were among the most dauntless fighters of the foreign legions during the great rebellion against Rome. The sages add: "The Galileans were more solicitous of their honor than of their property. The Judeans were more solicitous of their property than of their honor."[239]

3 / THE FAULTY PRONUNCIATION OF THE GALILEANS

The simple folk of Galilee spoke a faulty language and corrupted many words in their inaccurate speech. The sages of Israel rebuked them, saying, "The people of Galilee do not heed their pronunciation, therefore the knowledge of the Torah is not spread among them." (The Galileans could not distinguish between the letters "A," "'A," "Ha" and "Kha.")

A story is told of a Galilean who brought with him a sheep to sell at the marketplace. He called out: "Who wants an *'amar* [sheep]? Who wants an *'amar!?*" As he did not articulate well the "A" of *'amar,* the people could not understand his meaning.

They said, "You simpleton from Galilee! What do you have for sale? *Hamar*—a donkey for riding, or *hemar*—wine for drinking, or *'amar*—wool for spinning, or *'imar*—a sheep for slaughter?"

He answered, *"'Imar,* a sheep for slaughter."

Only then did the people know what merchandise he had for sale.[240]

4 / MAY A LION DEVOUR THEE!

The Galilean women used to cook a cheap bean named, in Hebrew, *halba.* To this day, Yemenite and Arab women eat the *halba* to gain weight and to fatten their domestic animals.

The women of Galilee could not pronounce well the word *halba* and they made it sound as *halabi*—the lion.

A woman said once to her neighbour, "Come, I shall give you *halba* to eat."

The neighbour thought she had said *halabi,* and she answered angrily, "May the lion eat *thee.*"[241]

5 / WHAT CAUSED THE RUIN OF UPPER GALILEE?

Galilee is widely covered with shrubs and bushes, which add beauty to the hills, refresh the air, and protect the soil from erosion.

The flocks of sheep and goats which graze in the groves gnaw at the young shoots and thus cause the diminution of the forests and of the brush. Erosion soon follows; the stony earth is uncovered, and thus the fertile soil is replaced by areas of naked rock.

In ancient times, the Israelites took good care of the forests, for they knew well their importance in the preservation of the land's fruitfulness. They forbade the grazing of small cattle, sheep, and goats in woodlands near their habitations.

The sages enjoined: "One is not allowed to breed small cattle in the Land of Israel, but they can be bred in Syria and in the wildernesses of the Land of Israel." They also said: "The breeders of small cattle never see a sign of blessing."

Legend tells: "Eclipses of the two great lights [the sun and the moon] are caused by four reasons. Two of these are the breeders of small cattle in the Land of Israel and those who fell good trees."

Rabbi Shimon Shazuri was a well-known sage of about the third century. His hometown was Shazur, in Galilee, now a new settlement on the side of the Zefat–Acco highway. Rabbi Shimon described the sad fate of his family: "My father's family," he said, "were great landlords in Galilee. And why were they ruined? Because they bred small cattle. We owned a forest near town and there was a field between the house and the forest. And the small cattle used to go in and out of the forest."

A similar tale was told by Rabbi Ishmael: "My father's family and kinsfolk were among the landlords of Upper Galilee. And why did they decline? Because they bred small cattle in the woodlands."

The Mishnah lists the obligations binding every man who joins the society of scholars: "Whoever takes upon himself to be a member, neither will he breed small cattle."

The well-known Galilean sage, Rabbi Judah son of Babba, was a very pious man. He was found guilty of only one sin. He kept a goat in his house for reasons of health; and his scholarly companions did not forgive this transgression.

"Of Rabbi Judah it was said that all his activities were for the sake of heaven except that he grew small cattle. And this is how it happened. Once Rabbi Judah fell ill and the doctors visited his bedside, and they told him: There is no remedy for you except warm milk (for he was coughing badly).

"What did he do? He bound a goat to the legs of his bedstead and whenever a coughing fit shook his body he would suck her warm milk. After his death, although they searched into all his deeds, they found in him no fault except the sin of keeping a goat in his house."[242]

6 / THE INHERITANCE OF ASHER IN GALILEE

The tribe of Asher settled in the western section of the mountains of Upper Galilee, a land rich in vineyards and olive groves.

The patriarch Jacob blessed his son, saying, "As for Asher, his bread shall be fat, and he shall yield royal dainties."

The sages expounded: "His bread shall be fat"—this refers to his handsome daughters. "And he shall yield royal dainties"—his daughters are worthy of kings.

"His daughters were handsome and were wed to the sons of priestly families who were anointed with olive oil, and were given in marriage to kings who were sanctified with precious ointments."

Moses too promised Asher affluence and prominence: "Blessed be Asher above sons," he said. "Let him be the favored of his brethren, and let him dip his foot in oil. Iron and brass shall be thy bars."

The ancients commented: "Blessed be Asher above sons" —there is no son more blessed than Asher. "Let him be the favored of his brethren"—teaches us that he satisfies his brothers' need for oil, and they satisfy his need for corn.

Others say: "Let him be the favored of his brethren"—with his daughters. "And let him dip his foot in oil"—namely, that in the land of Asher oil streams as from a fountain. "Iron and brass shall be thy bars"—indicates that the land of Asher was the bolt of the Land of Israel.

And ancient commentator adds: "The heroes [of Asher] sit in the border towns and lock them, so that the enemies should not enter it [the Land of Israel] as if it were closed with locks and bars made of iron and brass."

Foreign people lived on the borders of Asher and tried from time to time to invade the Land. But the sons of Asher were warriors; many of them joined the army of King David, as it is told: "And of Asher, such as were able to go out in the host, that could set the battle in array, forty thousand. All these, being men of war, that could order the battle array, came with a whole heart."

The olive tree growing profusely in the land of Asher was the symbol of the tribe. Asher's stone was the jasper, and thus it was represented in the breast-plate of the High Priest.

The sages said: "Asher is jasper, and his standard is the color of this precious stone that women use to adorn themselves. On it is drawn an olive tree."[243]

7 / THE TWO RIVAL VILLAGES

Among the mountains of Galilee, on the high road that descends from Zefat to Acco, there is a village called Parod. Here is found the holy grave of Rabbi Nahum Ish-[man of] Gimzo, a little town in the vicinity of Lod. Below Parod there stood another village named Kefar Hananiah, which was famous for its pottery. There was no spring in Kefar Hananiah, and the inhabitants received water from the neighboring Parod.

A Jewish traveler who visited Galilee in the year 1522 wrote: "In Kefar Hananiah there are about thirty Jewish families, most of whom are priests *(kohanim)*, and they have a synagogue. I prayed there at the grave of Rabbi Abba Halafta. About forty years ago, the inhabitants of Kefar Hananiah quarreled with the inhabitants of Parod over the waters of the spring. Each village claimed the water. The inhabitants of Parod said, 'The spring is within our borders; it is clear, therefore, that the fountain is ours.' The inhabitants of Kefar Hananiah said, 'It is well known that for many generations we have had the right to use the waters of this well.' In the end, they went to the court of justice, where judgment was given against the inhabitants of Kefar Hananiah because they possessed no title deeds.

"In the night, one of the Jews of Kefar Hananiah dreamed that he saw Rabbi Abba Halafta, who said to him, 'Search in my grave and you will find a casket of copper which contains title deeds describing how I bought the spring from Rabbi Nahum Ish-Gimzo. Take these documents and show them to the king, and you will win your case. Afterward, you will return the casket with the deeds to its place.'

"The inhabitants of Kefar Hananiah did as they were directed and won their case."[244]

8 / DO NOT BRING POTTERS TO KEFAR HANANIAH

Kefar Hananiah lies on the border line of Lower and Upper Galilee. Among its inhabitants were many skillful potters whose earthenware was famous. The common saying, "Bringing potters to Kefar Hananiah" was equivalent to today's "Bringing coals to Newcastle."

The ancients said: "The pottery of Kefar Hananiah, it is not its nature to break."

Here was made a special pot known in the Talmud as "*lepissa* of Kefar-Hananiah," of which it was said, "*lepissa* of Kefar Hananiah holds one measure of lentils."[245]

9 / THE AFFLUENCE OF ANCIENT GUSH-HALAV

Gush-Halav was an important Jewish townlet of Upper Galilee in ancient times. Situated in the vicinity of Zefat, it is today a large village occupied by a Christian-Arab population. It was renowned for the fertility of its soil and the excellence of its oil. The following story illustrates these facts:

"It is related that once the people of Laodicea [a city in Syria] were in need of oil. They appointed an agent, and instructed him, 'Go and purchase for us a hundred myriad worth of oil.' When he came to Gush-Halav, he was told, 'Go to so-and-so in that field.' He went there and found a man breaking up the earth around his olive trees.

"The agent said to him, 'Have you a hundred myriad worth of oil that I require?' 'Yes,' replied the other, 'but wait until I finish my work.'

"The agent waited until the other had finished his work, but the man threw his tools on his back and went his way, removing the stones from his path as he went. The agent, following him, thought to himself, Has this man really got a hundred myriad worth of oil? I see that the Jews have merely made game of me!

"As soon as he reached his hometown, the man's maidservant brought out to him a bowl of hot water, and he washed his hands and his feet. She then brought out to him a golden bowl of oil, and he dipped in it his hands and his feet. After they had eaten and drunk, he measured out to the agent a hundred myriad worth of oil, and then asked, 'Do you perhaps need any more oil?'

" 'I do, indeed,' replied the agent, 'but I have no more money with me!'

" 'Well, if you wish to buy more, take it, and I will go back with you for the money,' said the man. He then measured out for him another eighteen myriad worth of oil.

"It is said that he [the man form Laodicea] hired every horse, mule, camel, and ass that he could find in all the Land of Israel.

"When he reached his hometown, all the townspeople came out to meet him and to applaud him."[246]

10 / WHAT DID THE EMPEROR RECEIVE FROM GUSH-HALAV?

In ancient times, Gush-Halav was reputed not only for the quality of its oil but also for its manufacture of a fine silk designated by the Greek name *mettaksa*.

"Once, the Roman Emperor Hadrian—may his bones be ground to dust—addressed himself to Rabbi Joshua son of Hanina, saying: 'Is it not written in the Bible: "A land wherein thou shalt eat bread without scarceness, thou shalt not lack any thing in it"?' And he asked from him three rare things, one of which was *mettaksa*.

"Rabbi Joshua, son of Hanina, brought him *mettaksa* from Gush-Halav."[247]

11 / THE CHAIN OF KING DAVID AT GUSH-HALAV

King David was wont to sit in his tribunal* on the top of Mount Moriah, where later the Great Temple was erected. And there he would judge his people Israel, helped by the magic of a chain possessed of wondrous virtues that hung in front of him in the hall of justice.

An Arab legend tells that the chain was later concealed in a secret place in Gush-Halav. The Arab geographer Al-Mukaddasi the Jerusalemite, of the tenth century, wrote: "At Gush-Halab is preserved the chain of David, but the authenticity thereof is doubtful."[248]

12 / THE CAVERN OF THE BABYLONIANS

In the mountains of Upper Galilee, in the vicinity of Zefat, stands the village of Alma. In ancient times it was a Jewish townlet. A large well-cut stone found on the spot, a remnant of the synagogue, brings us a warm greeting from the community that lived here in the past. Along its lower margin is carved the following Hebrew inscription: "Let there be peace in this place and in all the places of His people Israel."

Numerous grottoes are found in this area. The largest of them was known as the "Cavern of the Babylonians" for, according to legend, the bones of Babylonian Jews were brought here for burial.

About the year 1769, Moshe the Jerusalemite mentions "the large grotto which includes many caverns, and one passes from one to the other every three steps." Describing his experience in this subterranean hollow, he adds, "It stretches a distance of three days' walking as far as Jerusalem, and it is named the Cavern of the Babylonians; the stranger who enters within it loses his way, for it lies in complete darkness.

"And I did not wish to believe this, so I entered carrying

* *Legends of Jerusalem,* p. 41.

two candles, and a man was with me. And we tied a rope of great length at the first cavern and we penetrated a very long way inside. And the beadle stood outside near the rope, lest someone undo it. But after we had gone through several caves, the awe of darkness fell upon us. And speedily we went out of the cavern, driven by fear, and only after a long time did we gather our strength again."²⁴⁹

13 / THE STRANGE INSCRIPTION IN KEFAR-BIRAM

Among the houses of Kefar-Biram, in Upper Galilee, there can still be seen the impressive ruins of an ancient synagogue. In the Middle Ages, Jewish pilgrims were shown in this place the purported tomb of Queen Esther.

FIG. 46. ANCIENT SYNAGOGUE OF KEFAR-BIRAM

The Italian pilgrim Moses Bassola, who visited the Land of Israel in 1522, wrote of Kefar-Biram: "At the entrance to this ancient site, the following inscription, cut in the stone in square Hebrew letters, can be read: "Do not be astonished if snow falls in Nisan [April]. We have experienced it even in Sivan [June]."[250]

14 / THE WONDER-CHILD OF KEFAR-BIRAM

In the twelfth century, there lived in Kefar-Biram a couple by the name of Pinhas and Rahel. "Rabbi Pinhas was a great scholar; he knew the 'Innefable Name' of the Almighty; he never committed a sin, and never used his knowledge of the great and terrible Name [for his own personal advantage]."

In time, a wonder-child named Nahman was born to him. When the baby was one day old, he started to speak and to give wonderful scholarly discourses. His father took fright, rebuked him, and silenced him.

At the end of twelve years, the child began to speak again, and to prophesy "Wars and ordeals and signs and omens until a redeemer comes to Zion to deliver the House of Israel."

After he had uttered his predictions, the child died, and was thereafter called "Nahman Hatufa," for he was carried off [Hebrew, *hatuf*] before his time by death.

In Aramaic, this child is known as *Yanuka*—the Infant. The Infant's prophecy is accepted by the Cabalists. It is purported to have been discovered in a ruin of the town of Tiberias, written in the Aramaic language on ancient dilapidated scrolls hidden in a lead vessel.

Traditionally, the grave of the *Yanuka* was indicated in Kefar-Biram: "And with him there are Forty Just Men [buried] in the cavern."

At a later period, the tomb of Nahman Yanuka was shown in the cemetery of Zefat, and the "Cavern of the Yanuka"— *Mearat Yanuka*, in Hebrew—is known there to this very day.[251]

15 / THE CITY OF REFUGE

"The sixth lot came out for
the children of Naphtali.
And the fortified cities . . . Kedesh."

In Upper Galilee once stood the city of Kedesh Naphtali, a town of importance mentioned several times in the Bible. Kedesh was a city of refuge for Galilee as Shechem was for Samaria and Hebron for Judah.

"The Lord also spoke unto Joshua, saying, 'Speak to the Children of Israel, saying: Appoint out for you cities of refuge, that the slayer that killeth any person unawares and unwittingly may flee thither, and they shall be your refuge from the avenger of blood. And when he that doth flee unto one of those cities shall stand at the entrance to the gate of the city and shall declare his cause in the ears of the elders of that city, they shall take him unto them into the city, and give him a place that he may dwell among them. And if the avenger of blood pursue after him, then they shall not deliver the slayer up into his hand, because he smote his neighbor unwittingly and hated him not beforetime."

The sages of Israel pondered: He who slays his neighbor unwittingly whether in the south or in the north, how is he to know where the city of refuge is situated; where he can find safety? On the crossroads leading to these cities was written, in Hebrew, *Miklat! Miklat!*—Refuge! Refuge!"

At the end of every mile, there stood a little tower with the figure of a man pointing with his hand in the direction of the city of refuge.

From the sages of Israel we learn that a footpath was four feet wide and the highroad sixteen, but the roads leading to the cities of refuge were thirty-two feet wide, so as to give the fugitive sufficient room to escape without stumbling in his flight.[252]

16 / WHAT DID THE EMPEROR RECEIVE FROM NIZHANA?

Nizhana was a Jewish townlet in Upper Galilee. Today it has been replaced by an Arab village situated beyond the northern border of Israel, in Lebanon, and called Zalhana, an obvious corruption of the ancient name.

It is told of the Roman Emperor Hadrian ("may his bones be ground to dust") that he once hailed Rabbi Joshua son of Hanina, saying, "Is it not written in the Bible, 'a land wherein thou shalt eat bread without scarceness, thou shalt not lack any thing in it'?" And he asked three things from him, and one of them was pepper. And Rabbi Joshua son of Hanina "brought pepper from Nizhana."

Wherefore it was said: "The Land of Israel lacks nothing, it even has pepper."[253]

XIX
IN THE VALLEY OF THE UPPER JORDAN

1 / AYELET-HASHAHAR—THE MORNING STAR

Years ago, some young pioneers set up a communal settlement in beautiful Galilee, opposite snowy Mount Hermon.

For a few years, the farmers lived happily in all simplicity
without giving their place a name. They lacked even a clock
to measure the time; and thus did they rise to work: When
the watchman saw that the morning star stood directly over
the courtyard of the farm, he knew that it was time to begin
the day's labor, and he went from house to house calling:
"Haverim! Haverim! Ayelet hashahar aleichem! La'avoda!"
—Comrades! Comrades! The morning star shines upon you!
Rise to work!

When the members of the settlement decided to name
their settlement, they all gathered to discuss the matter, but
not one of the names suggested seemed fitting.

While sitting and arguing late into the night, weary and
sleepy, they suddenly heard the call of the night watchman:
"Ayelet hashahar aleichem!" The whole company rose as
one man and said, "That is the name we want. Let us call our

settlement Ayelet-Hashahar, since this star has roused us to our work in our fields and groves for so many years!"

The name was adopted on the spot, and the settlement has been called Ayelet-Hashahar ever since.*[254]

FIG. 47. AYELET-HASHAHAR
A photograph of the settlement in its early days.

2 / JOSEPH'S PIT IN UPPER GALILEE

At a short distance from the road going from Tiberias to Zefat, near the village of Amiad, lie the ruins of a medieval inn, named by the Arabs *Jib Yusef*—Joseph's Pit. They say that this is the same pit into which Joseph was cast by his brothers, and that here passed the Ishmaelite caravan that gathered him in and took him to Egypt.

By the tenth century, an inn named Jib Yusef already stood on this spot, on the route of the caravans traveling from

* See legend XII: 1.

Damascus to the Bridge of the Daughters of Jacob, and thence to Gaza and Egypt.

Medieval Christian pilgrims mention the Pit of Joseph, as does the Karaite traveler Shemuel, who crossed here on his way to Damascus in 1642. He wrote: "And we came to the pit where Joseph the Righteous, may his soul rest in peace, was thrown. Over the well a small dome has been erected, standing on four marble pillars. We drew water from the well and we drank it with great delight. In front of the pit there is a prayer place and an inn for travelers."

Another pilgrim, Rabbi Simha, confirms the tale in 1764. He too mentions "the pit of Joseph into which Joseph's brothers cast him, and the Arabs call it Jib Yusef; on top of it there is a round cupola which rests on four small arcades."[*255]

3 / THE BRIDGE OF THE DAUGHTERS OF JACOB

A bridge spans the Upper Jordan, near its source in Upper Galilee, along the highway leading to the Heights of Golan and on to Damascus, capital of Syria.

In Hebrew, it is known as *Gesher Benot Yaakov*—the Bridge of the Daughters of Jacob—for, according to legend, at this spot the patriarch and his faithful daughters crossed into the Land of Canaan.

The Arabs of the surrounding territory used to point out the tombs of the mourning sisters of Joseph, under the shade of venerable holy trees in this vicinity.

At this same place, Jacob and his daughters first heard the grievous tidings of Joseph's death, wherefore it is known, in Arabic, as *Makhadat el-Hizen*—the Ford of Sorrow. A Moslem geographer of the thirteenth century mentioned a building next to the ford and named it *Beit Alahzan*—House of Lamentation—and he added: "They say it is the place where

* The true site of Joseph's Pit is in the mountains of Samaria, in the vicinity of Shechem. See *Legends of Judea and Samaria,* p. 263.

Jacob passed the days of his lamentation when he was separated from Joseph. It was rebuilt by the Franks, and they made it into a great fortress. Saladin took it in 575 [1179] and destroyed it."

In the Middle Ages, the bridge was named for the patriarch Jacob. Moses Bassola, who traversed it in 1522, wrote, when traveling from Zefat to Damascus: "One passes over the Jordan by a stone bridge that is named "Bridge of Jacob," for it is said that here passed the patriarch, may his soul rest in peace, on the way back from Haran."

A later pilgrim, Moses son of Eliahu, also mentioned it, in the year 1655: "The Bridge of Jacob, peace be upon him! The Arabs that were with us told us [that] these are the places of Benei [the sons of] Israel from days of yore. And we celebrated the Sabbath at the Bridge of Jacob, and the Ishmaelites said, 'This is the bridge that Yaakub [Jacob] built, and he also put up an inn [caravansary] here for the passersby.' And one Ishmaelite showed us a ruined house, which was no more than a heap of stones, and said, 'This was the house of Yaakub where he dwelt in winter days; the summer months he spent in the town of Zefat.' He said, 'This, forsooth, I hold from my father, and he heard it from his own father, for truly I am a native of this land.' "256

4 / THE TEARS OF THE DAUGHTERS OF JACOB

When the daughters of Jacob, coming from the east, were crossing the Jordan at the spot where today stands the bridge named for them, tidings reached them that Joseph had been mauled by a wild beast.

The maidens began to stray to and fro, and wandered amid hills and dales, seeking traces of their unfortunate brother. They wept and wailed and hot tears welled from their eyes. These tears were changed to black stones, and these are the blocks of dark basalt scattered through the numerous hills and vales of Galilee.[257]

5 / YESOD-HAMAALAH—WHY WAS IT SO CALLED?

On the eastern side of Upper Galilee stands Yesod-Hamaalah, one of the first pioneer settlements in Eretz-Israel. Its name is derived from the Book of Ezra, in the description of the return of the exiles from Babylon to the Land: "For upon the first day of the first month began he to go up [Hebrew, *yesod hamaalah*] from Babylon"; this marked the beginning of the ascent to Zion, toward the establishment of the Second Commonwealth.

Though the Bible here spells the word *yesod* defectively (that is, with a *yod, samekh,* and *dalet*), minus the penultimate *vav,* the residents of Yesod-Hamaalah are meticulous in spelling the name of their settlement with the missing *vav.* What prompts them to do so? According to Jewish tradition, prior to the advent of the Messiah in "the latter days," the settlements of Galilee will be laid waste. Our sages opined that "In the steps of the Messiah, impertinence will be on the increase and dignity will vaunt itself. Galilee will be laid waste, and the men of the border will wander round from city to city, but will find no favor."

However, the legend adds: "Whatsoever includes the Tetragrammaton *(yod, heh, vav, heh),* the 'Ineffable Name' of the Almighty, will not be destroyed but will remain eternal." In the Hebrew name Yesod-Hamaalah (when *yesod* is spelled with the missing *vav*), you have the letters *yod, heh, vav, heh.* Hence, this is a guarantee that the settlement will be secure in the bond of eternal life, and will exist even in the Messianic Age.[258]

6 / RABBI MEIR IN KEFAR-MAMLA

Mamla was a Jewish center in Galilee whose inhabitants never reached old age.

It apparently stood on the margin of the malarial swamps of the Hula Valley, and the disease claimed many victims.

It is possible that the name Mamla has survived, slightly altered, in the Arab *Malha,* which the large source is called that emerges near the Sea of Hula, by the side of the highway running today from Rosh-Pinna to Metulla.

Rabbi Meir, the famous Tiberias sage, once came to Kefar-Mamla. The inhabitants complained that while they were still young, "when the hair on the head is dark," they met untimely deaths.

Rabbi Meir said to them, "Perchance you are of the house of Eli, to whom the man of God said: 'There shall not be an old man in thy house . . . and all the increase of thy house shall die young men.' "

Said the people of Mamla, "Rabbi, pray for us!"

He said to them, "Go and see that charity is practiced, give alms, and you will be worthy of old age!"[259]

7 / THE ORIGIN OF THE NAME HULA

In the northern section of the Jordan Valley, there was a small lake called *Yam-Hula*—the Sea of Hula. In old Hebrew literature this name appears in the Aramaic form of *Hulata.*

Yakut, the Moslem geographer of the thirteenth century, held that Hula derived from Hul, one of the descendants of Shem, son of Noah.

Truly, the names of Shem's sons and grandsons were given to various eastern nations and countries. Genesis mentions a few: "The sons of Shem . . . Asshur . . . Aram. And the sons of Aram: Uz, and Hul . . ."[260]

8 / FROM JERUSALEM TO HULA

At the end of time, says legend, living waters will stream from the Holy of Holies in Jerusalem's Temple to Lake Hula.

As Zechariah prophesied: "And it shall come to pass in that day,/That living waters shall go out from Jerusalem:/Half of them toward the eastern sea,/And half of them toward the western sea."

Ezekiel adds: "These waters issue forth toward the eastern region."

"Eastern region," say the sages, "this is the Sea of Somho" —another name of the Sea of Hula.*[261]

9 / A TRADE OF THE SONS OF NAPHTALI

The Tribe of Naphtali inherited Upper Galilee, including the swamps of Lake Hula.**

Vast thickets of papyrus grew in the marshes, the same papyrus from which the ancients, especially the Egyptians, prepared paper. Many old manuscripts were written on papyrus sheets; some of them were brought to light in the excavations of the Holy Land.

The sons of Naphtali, it is said, learned to make paper out of the papyrus. They cut the pliant long stems into thin strips, then twisted and wove them into sheets.

How do we know that they did indeed practice this handicraft? "From their very name," say the sages. "Naphtali is derived from the Hebrew root *phatol*, meaning, 'to twist.' "[262]

---

* See legend XI:9.
** See legend XII:6.

10 / THE SOURCES OF THE JORDAN

At the foot of a hillock whereon once flourished the biblical town of Dan gushes forth one of the richest sources of the Jordan. Therefore the ancients derived the name of the river from the combination of the name Dan and the root "to descend"—in Hebrew, *yored*.

FIG. 48. MOUND OF ANCIENT DAN
The Arabs call this site *Tel el-Kadi*—Mound of the Judge.

Said the sages, "Why is it called Jordan? Because it descends [Hebrew, *yored*] from Dan."

In the Middle Ages, the Christian pilgrims thought that the

name Jordan was composed of the addition of the two words "Ior" and "Dan." They believed that the Jordan had two tributaries, one called Ior and the other Dan; several maps of that period depict the Jordan originating from two branches designated by these names.

In present days, the name Jordan is related to the Hebrew *yored,* for the Jordan flows down—descends—through the whole length of the Land of Israel from north to south, from the foot of the Hermon to the Dead Sea—a fall of about a thousand meters.[263]

11 / DAN WAS FORMERLY NAMED LESHEM

Many families of the tribe of Dan, which inherited the surroundings of Jaffa, wandered up north and settled at the foot of Mount Hermon, in the present Valley of Hula. Here they built the town of Dan, the northernmost city of the country in biblical times—whence the saying "from Dan to Beersheba" to describe the whole length of the Land of Israel. The town stood on the hill called by the Arabs *Tel el-Kadi,* next to the contemporary settlement of Dan.

The Holy Scriptures relate Dan's migration to the north, and tell of its town Dan, which was erected on the foundation of a more ancient city named, according to one version, Laish and to another, Leshem.

"And they . . . came into Laish . . . and smote them with the edge of the sword; and they burnt the city with fire. And they built the city, and dwelt therein. And they called the name of the city Dan, after the name of Dan their father."

Or, again, "The children of Dan went up and fought against Leshem, and took it, and smote it with the edge of the sword, and possessed it, and dwelt therein, and called Leshem, Dan, after the name of Dan their father."

The well-known commentator Rashi says, "Leshem—after a precious stone of that name which was found there and which was set in the breastplate of the High Priest as the symbol of Dan. In this way it was established that in truth this was their inheritance."[264]

12 / THE SYMBOL OF DAN

The stone representing Dan on the ceremonial breastplate worn by the High Priest officiating in the Great Temple was the jacinth—*leshem,* in Hebrew. God commanded Moses, saying: "And thou shalt make a breastplate of judgment, the work of the skillful workman. . . . And thou shalt set in it settings of stones, four rows of stones . . . and the third row a jacinth."

Why was it found appropriate to represent Dan by the jacinth? Because as this stone changes its aspect to the good or to the bad, according to the nature of its wearer, so was Dan wont to change its disposition—sometimes serving faithfully the Almighty God, blessed be He, and sometimes swerving from the right path and sacrificing to the Baals and the golden calves.

The *leshem* had the luster of a lion's eye. So Moses, the man of God, said: "Dan is a lion's whelp."

It was said: "Dan [is] jacinth; the color of his flag is like that of the sapphire, and a snake is depicted on it. Why a snake? Because Jacob said of his son: "Dan shall be a serpent in the way,/A horned snake in the path."

Legend adds: "Dan's bit is like the sting of a snake."[265]

13 / DAN IS A LION'S WHELP

"The lion, which is mightiest among beasts,
And turneth not away for any."

The territory of Dan spread in the northeastern section of the Valley of Hula, at the foot of the mountains of Bashan, rising in Transjordan. Many warriors were provided by the tribe to the armies of King David, as recorded in Chronicles: "And of the Danites that could set the battle in array, twenty and eight thousand and six hundred."

Of Dan, Moses said: "Dan is a lion's whelp, that leapeth from Bashan."

Why this comparison of Dan to a lion? "This teaches us that he [Dan] guarded the border, and whoever guards the border is like unto a lion."

Another commentator elaborates: "And he guards and protects Israel like a lion, that no enemies should penetrate into the Land."[266]

14 / THE HILL OF THE JUDGE

At the northern limit of the Land of Israel, at the foot of Mount Hermon, rises an ancient hill *(tel)* whereon sat the town of Dan. At its base surges a large stream, one of the main sources of the Jordan.

To the west of Tel Dan flows the brook Hatzbani, and to the east the Banias, both tributaries of the Jordan. The three branches—the Dan, the Hatzbani and the Banias—join to form the River Jordan.

Tel Dan is known to the Arabs as *Tel el-Kadi*—the Hill of the Judge—for they tell the following tale:

In ancient times, there was no Jordan in the land, but there were three streams, all flowing from the foot of Mount Hermon in various directions. A quarrel once broke out between them as to which was the largest and most important. The quarrel went on until finally the rivers invited the Lord of the Universe to descend and judge between them. The Lord of the Universe descended to earth and seated Himself on a small hill to judge the matter. But He could not settle their dispute, so, in the end, he said, "Rivers! Ye are dear to Me, all three. Hearken to

My counsel. Unite all three and together ye will indeed be the biggest river."

So the three rivers joined together and the Jordan was formed from them. And the mound whereon the Lord of the Universe sat in judgment is known as The Hill of the Judge to this very day. See fig. 48.[267]

15 / THE GOLDEN CALF IN DAN

When the town of Dan was established, the statue of Micah was put up in the city, as recorded in the Book of Judges: "And the children of Dan set up for themselves the graven image; and Jonathan, the son of Gershom . . . he and his sons were priests to the tribe of the Danites until the day of the captivity of the land."

At a later period, Jeroboam, King of Israel, introduced the cult of the golden calf in Dan: "Whereupon the king took counsel, and made two calves of gold . . . and the other put he in Dan. And this thing became a sin; for the people went to worship before the one, even unto Dan."

In the Middle Ages, since no traces of the ancient city had remained at its true location, the Jewish pilgrims called the nearby town of Banias by the name Dan. Here, at the foot of the mountains, one of the main sources of the Jordan streams form a grotto cut out of the rock.

Benjamin of Tudela, who visited the Land of Israel about the year 1170, also calls Banias by the name Dan, and he tells: "There is a cavern from where the Jordan issues, and before the cavern one can discern the site of the altar of Micah's image; the place of the altar of Jeroboam where stood the golden calf."[268]

16 / MAY THE WATERS OF PANIAS BE TURNED INTO
BLOOD

At the foot of Mount Hermon, in Upper Galilee, rests the village of Banias, on the site of the ancient town of Panias, or Pamias, named after the Greek shepherd god Pan, to whom the inhabitants sacrificed. Pan was the protector of flocks, herds, and pastures. He made the first shepherd's pipe from reeds, and taught men to play it. He was pictured with the horns, legs, and ears of a goat.

From among the thickets and the luxuriant bushes of the surroundings bursts forth an abundant spring, which develops into a turbulent river—one of the three main sources of the Jordan.

These waters stream from under the debris of a wrecked cavern, the famous grotto of Panias well-known to the ancients, where the rites of Pan's cult were practiced.

It was said: "The Jordan issues from the cavern of Panias."

Said Rabbi Kahana: "The virility of the Jordan comes from the cave of Panias."

Rabbi Yose son of Kisma, lived in the second century C.E. Jewish pilgrims of medieval times knew his tomb in Upper Galilee, and many came to prostrate themselves on his grave.

It is related: The pupils of Rabbi Yose asked him, "When shall Messiah, son of David, come?"

Said Rabbi Yose, "I fear you may ask me for a sign."

Said they, "We shall demand no omen from you."

Said the Rabbi, "Whenever this gate falls and is rebuilt, is wrecked again and erected anew, destroyed once more— then, before it is completed for the third time, the son of David shall appear."

Said the pupils, "O Master! Give us a sign!"

Said he, "Did you not say that you asked for no omen?"

Said they, "Nevertheless."

Said the Rabbi, "If so be it, may the waters of the cave of

Panias be turned into blood." And they were turned into blood.[269]

17 / THE SUFFERING OF PANIAS

The powerful Roman Emperor Diocletianus came to Eretz-Israel in the year 297 C.E., and, as it is told, he "suppressed the people of Panias." He burdened them with heavy taxes and caused them much distress.

Legend holds that in his youth, Diocletianus Caesar was a swinekeeper in Tiberias, and the Jewish boys there used to beat him. In time he became emperor, but he remembered the thrashings he had received from the children of Tiberias, so he settled in Panias and decreed harsh edicts against the sages of Tiberias.

To the words of the Torah: "The Lord bless thee, and keep thee," the elders added, "that thou may not come under the ruling of the country of Panias, be fined wrongfully, and be told, 'Pay gold!' "[270]

18 / THE MIRACULOUS STATUE IN BANIAS

According to the Christian legend, the woman who was cured by Jesus, as told in Matthew, originated from Banias: "And, behold, a woman which was diseased with an issue of blood twelve years, came behind him, and touched the hem of his garment: For she said within herself, If I may but touch his garment, I shall be whole. But Jesus turned him about, and when he saw her, he said, Daughter, be of good comfort; thy faith hath made thee whole. And the woman was made whole from that hour."

In memory of this cure, the Christian inhabitants of the past put up a statue of Jesus in Banias.

One of the fathers of the Christian Church, Eusebius, wrote in the fourth century that he saw with his own eyes this statue of Jesus, and around it grew a plant whose branches brushed against the holy image; from this touch the green boughs were imbued with the virtue of healing all ailments.

Julian the Apostate destroyed the image of Jesus, and erected in its place his own statue. God punished him by sending a thunderbolt which cleaved it into two; the head and the neck stuck in the ground while the trunk remained standing, marked by signs of the lightning.

St. Willibald, the English traveler of the year 954, described the Christian inhabitants of Banias and their church, wherein are kept the remnants of the ancient statue of Jesus.[271]

XX
ON THE HEIGHTS
OF MOUNT HERMON

1 / MOUNT HERMON

The precise origin of the name Hermon is unknown. According to one tale, it derives from the Hebrew *herem*—ban
—because, says legend, on these very heights the angels pledged to ban from their midst whosoever swerved from the oath they had sworn.*

Mount Hermon was blessed with many names. The Holy Scriptures said, "Hermon, the Sidonians call Sirion, and the Amorites call it Senir." The sages added: "Senir and Sirion are among the mountains of Eretz-Israel."

According to one explanation, the name Senir is a contraction of two Hebrew words, *soneh nir*—field hater. For, as explains the commentator, "Senir does not yield itself to the plough and to the hand of the sower." Its summit and higher slopes are covered with snow and ice all through the year, wherefore it was also known as *Har Hasheleg*—Mount of Snow.

Thus, four different names were conferred upon Hermon:

* See legend XX:3.

"It proves how precious the Holy Land was in the eyes of the nations. Every one wished to have a part in it—four empires ruled over it, and each gave it a name after its own choice."[272]

2 / MOUNT HERMON—SNOW MOUNT

Since Mount Hermon is coated with deep layers of ice all the days of the year, it was also known as Snow Mount—in Aramaic, *Tur Talga.*

The Aramaic translation of the Bible designates Mount Hermon by the name Senir and adds this brief description: "The mountain of snow which is never free from ice neither in summer nor in winter."

FIG. 49. SNOW-CAPPED HERMON

The famous scholar, Rabbi Joshua son of Hanina, who lived in the second century, jokingly referred to himself as "The Mount of Snow," for the white hair which topped his head.

The Arabs call Hermon *Djebel a-Talg*—Mountain of Ice. They also refer to it as *Djebel a-Sheikh*—Mountain of the Sheikh—for, like snow-capped Hermon, the sheikh, the chieftain of the village, covers his head with a white turban. Thus he stands out among his people, as Mount Hermon towers over all the heights of the Holy Land.[273]

3 / THE ANGELS ON MOUNT HERMON

"And it came to pass, when men began to multiply on the face of the earth, and daughters were born unto them, that the sons of God saw the daughters of men that they were fair; and they took them for wives, whomsoever they chose . . . and they bore children to them, the same were the mighty men that were of old, the men of renown."

This happened during the lifetime of Jared son of Mahalal, of whom the Bible says: "And Jared lived a hundred sixty and two years, and begot Enoch . . . and Enoch walked with God."

The Book of Enoch repeats the tale with further details: "And it came to pass that men multiplied in these times, and daughters comely and beautiful were born unto them. And the sons of heaven, the angels, saw them and coveted them. And they said one to another: Let us choose wives to ourselves from among the daughters of men and they shall bear us sons. And they all responded and declared: Let us take an oath one and all and swear under penalty of excommunication that we shall not swerve from our decision but shall fulfill this purpose. Then they swore the oath. And they were all together two hundred angels. And in the time of Jared they descended on a mountain which since then was called Mount

Hermon because here they pledged themselves under penalty of anathema [in Hebrew, *herem*]. And they took to themselves each one of them wives, and they became with child and gave birth to mighty men, three hundred ells high each, who devoured all the fruits of man's labor."[274]

4 / THE PLACE OF THE PROMISE

"Said the Holy One, blessed be He:
I shall bring Israel out of Egypt,
through the merit of the one with whom
I spoke at the Place between
the Parts—that is Abraham."

"The word of the Lord came unto Abram in a vision, saying, 'Fear not, Abram, I am thy shield, thy reward shall be exceeding great.' . . . And He brought him forth abroad, and said: 'Look now toward heaven, and count the stars, if thou be able to count them'; and He said unto him: 'So shall thy seed be.' . . . And He said unto him: 'I am the Lord that brought thee out of Ur of the Chaldees, to give thee this land to inherit it.' And he said: 'O Lord God, whereby shall I know that I shall inherit it?' And He said unto him: 'Take Me a heifer of three years old, and a she-goat of three years old, and a ram of three years old, and a turtle-dove, and a young pigeon.' And he took him all these, and divided them in the midst, and laid each half over against the other; but the birds divided he not. And the birds of prey came down upon the carcasses, and Abram drove them away. . . . In that day the Lord made a covenant with Abram, saying: 'Unto thy seed have I given this land.' "

"On the fifteenth of Nisan did He speak with our father Abraham at the covenant between the parts."

On one of the slopes of Mount Hermon which overlooks the Land of Israel, the place can be seen where God made this covenant with Abraham, and promised him the Holy Land.

According to Jewish pilgrims, in medieval times, a beautiful building with three domes stood on the spot; it was called, in Hebrew, *Maamad Avraham Avinu*—the Place of our Father Abraham—or *Maamad bein ha-Betarim*—the Place of the Covenant between the Parts—and by the Arabs *Mashad et-Tiyur*—the Holy Place of the Birds—in memory of the birds of prey that came down upon the carcasses and which Abraham drove away.

FIG. 50. PLACE OF OUR FATHER ABRAHAM

This is the spot which is now called *Makam Ibrahim el Khalil*—the Holy Place of Abraham, the friend of God—and it is situated in a dense forest of oaks, whose venerable trees have been preserved owing to the sanctity of the shrine in their midst.[275]

5 / THE SNOW-CAPPED HERMON

After the Almighty had given the Holy Law from Mount Sinai, all the other mountains appeared before the Lord with plaints and quarrelsome words, crying together, "Why didst Thou give the Holy Law from Mount Sinai and not from other mountains?"

The Lord answered, "Set yourselves in an orderly row and let Me hear each mountain in turn." The mountains tussled among themselves until they stood in order, from the most powerful to the weakest.

Mount Tabor approached first, and said to the Almighty, "Why was the Holy Law not given upon me? See my rounded peak. Am I not lovelier than all the mountains of the world?" And the Lord answered, "Indeed you are more beautiful; but I foresee that in days to come churches of the Gentiles will rise on your summit. I cannot give the Law to Israel from a mountain upon which there will be churches."

Tabor went forth with bowed head, and Mount Gilboa drew near, saying, "Why didst Thou not give the Torah from me?"

"Because I know that Saul, first of the kings of Israel, will perish upon you," replied the Lord.

Thus did all the mountains pass before the Lord of the Universe and were turned away.

Last of all came a small, lowly hill, and the Lord said, "Tell Me your name." In sorrow, it answered, "Hermon. Why didst

Thou not give the Torah from me? At the borders of the Holy Land am I, and from my feet flow the fountains of the Jordan that is so dear to Thee." And the Lord said, "Verily, it would have been fitting that the Holy Law should be given from you; but since it was not, I give you another gift. I shall make you loftier than all the mountains of the land, and upon your highest portions shall eternal snows rest. And all the mountains shall envy you."

Since then, Mount Hermon is the highest of the mountains of the land, and its summit is covered with an eternal cap of snow.[276]

6 / MOSES AND MOUNT HERMON

"For thou shalt see the land afar off;
but thou shalt not go thither."

The topmost summit of Mount Hermon is called Sion, from the Hebrew *si*—peak. Legend has evolved another etymology: *si*, it contends, is derived in this case from the root *lehasi* —to lift up and carry off—wherefore the following tale is told:

When he was standing on the threshold of the Land of Israel for which his soul had yearned so long, Moses came into the presence of the Almighty and begged to be allowed to enter into the land of His promise, saying, "I beseech Thee, O my Lord, do for me what Thou shalt do for Elijah the Prophet; lift me up as amidst a storm and carry me into Eretz-Israel so I need not cross the Jordan, since such is Thy wish."

Said the Almighty, blessed be He, "Let it suffice thee!"

Said Moses, "If Thou art not so disposed, pray allow me to go the way I wish and I undertake not to traverse Thy river Jordan."

What did Moses intend to do? He meant to climb Mount Hermon to its very top, cling to the peak, Sion, which would then lift him up and carry him off *(lehasi)* into the Holy Land.

But then the voice of God pierced his consciousness, saying sternly, "Let it suffice thee!"*277

7 / JERUSALEM WILL BE BUILT ON MOUNT HERMON

"And it shall come to pass in the end of days,
That the mountains of the Lord's house shall be
established as the top of the mountains."

At the end of time, with the advent of the Messiah and the redemption of Israel, Jerusalem and the Temple of the Lord will be built on top of the mountains that have been exalted by Jewish tradition.

The Book of Zerubbabel tells: "The Temple too will be built on the summit of five mountains, and I asked Him (the Almighty, blessed be He): What are their names? And He answered, saying: Lebanon, Mount Moriah, Tabor, Carmel and Hermon.**278

8 / THE HIVITES ON MOUNT HERMON

At the time of Joshua's conquest, the Hivites were among the small nations living in the Land of Canaan. Some dwelt on the mountains of Hermon and Lebanon. The Book of Joshua mentions them: "The Hivite under Hermon in the land of Mizpah." Also, the Book of Judges: "And the Hivites

* A similar story depicts Moses' attempt to penetrate into the Land of Israel by way of the underground tunnel of Caesarion, which ran underneath the base of Mount Hermon. See legend XXI:3.
** See legend II:18.

that dwelt in mount Lebanon, from Mount Baal-hermon unto the entrance of Hamath."

The origin of the name is unknown; legend derives it from the Aramaic *hivia*, meaning "snake."

"For," said the sages, "they [the Hivites] tasted the earth like a serpent [*hivia*] to ascertain its nature, whether good for cornfields, vineyards, or other plantations."

Others say: "It signifies that they were as expert in the knowledge of different kinds of earth as a serpent, for in Galilee a serpent is called *hivia.*"

Hivites also lived in the vicinity of Jerusalem and "their cities were Gibeon, and Chephirah, and Beeroth, and Kiriath-jearim."

When they saw Joshua prevail over their neighbors, fearing for their lives, they sent a delegation to him, footsore, as if it had come from a faraway land, and thus they tricked him into signing a covenant with them. The story is told at great length in the Book of Joshua and the commentator adds: "Why [are they named] Hivites? Because they acted treacherously, like the *hivia*"—the snake.[279]

9 / WATER FLOWS FROM MOUNT HERMON TO PERSIA

At the foot of Mount Hermon issue forth not only the sources of the Jordan but also, according to the legend, a large spring named Abulwair, whose waters once streamed through underground channels to the faraway land of Persia.

This tale is reported by an English traveler of the eighteenth century, and these are his words:

"A shepherd who fed his flock every day on the descent of the Mountain and was obliged always to carry water with him to drink, because there was none to be found upon the mountain, nor about it, one day perceived his dog coming from beneath a rock and shaking the water off his body. He followed his dog and observed that he slid under a great rock;

he found a cavity where he saw issue from under the rocks a surprising quantity of water. He took a fancy to stop one of the canals. About a year after, three Persian lords, sent on purpose, arrived in the Plain of Damascus inquiring the way to the head of the River Abulwair; they said they knew by tradition that it was in the plain, adding that the River which never ceased running before was lately become dry, and offered a liberal reward to any who should make the discovery." After many diversions the shepherd opened the canal, the river Abulwair started flowing as formerly, and he received his reward. The traveler ends his story on a skeptical note: "I do not pretend to warrant the truth of this story; but it is certain that it has been the occasion of calling the western part of Damascus the Plain of Persia"—a name which has remained to this very day.[280]

JORDAN

XXI
ON THE HEIGHTS OF GOLAN

Golan is the name of a mountainous range rising on the eastern coast of the Sea of Galilee and running northward along the Upper Jordan and the Valley of Hula as far as the mountains of Hermon. The Heights of Golan stand in Transjordan, facing the mountains of Galilee across the Jordan Rift.

The Golan is an integral part of the Land of Israel and of its history, as related in the Holy Scriptures. It was part of the inheritance of Manasseh, an Israelite tribe which settled in Transjordan. Many ruins of synagogues, as well, of the second and third centuries, testify to its dense population in ancient times.

1 / THE FORTRESS OF NIMROD

On the summit of a steep rocky mount rising between the heights of Mount Hermon and the plateau of the Golan, ruins of a mighty fortress stand out clearly against the skyline.

It was erected in the Middle Ages, during the crucial wars waged between the Crusaders and the Moslems, when the two great powers from the west and the east fought for supremacy in the Holy Land.

Legend holds that this stronghold was built by Nimrod, a descendant of Noah the Just, of whom the Bible says: "He began to be a mighty one in the earth. He was a mighty hunter before the Lord."

FIG. 51. POOL OF RAM
In the foreground are the heights of Golan; in the background, the Sea of Galilee.

Wherefore it is called in Hebrew *Metzudat Nimrod,* a translation from the Arabic *Kalat Nimrud*—Fortress of Nimrod.[281]

2 / FROM RAM TO PANIAS

On the heights of the mountains of Golan lies a small pool, the Pool of Ram. It is named from the Hebrew *ram*—high— because it is situated on a high mount more than a thousand meters above sea level. The Greeks called it *Phialar*—the bowl—because of the roundness of its circumference.

The ancients believed that the cavern of Panias continued deep into the bowels of the mountain, forming a tunnel which connected with the bottom of the small lake Ram, at a walking distance of about two hours. Through this channel, they held, the waters of the lake flow to the cave of Panias and join the river Jordan. Josephus Flavius wrote: "Panium is thought to be the fountain of Jordan, but in reality it is carried thither in an occult manner from the place called Phiala. Its waters continue always up to its edges, without either sinking or running over. The origin of the Jordan was formerly unknown, but was discovered by Philip, when tetrarch of the land of the Trachonites. He had chaff thrown into Phiala, and it was found at Panium by the water through the tunnel."[282]

3 / MOSES AND THE TUNNEL OF CAESARION

Panias was also known by the name Caesarion, after Augustus Caesar, Emperor of Rome. To distinguish it from the Caesarea on the seashore, Caesarea Maritima, the capital of Roman rule in Palestine, it was named Caesarea Philippi, after Philip, the son of Herod, who was the governor—tetrarch—of the district of Panias.

The name Caesarea Philippi is mentioned in the Gospels as one of the sites visited by Jesus and his disciples.

Legend holds that the tunnel of Panias, also known as Mehillah de-Caesarion—the Tunnel of Caesarea—continued deep into the mountains and penetrated beyond the river Jordan.

It is told that when Moses stood east of the Jordan, he asked the Almighty to be allowed to cross the river and to come into the Promised Land for which his soul yearned so fervently. And when God refused him, "Still Moses continued to pray and to beg the Almighty. He said, 'O Lord of the World, since the decree has been issued that I should enter it neither as a king nor as an ordinary man, let me then enter it by the cave of Caesarion which is below Panias.' But the Lord said, 'There thou shalt not pass!' "[283]

4 / HOW THE LAKE OF RAM CAME INTO BEING

Arab legend relates: In ancient times, on the site of the Pool of Ram, there was a rich and flourishing village; but the villagers were very stingy and bad-natured. They would not give food to the hungry, nor water to those who thirsted.

One day, a very holy man entered the village and could find no place to rest and refresh himself. All doors were barred against him and no one offered him food or drink, so all that night he remained in the street, hungry and without shelter.

When he went forth on the morrow, he turned to the village and cursed it, saying, "Ya Allah! May the village and its wicked inhabitants sink into the ground!" And the ground opened immediately and swallowed the village with all who dwelt there. And in its place appeared this lake, the blue Pool of Ram.[284]

5 / THE BIG EYE OF RAM

The Pool of Ram is likely the place called in Aramaic by the Talmud *Eina Rabati Debiram*—the Big Spring of Beit Ram. This was the name of the settlement by the side of the small

lake, probably on the site of the present Druze village Mas-
'ada. *Eina Rabati*—the Big Spring—can also be interpreted
the "Big Eye," as *ein* stands both for "spring" and "eye" in
Hebrew. This designation befits well the blue pond which
sparkles in the sun like a wide-open almond-shaped eye.

The Bible relates how the fountains of the deep sprang up
at the time of Noah the Righteous. When the deluge was
over, the torrential rains stopped and the fountains of the
deep were sealed, for it is written, "The fountains also of the
deep and the windows of heaven were stopped, and the rain
from heaven was restrained."

"But," adds legend, "not all the springs were closed; three
remained flowing." These are Balua of Gader—the hot
spring that streams close to the town of Gader in the Valley
of the Yarmuk—and also the hot springs of Tiberias and the
big spring of Beit Ram.[285]

6 / WHERE WAS THE LAND OF TOB

Of Jephthah the Gileadite, who ruled in Transjordan,
the Book of Judges says: "Then Jephthah fled from his
brethren, and dwelt in the land of Tob; and there were
gathered vain fellows to Jephthah, and they went out with
him . . . the elders of Gilead went to fetch Jephthah out
of the land of Tob. And they said unto Jephthah: 'Come
and be our chief.' "

According to the sages, the Land of Tob stretched to the
east of Lake Kinneret, within the area that later was known
as the Land of Golan. Its main city was Sussita, today a heap
of ruins on the heights of a steep mount towering above the
settlement Ein-Gev, on the eastern shore of Lake Kinneret.

Many Jewish villages flourished within the boundaries of
Sussita. But since they had a mixed population, the inhabitants were exempted from some ritual obligations.

"Why was it called Eretz-Tob—the Land of Good? Because

it was good to live there, for the inhabitants did not pay the tithe—the tenth part of the annual proceeds of the land.[286]

7 / THE TOMBS OF THE ISRAELITES IN GOLAN

To the east of the Sea of Kinneret soar the mountains of Golan, so rich in past memories of Israel. Their heights are strewn with many dolmens, the tombs of prehistoric times.

A group of such dolmens is scattered along the banks of the river Rukad, which crosses the mountains of Golan and descends into the waters of the Yarmuk, a tributary of the river Jordan.

The Arabs of the vicinity designate these dolmens by the name *Kubur Benei Israil*—the Tombs of the Sons of Israel. They believe them to mark the graves of the Israelites who dwelt in this vicinity in very ancient times.*[287]

* The name *Kubur Benei Israil* is also given by the Arabs to prehistoric tombs located near the village of Hizma, which has replaced ancient Azmut to the northeast of the nearby city of Jerusalem.

XXII

IN THE LAND OF BASHAN

1 / EDREI—THE CAPITAL OF KING OG

"And slew mighty kings,
For His mercy endureth for ever. . . .
And Og King of Bashan,
For His mercy endureth for ever."

In the Land of Bashan, today part of Syria, there is a townlet named, in Arabic, Dar'a. This is the site of Edrei, the
capital of King Og, who reigned over Bashan at the time of
the Israelite conquest.

As the Bible says: "And they [the Israelites] turned and
went up by the way of Bashan; and Og the king of Bashan
went out against them, he and all his people, to battle at
Edrei.

"And the Lord said unto Moses: 'Fear him not; for I have
delivered him into thy hand, and all his people, and his land.
. . . So they smote him, and his sons, and all his people . . . and
they possessed his land."

Legend embroiders on this tale, saying: Moses and Israel
came near to Edrei. Said Moses, "Let us wait here and enter

at the time of the morning prayer." The town was still enshrouded in darkness when Moses, lifting up his eyes, saw King Og sitting on the wall of the city. His giant feet were reaching down to the ground.

Said Moses, "I do not know what my eyes are seeing. These people must have built a second wall during the night."

Said the Almighty, blessed be He, "Moses, this that thou art looking upon is Og. His legs are eighteen ells long."

At these words, Moses' heart failed him and he was filled with great fear.

Said the Almighty, blessed be He, "Do not fear, I shall cause him to fall in front of thee."

Then King Og tore out a mountain and flung it upon Israel.

And Moses picked up a stone and threw it at him while uttering the Ineffable Name. And the giant king fell to the ground.

The sages of Israel said, "Whoever beholds the rock which Og King of Bashan threw at Moses should return thanks and praise to the Lord Almighty.*[288]

2 / HOW KING OG FOUGHT THE ISRAELITES

When Og, King of Bashan, saw the hosts of Israel, he asked, "The army of Israel, how large is it?" He was answered, "It stretches along three parasangs."

"I shall uproot a mountain three parasangs high," said he, "and throw it at Israel, and thus kill them all!"

The giant king went fortwith, tore out a mountain three parasangs high, lifted it upon his head, and hastened toward the advancing troops. At this juncture, the Almighty, blessed be He, sent an army of ants to dig a large passage through the bowels of the mountain. The hollowed hill sank upon Og's

* See *Legends of Jerusalem*, p. 230.

shoulders, imprisoning his head, and greatly incommoding him.

The heathen king tried to lower his burden. But by God's will, his teeth suddenly grew large and long, stuck out of his mouth on both sides, and were thrust deep into the mountain's sides, fastening it to its position; and all his efforts did not avail him to lift up the suffocating load.

What then did Moses do? He himself was ten ells high. He seized an ax ten ells long, jumped ten ells high, struck at Og's ankles, felled him, and killed him.

On this occasion the psalmist sang: "Arise, O Lord: save me, O my God;/For Thou has smitten all mine enemies upon the cheek,/Thou hast broken the teeth of the wicked."

The sages said, "Do not read, 'Thou hast broken' in—Hebrew *shibarta;* read instead *shirbavta*—'Thou hast enlarged and lengthened.' "[289]

3 / THE LAND OF THE PROPHET JOB

In the biblical story, Job and his family lived in the Land of Uz. According to legend, Uz was in the region of Bashan, in the northern part of Transjordan. To this day, the Arab inhabitants still hold to this belief, and they show in the mosque of the village of Sheikh-Saad a holy stone which they venerate under the name of *Sakhrat-Ayub*—the Rock of Job. Indeed, it can be identified as a fragment of an ancient Egyptian monument dating from the time of Pharaoh Ramses II, who ruled the Valley of the Nile about the year 1300 B.C.E.

Here, says the Arab legend, Job sat, afflicted with leprosy and resting his back on the stone, wherefore it is worshiped in Arab tradition. This is the spot, too, where Job's friends came to comfort him: "So they sat down with him upon the ground seven days and seven nights, and none spoke a word unto him; for they saw that his grief was very great."

Under Byzantine rule, there stood here a Christian church named for the prophet Job. The Arabs called it *Beit-Ayub*—the House of Job.

Rabbi Ashtori ha-Parhi, who lived in the Land of Israel in the fourteenth century, also mentioned "the Land of Uz, where there is a special place consecrated to Job, called *Deir Ayub.*"

Close to the Mosque of Job, there was a bath named after him—in Arabic, *Hammam Ayub.* It is told that here the stricken prophet washed his ulcerous body and was healed of his wounds. Alongside flows a rivulet, *Wadi Moyet Ayub*—the River of the Waters of Job.

In the same vicinity, the Arabs also show the tomb of Job and his wife within a mosque standing near Sheikh-Saad. Many are the pilgrims who come to pray piously at the grave of the upright and afflicted prophet.[290]

4 / KARNAIM—THE BIRTHPLACE OF JOB

Some hold that on the site of Sheikh-Saad stood ancient Karnaim, an important city of Bashan in olden times. Past generations already sought to find in Karnaim and its surroundings the famous town of Uz, the birthplace of Job who was "greater than all the men of yore."

The Arab legend relates that from Karnaim came the shepherds who tended to Job's numerous flocks. To the sentence of the Book of Job "and the Sabians made a raid, and took them [the shepherds] away," it was added, "They [the shepherds] came out of the village Karnaim."

The first Christians too associated these surroundings with the memory of the prophet. One of them mentions Karnaim, "Karneia," in his language, and says: "And there is shown according to tradition the house of Job."

John Chrysostom, the patriarch of Constantinople in the fourth century, tells of "That dunghill [of Job] more to be venerated than any kingly throne. For from seeing a royal throne no advantage results to the spectators but only a temporary pleasure, which has no utility; but from the sight of Job's dunghill, one may derive the greatest benefit, yea, much divine wisdom and consolation. Therefore to this day many undertake a long pilgrimage, even across the sea, hastening from the extremities of the earth, as far as Arabia, that they may see the dunghill; and having beheld it, may kiss the land, which was the arena of such a visitor and received the blood that was more precious than all gold."[291]

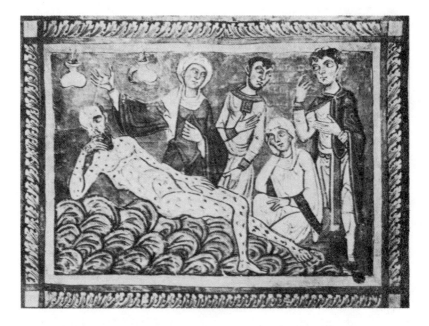

FIG. 52. JOB ON THE DUNGHILL
By Job's side are his wife and friends. This is an illustration from a twelfth-century Bible in manuscript.

5 / WHEREFROM CAME THE WICKED HAMAN?

Legend describes Haman the Wicked, or his father, as a barber and bath-attendant. According to one belief, he came from a village named Kefar-Kartzoum, or Kefar-Karynos.

It is said that before Haman the Wicked was hanged "the people said to him, 'Wicked man, thou art none but the former barber of Kefar-Kartzoum!' And we know that Haman was the barber of the village for twenty-two years."

Another source describes "Haman's father, may his bones be ground to dust," as bath-attendant and barber in the village of Karynos.

Some are of the opinion that the designation Kefar-Kartzoum or Karynos is a corruption of the name Kefar-Karnaim which lay in East Transjordan, within the borders of the Land of Bashan. There dwelt Job and his family.[292]

6 / WHEREFORE THE NAME ASHTAROT-KARNAIM?

In the most distant past, there was in the Land of Bashan an important city named Ashtarot-Karnaim. It is mentioned in the Bible as far back as at the time of the patriarch Abraham: "Chedorlaomer and the kings that were with him, smote the Rephaim in Ashtaroth-karnaim."

Ashtarot-Karnaim belonged to Og, King of Bashan. After its conquest by the Tribes of Israel, it was apportioned to the sons of Manasseh. Today, this site is occupied by a large mound still known to the Arabs as Ashtara (a slight variation of the biblical name), in the vicinity of Dar'a—obviously historical Edrei.

The ancient inhabitants belonged to the cult of Ashtarot, named for the principal female deity of the Canaanites, Ashtoret, to whom they dedicated their town. Probably to distinguish it from other places called after her, the name of the nearby city of Karnaim was added to identify it completely. The name Ashtarot-Karnaim—meaning Ashtarot-of the-Horns, in Hebrew—stirred the imagination of the commentators, and they pictured the town as set deep in a narrow valley flanked on both sides by tall mountains pointed like horns. In the Talmud, the name Ashtarot-Karnaim became a common expression denoting a place hidden deep between two great heights, and completely overcast by their shadow.

The talmudic scholars discussed whether "if a man made his *sukkah* in Ashtarot-Karnaim" it would be religiously valid.

Rashi expounds: "Ashtarot-Karnaim—two high mountains and a vale lie between them. And because of the tallness of the mountains, the sun never shines there in the valley."[293]

7 / THE STONES ON THE EASTERN BORDER OF ERETZ-ISRAEL

To the east of the plain of Bashan rise the mountains of Haran, their surface covered with heavy black stones of basalt. In ancient times, the highway from Babylonia to Eretz-Israel passed across the width of Haran, and many sages of Israel followed this route on their way back from captivity. When they left behind them the desert, with its glaring sunlight and white stones, and approached the limits of Eretz-Israel—Haran and Bashan—they met the dark basalt rocks, and then they knew that the desert had been crossed and their haven reached.

It was related: "When Rabbi Hanina the Great returned from Babylonia, he wished to ascertain whether he had entered Eretz-Israel, and for this purpose he used to weigh the stones on his way. As long as they were light, he said, 'I have still not penetrated the land of my desire.' Whereas he found them heavy, he said, 'These can be none but the stones of

Eretz-Israel.' And he kissed them and said over them the sacred verse [of the Book of Psalms]: 'For Thy servants take pleasure in her stones,/And love her dust.' "

Rabbi Hanina was noted for his strong love for the Holy Land. It was said: "He used to level and carefully remove all the stumbling blocks along the streets of the town, for in his deep love for the land he did his utmost that none should find fault with its perfection."[294]

XXIII

THE LAND OF GILEAD

1 / THE INHERITANCE OF GAD

The Land of Gilead stretches out in the central part of Transjordan, facing the mountains of Jerusalem and Samaria and the Valley of Jezreel.

The sons of Gad inherited the Land of Gilead. In their neighborhood dwelt the sons of Menasseh to the northeast and those of Reuben to the south.

On his deathbed, Jacob the Patriarch blessed Gad in these terms: "Gad, a troop shall troop upon him; but he shall troop upon their heel."

"For," said the sages, "when one of the tribesmen went out to war, he was always victorious."

It was added: "He [the Almighty] blessed Gad as the brave advance-guard that leads the nation of God in war."

When, in his turn, Moses, the Man of God, gave his blessing to the sons of Jacob, to Gad he said: "Blessed be He that enlargeth Gad, He dwelleth as a lioness, and teareth the arm, yea, the crown of the head."

The sages expounded: "Blessed be He that enlargeth Gad" teaches us that the borders of Gad's inheritance kept on stretching out to the east. "He dwells as a lioness," for Gad was settled next to the frontier, which he defended with the fierceness of a lioness protecting her cubs.

Some of the intrepid warriors of Gad joined David the shepherd in his wanderings through the Wilderness of Judah. As recorded in First Chronicles: "And of the Gadites there separated themselves unto David to the stronghold in the wilderness, mighty men of valor . . . whose faces were like the faces of lions, and they were as swift as the roes upon the mountains."[295]

2 / THE BANNER OF GAD

Tradition reports: "While in the desert of wanderings, there were distinctive signs for each and every one of the twelve chieftains, a flag and a color. Each flag had the color of one of the precious gems which adorned the breastplate of Aaron, the great priest. Gad had the agathe—in Hebrew, *shebo*. And his flag was neither black nor white, but black and white combined, picturing a camp, after the saying: "Gad, a troop shall troop upon him."

According to another version, the standard of Gad bore "Many figures of armed men going out to battle."[296]

3 / WHY IT WAS CALLED MAHANAIM

*"At the time when a man is in Eretz-Israel,
the angels of the Land guard and protect him."*

In eastern Transjordan, upon one of the high hills of Gilead, lies a ruin named by the Arabs *Mahana*. Apparently this is the site of Mahanaim, mentioned in the wanderings of the patriarch Jacob.

For it is written: "And Jacob went on his way, and the angels of God met him. And Jacob said when he saw them:

'This is God's camp.' And he called the name of that place Mahanaim."

"Why was this place called Mahanaim—Two Camps?" ask the sages of Israel. "When Jacob went from the Holy Land to Aram-naharaim [Mesopotamia], angels accompanied him and guarded him. But when he arrived at the borders of the Land, those angels disappeared and others came to accompany him and to guard him till he reached Aram-Naharaim.

"When he returned, the same angels accompanied him again till he arrived at the borders of the Holy Land. When the angels of Eretz-Israel became conscious of his approach, they went forth to meet him and accompany him, and the two hosts of angels stood by Jacob, for it is written: 'Mahanaim, two camps.' And sixty thousand angels danced in front of Jacob when he entered the Holy Land."

Mahanaim was situated near the river Yabbok, probably on the hills which now are called Tulul al-Dhahab—the Hills of Gold.[297]

4 / KING DAVID IN MAHANAIM

When Absalom rebelled against his father, King David, the latter fled from his capital, Jerusalem, eastward to Transjordan. And he came to Mahanaim as recorded: "And it came to pass, when David was come to Mahanaim, that Shobi . . . of Ammon, and Machir . . . of Lodebar, and Barzillai . . . brought beds, and basins, and earthen vessels, and wheat, and barley, and meal, and parched corn, and beans, and lentils, and parched pulse, and honey, and curd, and sheep, and cheese of kine, for David, and for the people that were with him."

The commentators describe fully David's stay in Mahanaim, which they designate by the Greek translation of the Hebrew name (Two Camps)—"Dismos," or, more correctly, "Distamos."

Of all that was offered to the king and his suite they give the following explanation:/"The beds were couches of down. The basins were jugs of wine. The earthen vessels came from Beit-Ramta.* The wheat and barley were of the usual varieties. The parched corn was *shattita,* a dish made of flour of roasted ears of corn mixed with honey. The beans and the lentils were of the usual kind. The parched pulse was roasted ears of corn. The honey, the curd and the sheep were of the usual kinds. The cheese of kine was a special kind of cheese made out of cow's milk and called *torin,* because not even a fly can keep its footing upon it."[298]

5 / THE FLAG OF REUBEN

The sons of Reuben settled in the southern part of the mountains of Gilead, between the inheritance of Gad in the north and the Land of Moab in the south.

The ancients recorded: "Reuben his stone was red. His flag was painted red and on it were drawn mandrakes," a reminder of the biblical tale: "And Reuben went in the days of wheat harvest, and found mandrakes in the field, and brought them unto his mother Leah."

The mandrake grows plentifully in the spring, and is easily recognized by its clusters of large leaves, vividly green, from whose center peep small violet flowers. These mature into yellowish-green round fruit, the size of small apples, which give off a sweet fragrance.

The root of the mandrake grows very deep into the ground and is usually divided in two, which often gives it the semblance of a tiny infant. Wherefore it has been interwoven into many popular tales as possessing the magic power of quickening the womb of barren women.**[299]

---

* An ancient town in the eastern Jordan Valley, in the vicinity of the Dead Sea.
** See legend XXIV:14.

6 / IN THE INHERITANCE OF GAD AND REUBEN

The inheritance of Reuben stretched out in Transjordan between the Gilead range in the north and the mountains of Moab in the south. Next to Reuben, northward, sat Gad. "Whereas," says legend, "the tribes of Reuben and Gad kept away from practices of theft, the Almighty, blessed be He, bestowed upon them their inheritance in parts where robbery was not to be found.

The Torah relates: "Now the children of Reuben and the children of Gad had a very great multitude of cattle; and when they saw the land of Yazer and the land of Gilead, that, behold, the place was a place for cattle, the children of Gad and the children of Reuben came and spoke unto Moses . . . saying: 'Atarot, and Dibon, and Yazer, and Nimrah, and Heshbon, and Elealeh, and Sebam, and Nebo . . . the land which the Lord smote before the congregation of Israel, is a land for cattle, and thy servants have cattle.' And they said: 'If we have found favor in thy sight, let this land be given unto thy servants for a possession, bring us not over the Jordan.' "

The ancients sought to interpret the meaning of the names of Reuben's towns by a study of their etymology, and said: "And why is it called:

aTaRoT? Because it was surrounded [Hebrew, *me'uTeReT*] with fruit groves.

DiBon? Because their fat cattle flowed [Hebrew, *DaB*] with milk.

YaZeR? Because it is a help [Hebrew, *oZeR*] to its owner.

NiMRah? Because of its variegated [Hebrew, *MNuMaR*] fruit.

SeBaM? Because its fruits had the smell of balsam [Hebrew, *BeSaMim*].

NeBo? Because it grew rich wheat [Hebrew, *TeBua*]."[300]

7 / THE TOWN OF REFUGE IN THE LAND OF REUBEN

"To three things did Moses devote all his soul
and the three bore his name:
the Torah, Israel, and the cities of refuge."

In the inheritance of Reuben stood the town Bezer, one of the three refuge cities in Transjordan. Its precise site is unknown, but it is surmised to have been situated at the place of the Arab village Um-Alamad—Mother of the Pillar—between Rabat-Amon and Madaba. The Torah relates:

"Then Moses separated three cities beyond the Jordan toward the sunrising; that the manslayer might flee thither, that slayeth his neighbor unawares, and hated him not in time past; and that fleeing unto one of these cities he might live: Bezer in the wilderness, in the tableland, for the Reubenites."

Bezer, in the east, was on one line with Hebron, in Western Palestine, another shelter city. The ancients expressed it thus: "Hebron in Judea is like to Bezer in the desert."

Bezer was the first town of refuge established in Israel. Legend asks: "Why did [Moses] find right to consecrate shelter cities first within the boundaries of Reuben? Because Reuben was the first man who endeavored to save a human life; as it is related [in the story of Joseph]: 'And Reuben said unto them: "Shed no blood; cast him unto this pit that is in the wilderness, but lay no hand upon him."' Therefore, shelter cities were first founded within Reuben's dominion."

On the words of Proverbs, "A man that is laden with the blood of any person shall hasten his steps unto the pit," the ancients commented: " 'Shall hasten his steps unto the pit'— that is, shall hurry into Reuben's inheritance. And there is no pit but in Reuben. For it is written: 'And Reuben returned unto the pit.' That is the shelter city within the boundaries of Reuben."[301]

8 / BEIT-GERES—THE GATE OF EDEN

The monumental ruins of an important city known to the Romans as Gerasa can still be seen in the heart of the mountains of Gilead. Under Roman rule, these, as well as the largest part of Transjordan, belonged to the "Province of Arabia." The Arabs call it "Djerash."

The talmudic sages knew Gerasa by the name Beit- (house of) Geres. The town stood in such luxuriant farmland that in a discussion among scholars as to the location of the Gate of Eden on earth one sage said: "And if it [the Gate of Eden] is in Arabia, Beit-Geres is its gate."*

Probably the name Geres, or Geresh, originates from the Hebrew *geresh,* meaning "abundant yield of the soil," as it is used in Moses' blessing of the children of Israel: "And for the precious things of the yield [Hebrew, *geresh*]."

The Roman variation of the name, Gerasa, gave rise to a different explanation: it would derive from the Greek *gerontos*—old man—for it was said that on this spot Alexander of Macedonia settled his veteran soldiers.[302]

9 / THE ORIGIN OF THE NAME BALKA

The southern section of Gilead is called by the Arabs, "Balka," and, according to their saying, this land spreads "from Zarka to Zarka"; from the river Zarka-in-the-South (the Arabic name for the Nahaliel, which flows down from the heights of Moab to the Dead Sea) to the river Zarka-in-the-North (the Arabic name for the Yabbok, one of the main tributaries of the Jordan, which starts its course in the mountains of Gilead).

The name Balka, in the form Balkin, appears in the Hebrew literature of the Middle Ages. Its meaning is unknown.

* See legend VII:1.

The Arab *Balka* translates into "variegated earth, both dark and light."

On the other hand, a Moslem geographer of the thirteenth century contends that Balka is named after Balak, son of Lot, who settled in Transjordan. There is no mention of such a person in Hebrew literature.

The Hebrew medieval legend connects the name with Balak son of Zipor, King of Moab, who was hostile to the tribes of Israel wandering through Transjordan on the way to the Promised Land.

Rabbi Ashtori ha-Parhi, who lived in Eretz-Israel in the fourteenth century, favors this last explanation: "Balka," he writes, "that is the land of Balak."[303]

XXIV
THE LANDS
OF AMMON AND MOAB

1 / AMMONITES AND MOABITES IN JERUSALEM

The lands of Ammon and Moab lie in Transjordan. Their inhabitants were hostile to the Israelites, and the Bible enjoins: "An Ammonite or a Moabite shall not enter into the assembly of the Lord."

It was said: "You find that at the time when enemies entered Jerusalem, Ammonites and Moabites entered together with them. They penetrated the Holy of Holies and found there the two cherubim, which they seized, placed on a chest, and carried around the streets of Jerusalem, exclaiming: 'Did you not declare that this people were not idolaters? See what we found belonging to them and what they were worshiping; behold, all faces are alike!' "

A different version relates: "And while all the others ran to plunder the silver and gold, the Ammonites and Moabites ran to plunder the Torah, for the purpose of expunging the sentence: 'An Ammonite or a Moabite shall not enter into the assembly of the Lord.' "[304]

2 / THE CLOUDS OVER AMMON AND MOAB

Rabbi Hiyya son of Luliani, a sage of the third century, tells that he once overheard the clouds whispering to each other, "Come, let us send a downpour over the land of Ammon and Moab."

Said the Rabbi: "Lord of the Universe! When Thou gavest the Torah to Thy people Israel, Thou addressed Thyself to all the peoples of the world, and none would receive it; and now Thou bestoweth upon them the blessing of rain?"

And He called out to the clouds and ordered: "Drop your waters here!" And the clouds obediently did so, and not even one drop reached Ammon and Moab.[305]

3 / IN THE WILDERNESS OF AMMON AND MOAB

Legend describes the advent of the Messiah and the great battle which will be fought at the gates of Jerusalem; and at first, the enemies will have the upper hand. Many Israelites will fall in this war and Nehemiah will perish with them: "And those who make good their escape flee to the desert of Moab and to the land of the sons of Ammon . . . and there they feed on the roots of the white broom for forty-five days. And there these fugitives stay, and God the Almighty performs for them miracles, and a fountain bursts out from the deep, and at the end of forty-five days God brings forth Elijah the Prophet and Messiah the King is with him, and Elijah brings to them the good tidings saying: "Why are you here Israel?"

And Israel answers, saying: "We are lost, we are destroyed!"

And Elijah says to them: "Stand up, for Elijah the Prophet am I, and this Messiah the King!" But they put no faith in his words, and he says to them: "Perchance you are like Moses and demand proof?"

And they answer: "Yea!"

At this moment, he performs seven miracles. The first miracle: He brings forward to them Moses and his uncle from the desert. The second miracle: He produces in front of them Korah and all his people. The third miracle: He raises from the dead Nehemiah the Prophet who had been killed. The fourth miracle: He reveals to them the hiding place of the Holy Ark and the jar of manna (Israel's food in the desert of wanderings) and the oil of ointment with which the High Priests were anointed. The fifth miracle: The Almighty, blessed be He, delivers into his hand the rod of might. The sixth miracle: He grinds all the mountains of Israel into powder. The seventh miracle: He reveals to them "The Secret."

The white broom commonly grows in the dry beds of rivers (wadis). As the ancients remarked: "It is the way of the white broom to germinate in the wilderness."

It became especially known for the good quality of the fuel made of its dried twigs; it retains heat a long time. In olden days the poet sang: "O Lord, deliver my soul from lying lips . . ./Sharp arrows of the mighty, with coals of broom."[306]

4 / ISRAEL IN THE DESERT OF AMMON AND MOAB

Legend depicts in very dark colors the lot of Israel before the advent of the Messiah: "And Israel shall be in great trouble and the people shall hide in caves and pits. And those that are left shall run away to the wastes of Ammon and Moab . . . and they shall roam over this wilderness for forty days and eat the fruit of the broom bush and of the salt plant [mallow]. For it is said: "They pluck salt-wort with wormwood;/And the roots of the broom are their food."

The salt plant is commonly found in the desert and in the saline wilderness of the Land of Israel. Its young shoots help sustain the nomads.

It is told how, after defeating his enemies, Janneus, the

Hasmonean king, fed the sages of Israel with sprouts of the salt plant: "And he assembled all the learned men of Israel and said to them: Our forefathers ate from the salt plant while they built the Temple. We too shall eat of the same in their memory. And on the tables of gold, salt plants were served, and they ate."

The bedouin too feed upon the soft shoots of the salt tree, which they call by the name *kataf.* They also like the cress, *houara,* in Arabic. Of these two plants the desert bedouin says: "Were it not for the cress and the salt plant the bedouin would live in hunger."[307]

5 / REDEMPTION SHALL BEGIN IN THE DESERT OF MOAB

> " 'Let mine outcasts dwell with thee;
> As for Moab, be thou a cover to
> him from the face of the spoiler.
> For the extortion is at an end, spoiling ceaseth."
> "Yet will I turn the captivity of Moab
> in the end of days."

According to one tradition, Israel's redemption shall begin in the wilderness of Moab in eastern Transjordan. And thus it is worded: "And God performs miracles for them and they see the Messiah standing at the top of the wilderness of Moab and with him there are four hundred men. And God brings salvation to them . . . and forgiveness is granted to them from the desert of Moab to Horeb [Sinai].

"And Israel advances, taking up the arms from the desert of Horeb where the 'Ineffable Name' is written, and they carry off Ammon and Moab. When the kings of the North hear that Ammon and Moab have been destroyed, they foregather and settle their rule in Damascus.

"And the kings of the West and the South gather, too, and take council in Midian, and the Messiah comes from Midian and loots her and [goes] to Damascus and loots her. And lo, the kings of the East assemble in Palmyra [Tadmor], and the Almighty, blessed be He, whispers in the wind and says to Israel: 'Return to Palmyra and overthrow the Kings of the East.' and the Messiah comes to Tyre and to Sidon; to Palmyra and to Biri [Beirut] And all the nations gather and come to Puja and to Acre, and they lament around Acre.

"And the Almighty, blessed be He, clefts open the firmaments and displays to Israel the throne of the Lord, and they pray toward Him and He receives their prayer."[308]

6 / THE ISRAELITE VICTORY IN TRANSJORDAN

Led by Moses, the Man of God, the tribes of Israel wandered through the lands of Ammon and Moab on their way to Caanan. When they reached the tip of the wilderness of Moab, they set their steps to the northwest, across the territory of Sihon, the Amorite king.

Sihon went out to wage war against Israel, but the tribes prevailed and, scoring their first victory, they took possession of his towns and of his capital, Heshbon, also known as Ir [town of] Sihon. Today, the small Arab village Hasban occupies this site.

The Israelites also conquered Ar-Moab, situated south of Heshbon on the banks of the river Arnon, which runs down to the Dead Sea amidst the "high places of Arnon." In this vicinity stood the town Dibon—today the Arab village Diban. The Israelites also subjugated Nophah, now unknown, which stood in the surroundings of Medaba, a village populated by Christians in our time.

After Israel's victory over Sihon and his towns, the tribes celebrated their success in the following verses: "For a fire has gone out of Heshbon,/A flame from the city of Sihon;/It hath devoured Ar of Moab,/The lords of the high places of Arnon./We have shot at them—Heshbon is perished—even

unto Dibon,/And we have laid waste even unto Nophah,/-
Which reacheth unto Medeba."

It has been taught: "He was called Sihon as resembling a
sayyah—a foal of the wilderness."

Sihon is truly *ayyar Sihon*—the young ass of Sihon. "This
refers to one who follows his evil inclination like a young
ass."[309]

7 / KING SOLOMON IN THE LAND OF AMMON

King Solomon took to himself for wife, Naamah, daughter
of the King of Ammon. "She was," says legend, "his chosen
mate since the sixth day of creation." Naamah the Ammonite
bore a son Rehoboam, who was to become King of Judah.
And this is how they met:

"King Solomon, peace be upon him, floated up to heaven
every day to learn the secrets of the Universe from the
mouths of Aza and Azel; and he knew no qualms and no fears.
And all the hosts of heaven bent the knee and prostrated
themselves before the Almighty God, blessed be He, and
praised Him for appointing such a king over Israel, and they
[the angels] fulfilled all his [Solomon's] wishes.

"He demanded, and they brought him, building materials
for the Holy Temple. And when he asked for the Shamir,
Ashmedai [King of the Devils] himself offered it dangling
from an iron chain.

"And Solomon possessed a ring carved with the 'Ineffable
Name'; and through its supernatural virtues he performed all
his miracles. However, when King Solomon sinned, it became within Ashmedai's power to snatch the ring away from
him and to throw it into the sea; and all Solomon's glory was
wiped away as if it had never been. And the Almighty God,
blessed be He, passed sentence upon him and sent him out
into exile: And he [Solomon] went from doorstep to doorstep

saying: 'I am Solomon who was King in Jerusalem!' And the people laughed in his face.

"At long last, the Almighty, blessed be He, was moved to compassion, 'for the sake of David, His slave, and for the sake of the pious Naamah, daughter of the King of Ammon, from whose lineage the Messiah, Son of David, shall be.' And the Holy One, blessed be He, brought him to the land of Ammon and there to the king's capital.

"After many hardships and many tribulations, Solomon became a servant of the King of Ammon and cooked for him all his meals: And the king's daughter, and her name was Naamah, saw him, and she told her mother that she wished to marry this man, the cook. Her mother rebuked her, saying: 'In thy father's kingdom there are many noble princes.' But nothing could prevail against her will, and the princess married the servant. In great wrath, the king of Ammon ordered one of his slaves to throw them into the wide desert that they should perish. And they went looking for nourishment to sustain their souls, and they came to a town on the seashore.

"And he [Solomon] went out to find food, and he met fishermen selling their catch. And he bought a fish from them and brought it to his wife to cook. When she opened its belly, she found among the entrails the ring carved with the 'Ineffable Name,' and she gave it to her husband, who recognized it and quickly put it on his finger. Forthwith his mind cleared, his spirit returned, and he proceeded to Jerusalem, drove Ashmedai away, and sat on the royal throne again."[310]

8 / THE THEATER OF KING SOLOMON IN RABAT-AMMON

Among the buildings of Rabat-Ammon (Amman, in Arabic), the modern capital of the Kingdom of Jordan, is an ancient Roman theater of the second or third century, among the loveliest and most complete of the Roman theaters which have survived in Palestine.

Medieval Arab legend attributed this theater to Solomon, King of Israel, and so the Arabs called it Malaab Suleiman—Solomon's theater. The Arab geographer Al-Mukaddasi mentioned it in the tenth century.[*311]

9 / WHEN THE PALM TREES OF RABAT-AMMON PERISH

The Arab legend holds that if the palm trees of Rabat-Ammon—Amman, in Arabic—die away, it will be a portent that the steps of el-Dajjal are nearing. El-Dajjal is the Antichrist, and he will appear before the coming of the true Messiah. These two will fight a great battle and the Messiah will gain the upper hand.

Meanwhile, el-Dajjal sits in a distant forlorn island and waits for the right hour to strike. A man once reached this lonely spot by accident and el-Dajjal asked him various questions: "And how are the palm trees in Rabat-Ammon?" said he. And the man answered: "The people are still collecting their fruit!" And el-Dajjal knew that his day had not yet dawned.[**312]

10 / THE POOLS OF HESHBON

The poet in Song of Songs, praising the beauty of the Beloved, compares her features and her limbs to famous sites of the Land of Israel: "Thy neck is as a tower of ivory;/Thine eyes as the pools in Heshbon,/By the gate of Bath-rabbim;/Thy nose is like the tower of Lebanon/Which looketh toward Damascus./Thy head upon thee is like Carmel."

* In the ruins of Baalbek, in Lebanon, there was a beautiful theater which the Arabs of the vicinity attributed to King Solomon. The Moslem geographer Idrissi mentions it about the year 1154.
** See similar legend in *Legends of Judea and Samaria*, p. 164.

Heshbon was an important city in Transjordan, famous for its beautiful pools. It stood in the vicinity of Rabbat benei-Ammon—capital of the children of Ammon—today, Amman. The city was called "Rabbah," for short, as told in the Book of Joshua: "And Moses gave unto the tribe of Gad . . . half the land of the children of Ammon . . . before Rabbah."

Playing on the word *rabbah*, the poet calls the city by the name Bath-Rabbim—Daughter of the Multitudes.

In medieval Hebrew literature, Barh-Rabbim is also a poetic designation for Jerusalem and for the Holy Land in its entirety.[313]

11 / THE CAVE OF RAKIM

The Moslem geographer of the tenth century, Al-Mukaddasi, relates the following story: "In the village of Rakim, which lies about a league distant from Amman [now the capital of Jordan] on the border of the desert, there is a cave with two entrances, one large and one small. Three men were once walking together when a heavy rain overtook them and drove them into the cave. Suddenly, there fell from the mountain above a rock, which blocked up the mouth of the cave and shut the three men in.

"Then one of them called to the others, saying, 'Now think of such good deeds as you may have done and call on Allah, beseeching him that for the sake of them perchance he may cleave this rock before us!'

"Then one of them cried out, saying, 'Allah! Of a truth, have I not my parents, who are old and feeble, and my children besides, of whom I am the sole protector? And when I return to them, I do milk the cows and give the milk first to my parents even before giving it to my children. So therefore cause this rock to cleave before us, that through the same we may perceive the sky.' Then Allah caused a cleft to split the rock, and through it they perceived the sky.

"Then the second one cried out and said, 'Allah! Was there not the daughter of my uncle, whom I loved passionately as only man can love? And when I sought to possess her, she refused me, saying that I should bring her a hundred pieces of gold. Then I made the effort and collected those hundred pieces, bringing them to her. And now, verily, as Thou knowest that I did this from fear of Thy face, so therefore cleave for us again a portion of this rock.' And Allah vouchsafed to cleave thereof another cleft.

"Then the last man cried out and said, 'Allah! Did I not hire a serving man, and when his task was accomplished, he said to me: "Now give me my fee." And I gave to him his fee; but he would not receive it and despised it. Then I ceased not to use the same for sowing till by its produce I became possessed of cattle. And after a long time, the man came to me and said, "Fear Allah, and oppress me not; but give me my fee." And I, answering him, said, "Go thou, then, to these cattle and their herdsmen and receive them." And he took them and went his way. And now, since Thou knowest how I did this thing in fear of Thy face, do Thou cause what of this rock remaineth to be cleft before us.'

"Then Allah caused the whole rock to become cleft before them, and the three men went out from the cave and saved their lives."[314]

12 / THE THORN-PALMS OF THE IRON MOUNT ARE VALID

Next to the eastern coast of the Dead Sea, on the mountain ridge of northern Moab, stands the peak named the Mount of Iron—in Aramaic, *Tur Parzelah.* On this height grew wild palm trees known as thorn-palms, common along the shores of the Dead Sea even today.

From the thorn-palms of the Iron Mount, branches (Hebrew, *lulav*) were taken for the Feast of Tabernacles. The sages of Israel state: "The thorn-palms of the Iron Mount are valid."

The sages of the Talmud, discussing the same subject, say of the Iron Mount: "And this is the entrance to Gehenna."

This last saying may contain a reference to the hot springs —in Arabic, *Hamam a-Zarka*—which emerge at the foot of the Mount of Iron, next to the Dead Sea.

The ancients were convinced that these hot waters streamed past the gates of Hell, where they were heated; and they named the spring Baara—Hebrew for "burning."*[315]

13 / JACOB AT THE BURNING WATERS

"Deliver me, I pray Thee,
from the hand of my brother,
from the hand of Esau;
for I fear him, lest he come and smite me."

In the mountains of Moab, by the side of the river Nahaliel, which flows down into the Dead Sea, burst forth the waves of a hot spring. The ancients appropriately named it Mei Baara—the Burning Waters. To the Arabs it is known as Hamam ez-Zarka—the Baths of Zarka (the blue)—the Arabic designation for the river Nahaliel.

In olden times, as in our days, many came to dip their aching bodies in the "Burning Waters" to find a cure in its mineral waters as in the hot baths of Tiberias.

The sages of Israel mention the "people who bathe in the burning waters and the waters of Tiberias."

It is told of Jacob the Patriarch, who fled for his life from his brother Esau, that he hurried to a certain hiding place

* Legend attaches the same belief to the hot springs of Tiberias, which are also said to gush forth at the entrance of the infernal regions. See legend XIV:1.

and "hastily did Jacob the Patriarch enter therein and lock himself from Esau. And the Almighty, blessed be He, dug for him an opening on another side and he came out safe."

"And," says legend, "testifying to this feat, Isaiah the prophet exclaimed: "When thou passest through the waters, I will be with thee,/And through the rivers, they shall not overflow thee;/When thou walkest through the fire, thou shalt not be burned,/Neither shall the flame kindle upon thee."

According to another tradition, Jacob the Patriarch ran away "to a cavern [Maarah]—a place of baths."

Said Jacob, "There is not one morsel of bread in my hand nor any other thing. Let me plunge and warm myself within these hot waters." But Esau and his men came and surrounded the baths that Jacob should not escape therefrom."

Apparently *Maarah* should be read *Baara*—the Baths of "the Burning Waters"—there did Jacob hide from the face of Esau.[316]

14 / BAARA—THE SPRING OF BURNING WATERS

Josephus, the Jewish historian of the first century, tells of the place named Baara that it produces a root: "flame-colored, and toward evening emitting a brilliant light." He adds, "It eludes the grasp of persons who approach with the intension of plucking it, as it shrinks up. Yet even then to touch it is fatal, unless one succeeds in carrying off the root itself, suspended from the hand.

"Another innocuous mode of capturing it is as follows: Dig all around it, leaving but a minute portion of the root covered; then tie a dog to it, and the animal, rushing to follow the person who tied him, easily pulls it up but instantly dies —a vicarious victim, as it were, for him who intended to remove the plant, since after this, none need fear to handle it.

"With all these attendant risks, the root possesses one virtue for which it is prized; for so-called demons—in other words, the spirits of wicked men that enter the living and kill them unless aid is forthcoming—are promptly expelled by this root, if it is merely applied to the victims."

The famous chronicler does not mention the name of the wonderful plant. It is, in all likelihood, the mandrake, whose root, vaguely resembling the shape of a newborn infant, has given rise to many legends in various countries.*[317]

15 / WHO HEATS THE HOT BATHS OF IBN HAMMAD?

According to the legend, King Solomon heats not only the Hot Springs of Tiberias but also all the thermal waters that issue forth to the surface of the Land of Israel.

On the eastern shore of the Dead Sea, near the peninsula nicknamed "The Tongue," emerges a hot source called, in Arabic, *Hamam Ibn Hammad*—Hot Baths of the Sons of Hammad—after the bedouin tribe which holds sway in the vicinity.

The ravine, running down from the heights of Moab within which the source appears, is also named after them—Wadi Ibn Hammad.

Bedouin come from far and wide to bathe in these curative waters.

The Czech traveler Aloys Musil, who visited the Dead Sea in 1898, told how he heard the voice of a bedouin dipping himself in the mineral spring, calling out to Suleiman ibn-Daud—Solomon, son of David—and begging him to heat the precious waters better.**[318]

---

* See legend XXIII:5.
** See legend XIV:6.

16 / THE SNEEZING GOATS IN
THE MOUNTAINS OF MACHOR

On the heights of Moab, beyond the eastern shore of the Dead Sea, rise the mountains of Machor (Macherus). Here once stood a town of the same name, which acquired renown at the time of the Jewish rebellion against Rome.

The flocks of goats belonging to its Jewish inhabitants grazed in the surroundings of Machor. Legend tells that the goats used to sneeze because of the smell of the incense reaching them from the Great Temple.

Said Rabbi Eleazar son of Diglai: "My father's house kept goats in the mountains of Machor, and they used to sneeze from the smell of the compounding of the incense" (in the Temple of Jerusalem).[319]

XXV
NEBO–BETH-PEOR–SHITTIM

1 / WHEREFORE THE NAME "MOUNTAINS OF AVARIM"?

The mountains of Avarim rise in Transjordan at the northern end of the Land of Moab. They overlook the Dead Sea and its shores, and one of their peaks is Mount Nebo at whose base the wandering tribes of Israel encamped: "And they . . . pitched in the mountains of Abarim, [read, 'Avarim'] in front of Nebo."

The meaning of the name Avarim is obscure and its origin unknown. According to one commentary, it is the plural form of the Hebrew *ever*, meaning "beyond," for the mountains of Avarim stand beyond the Jordan and the Dead Sea.

Others connect the name to that of the Hebrews, saying, "They [the Israelites] were called *Ivrim* [Hebrews], for they acted according to the Torah, which was written in *Ever-Hayarden*" (Transjordan, or *Ever*—beyond—the Jordan).

Still others propound that the mountains are called Avarim because they are mountains that the Hebrews [*Ivrim*] climbed.

About Isaiah's verses: "O thou that tellest good tidings to Zion,/Get thee up into the high mountain"; the Zohar interprets: "High mountain—this is the Mount of Avarim, which the Holy Providence will ascend at the end of time to proclaim redemption to the whole world."[320]

2 / MOSES ON MOUNT NEBO

From the summit of Mount Nebo, Moses, the Law-Giver, looked upon the Land he was not to enter. As it is written: "And the Lord said unto Moses: 'Get thee up into this mountain of Abarim, and behold the land which I have given unto the children of Israel. And when thou hast seen it, thou also shalt be gathered unto thy people.' "

"And Moses went up from the plains of Moab unto mount Nebo, to the top of Pisgah. . . . And the Lord showed him all the land . . . and all the land of Judah as far as the hinder sea. . . . And the Lord said unto him: 'This is the land . . . I will give it unto thy seed; I have caused thee to see it with thine eyes, but thou shalt not go over thither.' "

Legend adds: There were twelve steps leading from the wilderness of Moab to the top of Mount Nebo, and Moses took them all in one stride.

It was also expounded: Climbing up Mount Abarim was an elevation from which there was no descent, for there Moses died, and his tomb has remained unknown to men.

"And while he stood on Mount Nebo, the ministering angel Matatron, who brings men's prayers to the seat of the Almighty, pointed out to Moses with a finger the whole Land and explained: 'Until here shall stand the dominion of Ephraim, and there shall be the limit of Menasseh.' "[321]

3 / THROUGH THE GRACE OF PRAYER

The ancients said, "No power in the world is stronger than the power of repentance and prayer. Lo! Moses, the Man of God, was doomed never to enter the Land and never to see it, and nevertheless, whereas he prayed incessantly, the Almighty, blessed be He, was moved to leniency, and told him, 'Climb on the top of the peak!' And" say the sages, their memory be blessed, "the Almighty unrolled the whole Land in front of Moses and showed him every generation and its sons; each age and its means of livelihood, until the last sea. (Do not read 'the last sea,' Hebrew; *yam*, but 'the last day,' Hebrew, *yom.*)"

The sages wondered: "Why did Moses have such a strong desire to enter the Land of Israel? Was he hungry for its rich fruits? Or did he wish to be satiated with its good things? No, for these were the words of the Holy Man: 'Many commandments have been enjoined to Israel, and they cannot be performed except within the limits of the Holy Land. O, would that I might enter the Land, and these good deeds be fulfilled through me.' "

Said Moses to God Almighty, "Let me come into [the Land] borne through the air or carried along tunnels."

He was told: "But thou shalt not pass! For thou shalt not cross this Jordan, not even thy bones."

"The Jordan was in front of him like a wall that he might not penetrate into the Land."[322]

4 / MOSES WISHED TO ENTER THE HOLY LAND

Thus it is related: After the Almighty, blessed be He, refused to allow Moses to penetrate into the Land of Israel, the Holy Man entered the presence of the Lord and said: "If Thou wishest not to let me come into the Holy Land, would that I were left in this world to live on and know not death."

Said the Almighty, blessed be He, "If thou never dieth thou shalt not enjoy resurrection in the next world!"

Said Moses: "Lord of the Universe! Would then that I were like the hart on the heights and the deer of the mountains, which browse the grass, drink the waters of the rains, and set foot everywhere! Oh, that my soul were like unto one of them!"

Said the Almighty: "Let it suffice thee! Thou mayest not add another word upon this matter!"

Said Moses: "Lord of the Universe, take one of my two eyes and place it under the hinge of Thy Sanctuary's door. And let the door be fixed into the socket of my eye. That I may only see Eretz-Israel with my second eye and die satisfied!"

Said the Almighty, blessed be He: "Have I not told thee, do not add anything more!"

Forthwith did Moses start praising the Lord, blessed be He. And he faced the Holy Land, saying, "Oh Land! Oh Land! I beseech thee, beg for pity from the Holy One, blessed be He; maybe for thy sake He shall relent and be moved to compassion."[323]

5 / MOSES' EYE AND THE TEMPLE'S PORTAL

Moses, the Man of God, was willing to sacrifice one of his eyes to be used to fix the hinge of the Temple's portal if the Almighty would only allow him to see the Holy Land with his second eye.

Legend explains how the eye, whose socket serves as a hole to the door's pivot, suffers agonies every time the door is opened. The Pharaoh of Egypt is described in a similar position in Gehenna, supine on the ground, his head beneath the threshold of the entrance, with the door's axis turning in the socket of one eye. And the door swings incessantly, pushed by every soul who enters Hell.

A comparable tale is told of a woman named Miriam, daughter of Alei-Bezelim, who is in Gehenna: "And the hinge of the gate of Gehenna is set in her ear."*[324]

---

* Assyrian kings used to represent an enemy as prostrate on the threshold of their palace, crushed under the weight of the door whose socket is fitted into his back (see fig 53)

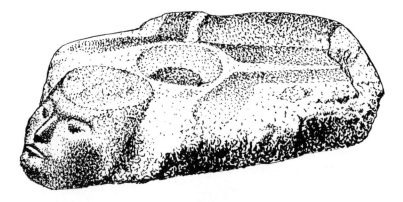

FIG. 53. DOOR SOCKET
This black stone dates from about 3,000 B.C.E. It was found in Hierokonpalis and is now in the University of Philadelphia museum.

6 / THE TREASURES HIDDEN ON MOUNT NEBO

Tradition holds that the prophet Jeremiah concealed the most precious possessions of the Great Temple within a cavern on Mount Nebo, the very mountain from whose heights Moses looked upon the Land of Canaan.

The book of the Maccabees relates how Jeremiah went up "the mountain upon which Moses climbed and saw the inheritance of the Almighty. And on his way Jeremiah found a cavern, and he brought there the Tabernacle and the Ark and the Altar of Incense and fastened the door upon them. And those who went with him tried a second time to follow the path along which they had come but they could not find it. And when this came to be known to Jeremiah, he rebuked them, saying that the place was to remain secret until the Almighty gathers His people and shows His favor again, and then He shall disclose all these treasures."[325]

7 / MOSES, THE MAN OF GOD, AND BETH-PEOR

Ancient Beth-peor was situated in Transjordan, in the heights of Moab. In their wanderings, the Israelites camped opposite the place. As it is written: "These are the testimonies, and the statutes, and the ordinances which Moses spoke unto the children of Israel . . . beyond the Jordan, in the valley over against Beth-peor."

When after some time Moses passed away, "he was buried in the valley in the land of Moab over against Beth-peor."

And when "the Lord was kindled against Israel" because they had worshiped Baal-peor, Moses, the Man of God, entered the presence of the Almighty, blessed be He, and entreated Him, saying, "For the sake of the oath Thou hast made to me, withhold Thy anger from Israel, as it is said: 'Turn from Thy fierce wrath.'"

And what did Moses do? "Within the land of Gad he dug [a cave] into the ground the size of a large house, and concealed therein the wrath of God, and it was there like a man imprisoned.

"And whenever Israel sinned, he [the wrath of God] came up and opened wide [Hebrew, *peor*] the mouth to blow his evil wind and to destroy Israel, wherefore it is called 'peor.'

"And then Moses uttered over him the 'Ineffable Name' of the Almighty, and the evil wind was pushed back into the ground.

"And when Moses died, what did the Almighty do? He set the tomb of the Holy Man opposite the cave of the Rock of God. And when Israel sins and the evil spirit opens again his mouth to blow his breath and put an end to Israel, he sees the grave of Moses opposite him, is seized with fear, and recedes back into the depth of the earth."[326]

8 / WHEREFORE THE NAME BETH-PEOR?

Beth-peor was a town in the mountains of Moab. It stood at the limit of Reuben's inheritance, in the vicinity of the dominion of Gad, which spread northward.

The town was named for Baal-peor, the main deity of the ancient Moabites. The Israelites, wandering through the land of Moab, were induced to worship the local god, as told in the Book of Numbers: "And Israel joined himself unto the Baal of Peor; and the anger of the Lord was kindled against Israel."

The Book of Joshua recalls the same shameful event: "Is the iniquity of Peor too little for us, from which we have not cleansed ourselves unto this day?"

The prophet Hosea too reminds Israel of its sin: "I saw your fathers. . . . But so soon as they came to Baal-peor, they separated themselves unto the shameful thing, and became detestable like that which they loved."

The cult of Baal-peor subsisted among the gentile inhabitants of Bashan. The ancients knew it well in the time of the Mishnah and the Talmud, and they warned the Jews against its practice. They said, "If a man excretes to Baal-peor [he is to be stoned because] this is how it is worshiped."

The story is told of "Sabta, a townsman of Avlas, [who] once rented an ass to a gentile woman. When she came to Peor, she said to him, 'Wait till I enter and come out again.' On her return, he said to her, 'Now do you wait for me until I go in and come out again.' 'But,' said she, 'are you not a Jew?' He replied, 'What does it concern thee?' He then entered, uncovered himself before the idol, and wiped himself on its nose, whilst the acolytes praised him, saying, 'No man has ever served this idol thus!' "

But the sages of Israel did not condone this behavior. They admonished: "He that uncovers himself before Baal-peor thereby serves it, even if his intention was to degrade it."

According to a different version, Sabta, the owner of the ass, was not of Avlas but of Ulam, possibly a town which stood on a site still called by the same name in Arabic, and situated in eastern Galilee.[327]

9 / THE CULT OF PEOR

The sages tell various stories about Peor and his cult: "A gentile woman once fell sick. She vowed, 'If I recover, I will go and serve every idol in the world.' She recovered, and proceeded to serve all idols. On reaching Peor, she asked its priests, 'How is this worshiped?' They replied, 'People eat beets, drink strong drinks, and they uncover themselves before it.' She replied, 'I would rather fall sick again then serve an idol in such a manner.'"

Another tale concerns a man named Menahem, a native of Govta de-Ariah, who was by profession a cooper. In his dream one night appeared the idol Peor. What did he do? He took a skewer and attacked him with it, and Peor escaped.

The following night, Peor came again and asked, "Why do you execrate me?" Menahem was frightened, and said, "I shall not curse you any more."

Govta de-Ariah was the name of a townlet probably situated in the Jordan Valley at the foot of the mountains of Lower Galilee.

A story is also told of a ruler who came from overseas to worship Peor. He said to his people, "Bring me an ox, a ram, and a lamb, and I will sacrifice them to Peor." He was told, "You have no need for all these."[328]

10 / ABEL-SHITTIM—THE PLACE OF FOLLY

At the foot of the Moab range, on the border of the Valley of Jordan and alongside the Dead Sea, lies Abel-Shittim, where the tribes of Israel encamped before they crossed the

Jordan west into the Land of Canaan. It is written: "And they pitched by the Jordan . . . unto Abel-Shittim in the plains of Moab."

This place is also referred to summarily as Shittim: "And Israel abode in Shittim, and the people began to commit harlotry with the daughters of Moab. And those that died by the plague were twenty and four thousand."

Undoubtedly, Shittim was named after the acacia trees (in Hebrew, *shittim*) that grow in these surroundings. From the wood of the acacia trees the Israelites in the desert built the Ark of the Covenant, the columns of the Tabernacle, the table of libations, and the altar.

Legend gives a different interpretation. It connects the name Shittim with the Hebrew *shetut*—folly. Rabbi Joshua says: "Because they engaged in improper actions. And Israel abided in Shittim, that is, in the place of folly."

FIG. 54. ACACIA TREE (ACACIA SPIROCARPA)

The Aramaic translation, too, says of Shittim: "Named Shittim—for the folly and corruption that were among the sons of Israel."[329]

11 / WHY WAS IT CALLED SHITTIM?

Legend says: "They [the children of Israel] sinned in Shittim, they were afflicted in Shittim, and they were healed in Shittim."

"They sinned in Shittim," for it is said, "And Israel abode in Shittim to commit harlotry."

"They were afflicted in Shittim," for it is written, "Those that died by the plague were twenty and four thousand."

"They were healed by Shittim," for it is said "And thou shalt make the altar of acacia-wood" (in Hebrew, *shittim*).

When the Israelites sinned in Shittim, God said to them, "By your lives! You shall be saved by where you have sinned. You erred in Shittim, you shall atone through Shittim, for it is written: 'And Bezalel made the ark of acacia-wood.' "

It was added: "The name 'Shittim' is made up of the following:

'Sh' for *shalom*—peace.
'T' for *tova*—favor.
'I' for *ishua*—salvation.
'M' for *mekhila*—forgiveness."[330]

12 / THE FOUNTAIN AND THE RIVER OF SHITTIM

Of the river that flowed at Shittim, legend says, "And the fountain of Shittim was a fountain of harlotry and a drink of the land of Sodom. Therefore they [the sons of Israel] were spoiled when they drank of its waters."

But in the end of time these waters of folly shall be turned into waters of blessing, as Joel prophesies: "And it shall come to pass in that day,/That the mountains shall drop down sweet wine,/And the hills shall flow with milk,/And all the brooks of Judah shall flow with waters;/And a fountain shall come forth of the house of the Lord,/And shall water the valley of Shittim."[331]

13 / KORAH AND HIS PEOPLE AT THE RIVER SHITTIM

Legend depicts at great length the beginning of the Messianic times and the advent of the Redeemer Menahem son of Amiel: "And in the second month, that is, the month of Iyar, Korah and his people whom the earth had swallowed—they and their houses and their tents—shall rise up in the wilderness of Jericho, by the river Shittim, and on the eighteenth of the month the mountains and the heights shall tremble and the earth shall quake.

"And on the first day of the third month, those who died in the desert shall come and make one party with their brethren on the river Shittim.

"And on the eighteenth of the month of Sivan, the houses, the walls, and the towns shall shake and the earth and its inhabitants shall be greatly agitated, and Menahem son of Amiel and Nehemiah son of Hushiel, and Elijah the Prophet, and all Israel, the near and the far, and those whom God shall awaken to eternal life shall proceed to Jerusalem.*[332]

14 / MATTANAH, NAHALIEL, BAMOTH, HAGAI

Before they entered into the land of Canaan, the tribes of Israel roamed over the mountains of Moab in Transjordan. On their way, they made several stations, as the Holy Scriptures relate: "And from the wilderness to Mattanah; and from Mattanah to Nahaliel; and from Nahaliel to Bamoth; and from Bamoth to the valley that is in the field of Moab, by the top of Pisgah, which looketh down upon the desert."

The sages of Israel liked to use these names to describe a learned and pious scholar who studies the Torah—the Divine

---

* A different version of the Book of Zerubbabel describes the advent of the Messiah in the following words: "And a great and severe hunger shall prevail on the face of the earth and all Israel shall go out to the wilderness of Judah and to the river Shittim and they shall eat of the salt plant, and gather roots of the white broom for a livelihood."

gift (Hebrew, *mattanah*); by her virtues he will acquire the revelation of God (Hebrew, *nahal El*); and there he will stand exalted far above other men, as upon a high stage (Hebrew, *bamah;* plural, *bamot*).

The Talmud adds to this description, saying: "Since in the wilderness man is prey to all evil powers, for his protection the Torah was given to him as a gift, for it is said: "From the wilderness to Mattanah" (gift). And since it was given to him as a gift, the inheritance of God *(Nahaliel)* was bestowed upon him, for it is said: "From Mattanah to Nahaliel." And because he enjoys the divine knowledge, he is aloof above all, as upon a high stage *(bamoth)*. For it is said: "From Nahaliel to Bamoth." And if he elevates himself and shows pride, God humbles him, for it is said: "From Bamoth down into the valley" (Hebrew, *hagai*).[333]

XXVI
THE LAND OF EDOM

1 / THE HORITES—THE ANCIENT EDOMITES

The Land of Edom lies in the southernmost part of Transjordan. In Edom lived the sons of Esau, the brother of the patriarch Isaac.

It was asked: "Why is it called Edom [red, in Hebrew]?" "[Because] he [Esau] is red-headed, his food [the plate of lentils for which Esau sold his birthright to Isaac] is red, and his land is red." The mountains of Edom are indeed tinted all shades of red, varying from pink to maroon.

The inhabitants of Edom, or Seir, as it was formerly called, were named Horites. The Bible mentions them as early as in the story of the patriarch Abraham: "And the Horites in their mount Seir." . . . "And in Seir dwelt the Horites aforetime, but the children of Esau succeeded them; and they destroyed them from before them, and dwelt in their stead."

Legend explains the name Horites as deriving from the Hebrew *reah*, meaning "smell," for the Horites, it was said, could identify the quality of each kind of soil by smelling it, and thus establish for what crop it was best suited for cultivating: "And *Horites* implies that they smelled [*merihim*, in Hebrew] the earth."

"They were thoroughly versed in the cultivation of the soil. For they used to say: This complete [measuring] rod [of land is fit] for olives; this complete [measuring] rod [is fit] for vines; this complete [measuring] rod for figs."[334]

2 / THE BOON OF RAIN ON MOUNT SEIR

*"Because I have given mount Seir
unto Esau for a possession."*

After the patriarch Isaac had blessed his son Jacob, Esau too asked for his father's benediction, saying, " 'Hast thou but one blessing, my father? Bless me, even me also, O my father,' and wept. And Isaac his father answered and said unto him: Behold, of the fat places of the earth shall be thy dwelling, And of the dew of heaven from above."

It was said that Esau was among "the three who wept and the Almighty, blessed be He, hearkened to their weeping."

What was Esau's reward for shedding two tears? He was given the mount of Seir, which is always blessed with rain. And the inhabitants of Seir who received Esau hospitably were rewarded too by the Lord. What was their reward? From among their descendants were born kings even before there were kings in Judah and Israel, as it is written: "And these are the kings that reigned in the land of Edom, before there reigned any king over the children of Israel."[335]

3 / IN THE MOUNTAINS OF GEBAL

The northern part of the Land of Edom was called Gebal in ancient times. The psalmist lists its inhabitants among the enemies of Israel, and he exclaims: "O God, keep not Thou silence;/Hold not Thy peace, and be not still, O God./For, lo,

Thine enemies are in an uproar . . ./They have said: 'Come, and let us cut them off from being a nation;/That the name of Israel may be no more in remembrance.' . . ./Against Thee do they make a covenant . . ./Gebal, and Ammon, and Amalek."

The villages situated among these mountains suffered continually from the attacks of the nomad Arabs who roamed the neighboring desert. These wanderers used to descend upon them and pillage their fruit groves. The Land of Gebal as well as the whole of Edom was renowned for its luxuriant grape plantations.

Rabbi Joshua son of Levi once went to Gebal, where he noticed that the clusters of grapes growing in the vineyards were so big that they looked like calves, and he asked, "Are there calves among the vines?" To which the inhabitants replied, "These are not calves but bunches of grapes." Whereupon he exclaimed, "O Land! O Land! Shrivel thy fruit! For whom art thou producing fruit? Is it not for the Arabs, who rose against us because of our sins?"

A year later, Rabbi Hiyya visited the same place. When he saw the clusters as large as goats, he said, "Are there goats among the vines?" The prompt reply was, "Away with you! And do not serve us as your friend did last year!"[336]

4 / THE TORAH WAS OFFERED TO THE SONS OF ESAU

Extending his blessing to the Israelites, Moses, the Man of God, said: "The Lord came from Sinai, And rose from Seir unto them";

The Aramaic translation of the Bible adds that from the heights of Mount Gebal the Almighty, blessed be He, first offered the Torah to the sons of Esau. But they refused to receive it.

Said the Almighty, "Will you receive My Holy Word?"

Said they, "Lord of the Universe, what does it proscribe?"

Said the Holy One, blessed be He, "Thou shalt not kill!"
Said they, "It is beyond us to fulfill Thy Commandments!"*337

5 / MOSES AND AARON ON MOUNT HOR

Aaron's death, on a forlorn height away from the eyes of
the congregation, apparently gave rise to grave suspicions;
and the biblical story is reflected in tradition in the following
way:

"Once, when Israel camped by the land of Edom, Moses
and Aaron went forth to walk upon a mountain. When they
reached the summit, they saw a cave whence shone a bright
light. They entered and found a gold chair on which was
written, 'To him unto whom the place is fitting.'

"Moses tried to sit in it, but it was too small. Then Aaron
sat there, and the Angel of Death appeared, seized his soul,
and vanished. And Moses descended, and the Children of
Israel asked, "Where is Aaron?" So he told them what had
happened, but they did not believe him and suspected that
he himself had slain Aaron. Then the Lord gave Aaron's
coffin to angels, who flew over the camp with it. And a Divine
Echo cried out, 'Do not suspect Moses!'

"Aaron's grave is in an ancient cave. On certain well-
known nights, a mighty, awesome voice, inspiring dread in
all flesh, is heard from it."338

6 / THE SHRINE OF AARON THE PRIEST

"And they [Moses and Aaron] went up to Mount Hor [*Hor
ha-Har,* in Hebrew] before the eyes of all the congregation.
And Moses took off the robes of Aaron and set them on
Eleazar his son, and Aaron died there, on the top of the
mountain."

* See legend XXVII:9.

Why is it called Hor ha-Har—Mount of the Mountain? Because it was a small mount on top of a large one, like a little apple on top of a big one.

Jewish and Arab tradition alike place Mount Hor in the land of Edom, in Transjordan, not far from the ruins of Petra. On Hor's peak, a small edifice topped by a white dome can be seen from afar. Both Jews and Arabs believe that this is the tomb of Aaron the Priest—in Arabic, *Nebi* (prophet) *Harun.*

In past centuries, in spite of the dangers of the journey, pious Jews undertook the pilgrimage to the tomb of Aaron, and left their names carved into the stone of his cenotaph.

The bedouin of the vicinity also venerate the tomb. They often climb the steep rocky slope to prostrate themselves at the saint's sanctuary. They invoke his name in their solemn oaths, and, to honor his memory, they frequently bestow his name on their children.[339]

7 / THE SPRING OF MOSES IN EDOM

In the mountains of Edom, by the side of the highway leading from Maan to Petra (the ancient Sela), there flows a copious spring known to the Arabs as *Ein Moussa*— the Spring of Moses.

Arab legend describes Moses, the Man of God, encamping around this fountain with the tribes of Israel.

Yakut, the Moslem geographer of the thirteenth century, relates in great detail the wonders performed by Moses in this place, and these are his words:

"This valley is called after Moses the son of Amram. It is a fine valley, full of olive trees, and it is so called in memory of Moses, who came out of the desert, leading the children of Israel with him.

"And Moses had with him the rock mentioned by Allah in the Koran, in the verse: 'And when Moses asked drink for his people, we said: Strike the Rock with thy rod, and from it there gushed twelve fountains, and as he marched he carried this Rock with him, and fared forth.

" 'And when he halted he threw it on the earth, then there would gush out from it twelve springs, according to the number of the tribes, so that each man knew his drinking place.'

"Now when Moses came to this valley, and knew that his end was near at hand, he took thought for the Rock, and he fixed it on the mountainside there. From it came forth twelve springs, which divided among twelve villages, a village for every one of the tribes. Then Moses died, but by his command the Rock remained there.

"Now this has been related to me, Yakut, by the judge Jamal ed-Din Hassan, that he saw the Rock in this place, and it is of the size of a goat's head, and there is nothing else on the mountainside like to it."[340]

8 / PETRA AND ITS INHABITANTS

The ruins of Petra and the nearby bedouin village are called, in Arabic, *Wadi-Musa*—the Valley of Moses.

In the caves and among the ruins of Petra, there lives at the present time a small tribe of bedouin called al-Badul. They are the poorest of all the bedouin tribes in Transjordan, and they derive their miserable pittance by showing tourists around the beautiful remains of Petra.

The Arabs of the vicinity explain the origin of the name al-Badul by the following story:

When Moses and the children of Israel surrounded Petra, Moses declared war against the inhabitants because they refused to accept his religion. He conquered and slaughtered them all, except for twelve who hid themselves in a cave on the top of the mountain, which is now called Umm al-Biyarah.

Moses ordered them to come down. They answered in

Arabic: *"Inna abdalna, ya Nabi Allah!"* ("We have changed, O Prophet of God!")

"What have you changed?" asked Moses.

"Our religion, for we accept yours," was the answer.

Since that time, they are known as *al-Badul*—the people who became changed or altered.[341]

FIG. 55. PETRA—ROMAN THEATER (1828)
The theater was carved out of the side of a mountain.

9 / THE TREASURE OF PHARAOH IN PETRA

According to Arab legend, Pharaoh, ruler of Egypt (in Arabic, *Pharaoun*), sojourned in Petra, where he erected many buildings named after him. One of the most superb monuments of Petra is known to the Arabs as *Khaznat-Pharoun*—the Treasure of Pharaoh—for short, *el-Khazne*—the Treasure.

The top is surmounted by a rock shaped like a water pitcher. The bedouin Arabs believe that it contains the treasures of Pharaoh. They therefore shoot at this "pitcher" from time to time, hoping to pierce it and to uncover the great wealth it conceals. The rock is covered with bullet-holes,

FIG. 56. PETRA—*EL-KHAZNE* (1828)
This illustration shows the pitcher-shaped rock at the top of the ruin that the Arabs thought contained the Pharaoh's treasure.

but so far it has not been broken, to the great sorrow of the treasure hunters.*[342]

10 / THE PALACE OF PHARAOH'S DAUGHTER

Amidst the ruins of Petra, there is a temple dating from the second or third century—the time of Roman rule in the Land of Israel. The Arabs call it *Kasr Bint Pharaoun* or *Kasr el-Bint* —the Palace of Pharaoh's Daughter.

It is related that the unmarried daughter of Pharaoh, who was not allowed by her father to leave the palace, announced one day that she would marry the man who would divert the water of a spring to her dwelling.

Two young princes set to work, and succeeded in bringing the waters of two springs on one and the same day to the palace.

Pharaoh's daughter asked the first prince: "How did you bring the water in such a short time?"

He answered: "With my power and the power of my men."

To the same question, the second prince replied: "With God's power, my power, the power of my men, and that of my camels." And she married the second, because he showed more faith in God.

As the princess was making her decision, the wing of a locust fell into the aqueduct made by the first man, and completely stopped the flow of water. No one could remove this obstruction, although it was very tiny and insignificant.

This accident was divine proof that she had made the right choice.[343]

* The name Pharaoh is also attached to a small island—*Djezirat Pharoun,* in Arabic—lying a small distance offshore in the Gulf of Eilat.

SINAI

XXVII
THE DESERT OF SINAI

1 / THE WILDERNESS OF SNAKES AND SCORPIONS

After the crossing of the Red Sea, the Israelites roamed over the desert of Sinai, where snakes and scorpions crawl in great number. The Torah praises the Almighty, blessed be He, who knew how to protect Israel from this deadly scourge as He "led thee [Israel] through the great and dreadful wilderness, wherein were serpents, fiery serpents, and scorpions, and thirsty ground where was no water."

And this is how He accomplished this feat: "When Israel walked in the desert, the ark of the covenant went in front of them, and darts of fire flashed between the two poles of the ark. And they scorched snakes which were as large as the beams of an olive-press, and scorpions the size of tree-branches.

"And they burnt ahead of Israel all the thorns and thistles which encumbered their path. And the people of the world looked on and wondered."

To this day, the central part of the Desert of Sinai is called by the Arabs, *Tih Beni Israil*—the Desert of Wanderings of the Sons of Israel. The Arabic *tih* is similar to the Hebrew *tohu,* meaning waterless, desolate region."[344]

2 / MOSES SET THE TIME FOR MEALS

About Israel's customs in the desert, the sages tell: "At first, Israel was like cocks that pecked messily among the rubbish until Moses fixed the usage and set the time for meals, as it is written, 'Moses said: The Lord shall give you in the evening flesh to eat, and in the morning bread to the full.' "[345]

3 / THE MANNA—THE FOOD OF ISRAEL

On the arid soil of Sinai, where no wheat and no corn grew, the Israelites fed on the manna, as it is told:

"And when the layer of dew was gone up, behold upon the face of the wilderness a fine, scale-like thing, fine as the hoar-frost on the ground. And when the children of Israel saw it, they said one to another: 'What is it?' For they knew not what it was. And Moses said unto them: 'It is the bread which the Lord hath given you to eat.' And they gathered it morning by morning, every man according to his eating; and as the sun waxed hot, it melted. And the house of Israel called the name thereof Manna; and it was like coriander seed, white; and the taste of it was like wafers made with honey. And Moses said: 'This is the thing which the Lord hath commanded: Let an omerful of it be kept throughout your generations.' And the children of Israel did eat the manna forty years, until they came to a land inhabited; they did eat the manna until they came unto the borders of the land of Canaan."

Legend describes the Almighty, blessed be He, holding keys of the various parts of heaven: "And He has a key of manna, and He gives them [the Israelites] manna, for it is written: "And He commanded the skies above,/And opened the doors of heaven;/And He caused manna to rain upon them for food,/And gave them of the corn of heaven."

The sages said: During all the forty years that Israel spent in the wilderness no Israelite woman had need for perfumes; she scented her body only with manna.

It was added: "Together with the manna, Israel also received women's trinkets and ornaments."

After the Israelites crossed the river Jordan into the Promised Land the manna was discontinued: "And the manna ceased on the morrow, after they had eaten of the produce of the land; neither had the children of Israel manna any more."

Many beliefs have remained attached to the memory of the miracle of the manna. It was said: "A jar filled with manna was preserved in the Great Temple of Jerusalem in memory of the Almighty's benefaction in the desert of Exodus. When the Temple was destroyed, the jar was hidden away with the other sacred utensils. Some add, more specifically, 'When the holy ark was concealed, the oil of ointment and the jar of manna were hidden away, too.'"

In the end of days, when Redemption draws near, the Prophet Elijah will restore the jar of manna to Israel, together with all the holy vessels.

Of the firmament and the heavens legend says: "Therein are mills which ground manna for the Righteous."

And, in the Middle Ages, it was customary to pay homage to a learned rabbi by addressing him by the Hebrew title *"Zinzenet ha-Man"*—Jar of Manna.[346]

4 / THE MANNA-CARRYING TAMARISK BUSH

Modern scientific observation has uncovered a new aspect of the biblical narrative.

Some of the numerous tamarisk bushes growing in the riverbeds of Sinai are covered at night and in the early morning with tiny irregular flakes as white and soft as snow and sweet to the taste. These are drops of the shrub's sap, brought to the surface by the prick of a small insect, and frozen by the cold desert night air. With the sunrise, they melt and disappear. This phenomenon fits the biblical description of the manna so closely that this species of tamarisk bush has the botanical name *Tamarix mannifera*—the manna-carrying tamarisk.

FIG. 57. MANNA-CARRYING TAMARISK
The botanical name of the bush is *Tamarix mannifera.*

The Arabs call the sweet drops *Mann el-Yahud*—the manna of the Jews. They used to collect them to sweeten their food.

In the past, the monks of the Sinai monasteries collected the drops in small jars and sold them to the pilgrims as "the Manna of the Israelites."[347]

5 / THE QUAIL IN THE DESERT OF SINAI

"He caused flesh also to rain upon them as the dust
And winged fowl as the sand of the seas."

Every year, by the end of the summer, quail come in boundless flights to the southern shore of Eretz-Israel and to the Sinai peninsula. The Arabs stretch high nets along the seashore, and the exhausted birds are caught by the thousands. The Arab inhabitants relish their meat, and great numbers are also sold in the local markets.

In their wanderings through Sinai, the Israelites fed on the quail, as it is related: "And there went forth a wind from the Lord, and brought across quails from the sea, and let them fall by the camp, about a day's journey on this side, and a day's journey on the other side, round about the camp, and about two cubits above the face of the earth. And the people rose up all that day, and all the night, and all the next day, and gathered the quails; he that gathered least gathered ten heaps."

"Why is this bird called *shelav?*" (Hebrew for quail.)

"Because the righteous eat them with contentment" (*shalva,* in Hebrew), said the sages.

In the captivity of Babylon, the Israelites recalled with longing the softness of the quails' flesh. Said one scholar: "Why dost thou call the fowls of Babylon fat? Betake thyself to the wilderness of Gaza and I will show thee fleshier birds!"[348]

FIG. 58. QUAIL
The quail's botanical name is Coturnix communis.

6 / IN THE WILDERNESS OF SHUR

*"And they went into the wilderness of Shur—
that is the wilderness of Cub."*

Within the limits of the desert of Sinai there stretches a desolate and waterless land known as the Wilderness of Shur. The Israelites penetrated into this desert, too, as it is written: "And Moses led Israel onward from the Red Sea, and they went out into the wilderness of Shur, and they went three days in the wilderness, and found no water."

Legend sometimes designates this region by the name of Cub. "It has been said of the waste of Cub that it covered nine hundred square parasangs of land, and was overun by snakes and scorpions."*

The enormous size of these formidable and harmful creatures is described at length: "The wilderness of Shur," said the sages, "stretched over eight hundred square parasangs. And it swarmed with snakes, scorpions and other evil creeping creatures."

Said Rabbi Yossi, "There were serpents the size of the beams of an oil press, and scorpions with legs as thick as the fingers of a man's hand."

The story is told of King Shahur, who was making his way through this wilderness and lo and behold! his first caravan passed and was swallowed by a snake; a second caravan came along and was gulped up, too. A third caravan shared the same fate.

And the king sat down and tried to think out a solution.

And there were sages with him, and they said: "Why do you tarry? Ask for ten warriors." And they came.

They told the king, "Let these men fill big sacks with straw."

And the men filled the straw into bags and rolled them in front of the serpent, and he swallowed them up until his belly was full to bursting and he could not budge. Then they stood over the beast and killed him.

"A man once passed through this wilderness of Cub and saw a serpent asleep, [as thick] as the beam of an olive press. He saw the serpent but the serpent did not see him. Yet from the great fright he had, he became so terrified that his hair began to fall out, and they called him 'baldhead.' "349

---

* Cub, is the name of a people who lived on the border of the Land of Israel. The prophet Ezekiel mentions them: "Ethiopia . . . and Cub . . . shall fall with them by the sword." Cub is also the name of a thorn growing in the wilderness; possibly the desert was named for it.

7 / THE NAME "DESERT OF SHUR"

Legend connects the name Shur with the Hebrew *shura,*
meaning "row," for in the Wilderness of Shur, "Israel
yearned to form themselves in rows arranged under separate
banners, according to the tribes."

Others explain the name Shur as menaing "wall," and thus
we are taught: "What is the meaning of the Wilderness of
Shur? As long as Israel was in bondage in Egypt, the world
was a wilderness; when they came out, the world became
walled [secure, as if it were surrounded with a rampart]."

Another explanation: "Until Israel received the Torah, the
world was like unto a wilderness; since they received the
Torah, the world became walled."

"For I, saith the Lord, will be unto her a wall of fire round
about, and I will be the glory in the midst of her."[350]

8 / ISRAEL IN THE DESERT OF PARAN

"The Lord came from Sinai . . .
He shined forth from mount Paran."

The wilderness of Paran stretches within one of the most
barren sections of the desert of Sinai. By its side extend the
wilds of Zin and Kadesh. Eastward, at the extremity of Transjordan, spread the wastes of Kadmot.

Trekking from Egypt to the Promised Land, the Israelites
wandered through all these deserts.

The sages interpreted the meaning of these names thus:
"The desert of Zin," because there God ordered [Hebrew,
ziva] Israel to keep His commandments.

"The wilderness of Kadesh," because there God sanctified
[Hebrew, *kidesh*] Israel.

"The waste of Kadmot," because there was given the time-
honored [Hebrew, *keduma*] Law.

"The wilderness of Paran," because there the Israelites were fruitful [Hebrew, *peru*] and multiplied, according to the biblical saying *"peru u revu*—be fruitful and multiply."[351]

9 / HE APPEARED ON MOUNT PARAN

On his death bed, Moses, the Man of God, blessed his people, saying, "The Lord came from Sinai,/And rose from Seir unto them;/He shined forth from mount Paran."

It was asked: "What about Seir, and what about Paran?" This teaches us that the Almighty proposed (the Torah) to every people and nation of the world, and none would have it until he came to Israel, and they accepted it.

Rashi expounds: "He shined forth from mount Paran": That is, the Almighty went to the Children of Ishmael and endeavored to persuade them to receive the Torah, but they rejected it.*[352]

* See legend XXVI:4.

XXVIII
STATIONS AND SITES IN SINAI

1 / BAAL-ZEPHON—A STATION IN THE WANDERINGS

Baal-zephon was an important station of the Israelites in the desert of Sinai. The Bible mentions it in Exodus: ". . . and encamp . . . before Baal-zephon, over against it shall ye encamp by the sea."

Probably Baal-zephon stood on the shore of the Mediterranean Sea, at the site later known as Cassion. It was named after the Canaanite idol whose worship it practiced. Instead of Baal-zephon, the Aramaic translation of the Bible writes: *Taavuta,* meaning "idol-worship."

Legend tells: "Baal-zephon was left of all the deities to mislead the mind of the Egyptian."

It is also added: "When Pharaoh saw the Israelites encamping by the sea, he said, 'I had planned to destroy them in water and now Baal-zephon approves my decision to destroy them in water.' He then began to sacrifice, to offer incense and libations, and to prostrate himself to his idol. In this sense it is said, 'And Pharaoh drew nigh to sacrifice and offer incense.' "353

2 / PI-HAHIROTH—A STATION IN THE WANDERINGS

Pi-hahiroth was another station of the wandering Israelites in the desert of Sinai. God instructed Moses, saying, "Speak unto the children of Israel, that they turn back and encamp before Pi-hahiroth, between Migdol and the sea."

According to legend, the name Pi-hahiroth derives from the word *hirah,* which designates in Hebrew a large mass of rock shaped in the form of an idol, similar to the sphinx of the ancient Egyptians.

"What were these *hiroth?* They were not leaning but tapering to the apex. They were not rectilinear but slightly convex. They were not round but square. They were not the work of man but the work of heaven. They had eyes as openings. They were a sort of male and female."

Others say: "*Hiroth* only means the place of the licentiousness of the Egyptians, their market place, the place where idols were. It estranged its worshipers."[354]

3 / MARAH—A STATION ON THE WAY OF ISRAEL

After the Israelites crossed the desert of Shur they came to a place named Marah, because its waters were bitter (Hebrew, *mar*):

"And they went three days in the wilderness, and found no water. And when they came to Marah, they could not drink of the waters of Marah, for they were bitter. Therefore the name of it was called Marah. And, the people murmured against Moses, saying: 'What shall we drink?' And he cried unto the Lord; and the Lord showed him a tree, and he cast it into the waters, and the waters were made sweet."

The sages deliberated among themselves on the nature of this tree.

Said Rabbi Joshua, "It was a willow tree."

Said Rabbi Eliezer from Modiim, "It was an olive tree, because there is none more bitter."

Said Rabbi Joshua son of Karkha, "It was an oleander, because it is the most acrid of all trees."

Said Rabbi Nathan, "It was a cedar tree."

And some said, "It was the root of a fig tree, or of a pomegranate."

Legend exclaims in conclusion: Behold how wonderful are the miracles wrought by the Almighty, blessed be He! Human beings remedy bitterness by adding sweet; not so the Almighty, blessed be He. He remedies bitterness by even more bitterness.[355]

4 / MITHKAH AND MARAH

After the Israelites left the station named Marah, for its bitter (Hebrew, *mar*) waters, they encamped in a place named Mithkah—the Sweet Waters, as recorded: ". . . and pitched in Marah. And they journeyed from Marah, and came . . . and pitched in Mithkah."

Therefore, when one wishes to describe the tribulations of a man who has lost his wealth, and subsists in straitened circumstances after a life of great luxury and comfort, it is common to use the biblical text allegorically and say, "And he journeyed from Mithkah and pitched in Marah!"[356]

5 / ALOSH—A STATION IN THE WANDERINGS

Alosh was one of the places where the Children of Israel made camp during their forty years of wanderings in the desert of Sinai. Its site is now unknown.

According to tradition, the manna started to fall at Alosh, for this name, it is said, derives from the Hebrew *lush*, meaning "to knead bread," and the manna is "the bread which the Lord hath given you to eat."

We are taught: "And where did it [the manna] fall?" In

Alosh. "And why in Alosh?" Because it is written, in the words of Abraham to Sarah, "Knead [Hebrew, *lushi*] . . . and make cakes."

Thus did the Almighty, blessed be He, keep the promise He had made to His people: "I will cause to rain bread from heaven for you."[357]

6 / REPHIDIM OF THE SINAI DESERT

Rephidim was one of the most important stations of the Israelites in the desert of Sinai. Its exact site is unknown. Some surmise that it is the picturesque oasis named today, in Arabic, *Firan,* which is situated on the way to the high core of Sinai and its renowned monastery of St. Catherine: "And all the congregation of the children of Israel journeyed, and encamped in Rephidim. Then came Amalek and fought with Israel in Rephidim."

Of Amalek, legend says: "He came from the mountains of Seir [Edom]. He paced four hundred parasangs and came and waged war on Israel. He used to approach under the cover of clouds, catch people from Israel, and slay them."

The sages connected the name "Rephidim" to the Hebrew *Raphe* or *Riphion,* meaning "feebleness" or "laxity."

Why was it called Rephidim? Said Rabbi Joshua, "Because they [the Israelites] cast off the commandments of the Torah."

Some commentators say, "Rephidim means nothing else but 'feebleness.' " Because the Israelites slackened in the fulfillment of God's law, an enemy rose up against them. For the foe comes only as a punishment for sin and for transgression.

But inasmuch as Amalek injured Israel, he lost his place in this world and in the world to come. For what was Amalek like? As the fly that feeds on an open wound, so was Amalek avid after Israel.[358]

7 / TOPHEL—LABAN—DI-ZAHAB

As recorded in the opening sentence of Deuteronomy, when the tribes of Israel left Egypt on their way to the Promised Land, they went through Tophel, Laban, and Dizahab, among other places, as it is written: "These are the words which Moses spoke unto all Israel beyond the Jordan; in the wilderness, in the Arabah, over against Suph, between Paran and Tophel, and Laban, and Hazeroth, and Di-zahab."

Tophel, it is surmised, stood in the mountains of Edom, at the place of today's townlet Tephila, a likely corruption of the Biblical name.

Laban (Hebrew for "white") is probably the same as Libnah, one of the stations where Israel set up camp. Possibly this is today the site of Wadi Albaida, meaning "the White Brook" in Arabic.

Di-zahab (Hebrew for "of Gold") was conceivably in eastern Sinai, on the shore of the Gulf of Eilat, in a small bay still known in Arabic by the name *Minat a-Dahab*—the Harbor of Gold. A new settlement called by the biblical name is now established on this spot.

Legend holds that Tophel, Laban, and Di-zahab are not place names but words suggestive of the transgressions committed by the Israelites during their wanderings.

"We searched through all the Holy Scriptures and found no places named Tophel, Laban, and Di-zahab, but these are expressions of the Almighty's anger because of Israel's sins."

Tophel refers to Tiphla [Hebrew for folly], for when they were given the manna from heaven for food: "The people spoke against God, and against Moses: 'Wherefore have ye brought us up out of Egypt to die in the wilderness? for there is no bread, and there is no water; and our soul loatheth this light bread.' "

Laban—this is the manna whose color was white, as is

written: "Manna; and it was like coriander seed, white; and the taste of it was like wafers made with honey."

Di-zahab—that is the golden calf that the Israelites put up in the desert, to God's great wrath.[359]

8 / EL-ARISH—THE CAPITAL OF SINAI

El-Arish is the capital city of Sinai. It stands by the main highway that has linked the Holy Land and Egypt from the most ancient times. At the beginning of this century, a railway line was built through Sinai. It has not reduced the importance of its capital town, for the railway track follows the ancient route, and El-Arish has remained the main station of Sinai.

El-Arish is an Arabic word meaning "the Booth." Most likely, the name retains the fact that its first inhabitants dwelt in huts made of branches of palm trees common to the surroundings even today.

Legend has developed a different explanation: It holds that when the Patriarch Jacob traveled south from the Land of Canaan into Egypt, following the age-old trail, he wished to rest from the strain of the journey. So he built a booth by the side of the road on the spot where El-Arish was to be erected in a later age.

In the year 1481, Rabbi Meshullam, from Volterra, Italy, repeated the tale, as follows:

"We came to a place named Arish—that is, *Succoth* [booths], for in the language of Ishmael, *Arish* means "booths." And this is the place which was built by Jacob the Patriarch, peace be upon him."[*][360]

* Indeed, describing Jacob's wanderings, the Bible says: "And Jacob journeyed to Succoth, and built him a house, and made booths for his cattle. Therefore the name of the place is called Succoth (booths)." From the context, it appears that the Succoth mentioned here was situated in Transjordan.

9 / A BIGGER TRAITOR THAN THE GOVERNOR OF EL-ARISH

In the Middle Ages, there was current among the Arab population of Sinai the expression, "A bigger traitor than the governor of El-Arish" to designate a man who betrays the guest who rests under his roof.

And this is how the saying was born, in the year 658 C.E., about twenty years after the Arab conquest of Palestine.

The Caliph Ali ibn Abu-Taleb entrusted Ash-har en-Nahi with the governing of Egypt, and sent him there with a large army. This did not please Muawiya, Ali's archenemy, and he decided to put an end to the life of the prospective ruler.

He secretly sent a message to the governor of El-Arish, saying, "If thou succeedeth to poison Ash-har and bring about his death, I shall exempt thee from the payment of taxes to my treasury for twenty successive years."

On his way to Egypt, Ash-har rested in El-Arish. The governor of the town came to greet him and asked, "What is thy favorite food?" He replied, "Honey!"

The governor brought him honey, and when Ash-har tasted it, he fell dead on the spot. His infuriated men pounced on the governor and his people, and killed them all.

Since then, the man who betrays his guest is called "a bigger traitor than the governor of El-Arish."[361]

10 / RHINOCORURA—ANCIENT EL-ARISH

At the site of El-Arish, there existed in olden days a townlet with the Greek designation *Rhinocorura,* an odd name, meaning "the [people with the] cut-off noses."

The ancient Greek historian Strabo explains the origin of the name thus: "So called from the people with mutilated noses who had been settled there in early times, for some

FIG. 59. PALM GROVE OF EL-ARISH

Ethiopian invaded Egypt and, instead of killing the wrongdo-
ers, cut off their noses and settled them at that place, assum-
ing that on account of their disgraceful faces they would no
longer dare do people harm."

Epiphanius, the Greek historian of the fourth century, tells
that at precisely this spot Noah the Righteous divided the
world among his three sons: Shem, Ham, and Japheth.[362]

11 / WHO SAVED THE TOWN PELUSION?

Pelusion, or Pelusium, was an important city of Sinai, on
the ancient highway linking the Land of Israel with Egypt,
the Via Maris (the Way of the Sea) of the Romans.

Pelusion was famous for the manufacture of a fine linen
which was named after the city, as well as for the clothes
made from it. The ancients mention it among the ritual robes
worn by the High Priest performing at the Great Temple of
Jerusalem: "At dawn," they say, "he wore a pelusion."

In 701 B.C.E., Sennacherib, king of Assyria, invaded the
Holy Land; conquering many cities of Judah in this campaign, he took the Way of the Sea toward Egypt, his true goal.
His plans of expansion went for naught at Pelusion, where his
forward thrust was crushed by the stubborn defense of the
city, thus saving Egypt from the common foe.

Herodotus recorded this episode, attributing the Assyrian
king's change of fortune to divine interference. And Josephus Flavius repeats the tale in the following words: "After
he [Sennacherib] had spent a great deal of time on the siege
of Pelusium, and the earthworks which he was raising against
the walls had already reached a great height, and he was on
the point of attacking, the king of Egypt prayed to God, and
God hearkened to his prayer and in one night a host of mice
ate through the bows and other weapons of the Assyrians,
and, as the king on that account had no bows, he withdrew
his army from Pelusium."[363]

XXIX
SINAI–THE MOUNT OF GOD

1 / THE VARIOUS NAMES OF MOUNT SINAI

"The Almighty, blessed be He, appraised
all the mountains and did not find one worthy
of conveying the Divine Torah except Sinai."

Mount Sinai has been blessed with many names. It is told
that it was originally called "Horeb," meaning "dryness,"
because it has no water and is barren of vegetation.

"After water and earth were created," says legend, "this
mountain was named Horeb. But since the Almighty, blessed
be He, revealed himself to Moses from amidst a bush [in
Hebrew, *sneh*], this mountain was named Sinai, after the
bush."

And thus are the various names of Sinai explained: "The
Mount of God," because there did the Israelites recognize
the Godliness of the Almighty, blessed be He. "The Mount
of God," because the Lord rested upon it, as it is written:
"And the Lord came down upon mount Sinai."

"Mount Horeb," because from here the Sanhedrin, the
Supreme Court of Israel, acquired the right to sentence to

death by the sword—*hereb.* "Mount Horeb," because desolation *(hurbah)* to idolaters descended thereon.

"Mount Sinai," because hostility—*Sinah*—descended thereon toward idolaters.

The rabbis deliberated further on the meaning of the name "Sinai." Said one, "The mountain whereon miracles— *nissim*—were performed for Israel. Then it should be called Mount Nissai?"

Said another, "But [it means] the mountain whereon a happy augury—*siman*—took place for Israel. Then it should be called Mount Simanai?"[364]

2 / SINAI IS ALSO NAMED BASHAN

"Seven mountains has the Lord created and He did not choose any of them but Mount Sinai."

One of the names of Mount Sinai is Bashan, and thus it is designated in the Psalms:/"A mountain of God is the mountain of Bashan . . ./Why look ye askance, ye mountains of peaks,/At the mountain which God hath desired for His abode?/Yea, the Lord will dwell therein for ever."

The ancients expound: "Why look ye askance? [in Hebrew, *tirazdun*] that is, why do you wish [*tirezu*] to contend [*dun*] with Sinai? You are all peak-backed mountains. The peak-backed is blemished and he should not approach the altar of the Almighty, as the Torah dictates: 'For whatsoever man he be that hath a blemish . . . a blind man, or a lame . . . or a man that is . . . crook-backed . . . he shall not come nigh to offer the bread of his God.' "

The ancients explained the verse of Proverbs: "Better it is to be of a lowly spirit with the humble" as referring to Mount Sinai, for it humbled itself before the Lord and thus was found worthy to receive the Holy Law.

Rabbi Ashi observed: "You can learn from this that if a man is arrogant, this is a blemish in him."*[365]

3 / WHEREFORE THE NAME SINAI?

Sinai is named after the bush-tree—in Hebrew, *sneh*—where: "The angel of the Lord appeared unto him [Moses] in a flame of fire."

It is also said that stones in Sinai are streaked with branching veins resembling the twigs of the *sneh*. Rabbi Moshe of Narbonne related, in the fourteenth century, "And it may be known to you that all the stones in Mount Sinai, as has been testified, picture the bush, wherefore Sinai is named after this plant, for the Almighty, blessed be He, revealed himself to Moses from amidst a bush."

And one of Barcelona's Jewish notables brought back with him this description of the stones: "And the bush was seen pictured in full detail, and the drawing was godlike in its perfection, the work of divine hands, and I split the stone in two and the bush appeared on each half. And I cracked each part again into two and the bush was found on the innerside surface of each piece, and so on many times, until the smallest fragments still showed the bush within all. And I wondered and rejoiced in it."

Another learned rabbi, at the end of the fourteenth century, took great interest in these stones. He wrote: "And when I went to Barcelona, I asked the students about the Sinai stones, and they answered me that even today these stones exist, and the man in whose possession they are ran away from the plague in Barcelona to Perpignan [France]. And when I came to Perpignan, many testified to having seen these stones."[366]

* For further accounts of the quarrels among the mountains when the Torah was given from the top of Mount Sinai, see legends II:11 and XX:5.

4 / WHEREFROM CAME MOUNT SINAI?

"Mount Sinai—the abode of the Divine Presence."

Legend says of Mount Sinai: From Mount Moriah it was wrenched from the mass like a handful of paste is torn off the dough. From the very place where Isaac the Patriarch was to be sacrificed it was taken.

The Almighty said: "Whereas Isaac, the father, was ready to be sacrificed upon this rock, it is becoming that the Holy Law should be conveyed to the sons from its heights."

And when the psalmist sings: "His foundation is in the holy mountains," the rabbis teach that this means "His foundation of the world [is] by virtue of two holy mountains, Mount Sinai and Mount Moriah."[367]

5 / WHY WAS THE LAW GIVEN FROM SINAI?

"And the Lord came down upon mount Sinai."

When the Almighty, blessed be He, resolved to bestow the Holy Law on Israel, he looked for a high peak from which to convey His commandments to His chosen people.

The Almighty reviewed all the mountains and found none as worthy of His Divine Presence as Mount Sinai.

And why of all heights was Mount Sinai chosen for such a distinction? Because of its modesty and humble demeanor.

While Mount Hermon and Mount Shirion provoked each other, one saying, "Upon me He shall rest," and the other protesting, "No, on me alone shall the Divine Presence repose"—both exalting their merits—Mount Sinai kept modestly aside and humbled itself before the Lord.

Whereupon the Almighty rested His Divine Presence upon Mount Sinai's peak.[368]

6 / WHY WAS THE HOLY LAW GIVEN IN A WILDERNESS?

The Book of Exodus describes Israel's wanderings, saying: "And when they . . . were come to the wilderness of Sinai, they encamped in the wilderness; and there Israel encamped before the mount."

In that wilderness the Holy Law was given to the Children of Israel. And why in a wilderness? Because if it had been given in the Land of Israel, the Israelites would have said, "It is ours, and only ours."

If it had been given in some other land, the people of that land would have said, "Ours it is, and ours only."

Therefore it was given in a desert, so that whosoever wishes to partake of it is free to do so.

Others say: That the nations of the world should not be able to say, "Since the Torah was given within His own land, we are not called upon to accept it."

Another explanation: Not to create dissension between the tribes, lest one should say, "In my portion the Torah was given," and the other counter, "No, in my portion the Torah was given."

Therefore it was given in a desert, in a land belonging to no one.[369]

7 / MOSES ON THE HEIGHTS OF MOUNT SINAI

"And the Lord came down upon mount Sinai . . . and the Lord called Moses to the top of the mount; and Moses went up."

"And the Lord said unto Moses . . . 'Thou canst not see My face, for man shall not see Me and live.' And the Lord said: 'Behold, there is a place by Me, and thou shalt stand upon the rock. And it shall come to pass, while My glory passeth by, that I will put thee in a cleft of the rock, and will cover thee with My hand until I have passed by. And I will take away My hand, and thou shalt see My back; but My face shall not be seen.' "

The Mount of Moses—*Djebel Mussa,* in Arabic—rises some twenty-two hundred meters above sea level, and its peak dominates all the surrounding mountain ranges. On its heights, a depression is shown on the face of the rock. This, it is said, is the sign left by the body of Moses, who retreated humbly from the glory of the Lord when the Almighty revealed Himself to him in all His splendor.[370]

FIG. 60. MOSES WITH THE TABLETS OF THE LAW
This illustration from the fourteenth-century Passover Haggadah of Sarajevo, Yugoslavia, shows Moses bringing the Tablets of the Law to the Israelites.

8 / SINAI UNITES ISRAEL

When the Bible describes the wanderings of the tribes in Sinai, and their various stations, it always refers to Israel in the plural: "They journeyed from . . . they pitched in . . .". The plural implies that the tribes were disunited. "They journeyed in dissension," said the sages, "they rested and encamped in dissension."

FIG. 61. MOSES WITH THE TABLETS OF THE LAW
This 1723 drawing shows Moses receiving the Tablets of the Law.

But it is added: "When they came in front of Mount Sinai, they all became one . . . and it is no longer written "and they pitched" but "and there Israel encamped [singular form] before the Mount.'"

And when the Master of the Universe saw from the heights of Mount Sinai all the tribes united in front of Him, the Holy

One, blessed be He, said, "This is the hour at which I am giving the Torah to My children!"[371]

9 / HOW DID THE LORD APPEAR ON SINAI?

"And when the Holy One, blessed be He, appeared on Mount Sinai to give the Torah to Israel, He faced them as an old man, for the Torah is at its best when it comes from the mouth of an old man. What is the proof? The verse of Job: "With aged men is wisdom, and understanding in length of days."[372]

10 / THE DIVINE PRESENCE EXALTED MOUNT SINAI

"It is not the place that honors the man but it is the man that honors the place, for thus we find that as long as the *Shekhinah* [the Divine Presence] was present on Sinai, the law was 'Neither let the flocks nor herds feed before that mount,' but as soon as the *Shekhinah* departed from there, lepers were permitted."[373]

11 / A VOICE FROM MOUNT SINAI

"At Sinai, Israel possessed weapons upon which the Tetragrammaton was inscribed, but when they sinned, He removed the inscription from them . . . an angel descended and erased it."

Every day a divine voice goes forth from mount Horeb (Sinai), proclaiming and saying, "Woe to mankind for their contempt of the Law."[374]

12 / ISRAEL'S REWARD ON MOUNT SINAI

Legend tells: "At the time Israel stood at Mount Sinai and said, 'All that the Lord hath spoken will we do and obey,' at that time, splendor from the splendor of the *Shekhinah* above was bestowed upon them. And the proof? The words of the prophet Ezekiel: 'Thy renown went forth among the nations for thy beauty; for it was perfect, through My splendor which I had put upon thee, saith the Lord God.' "[375]

13 / WHEN WAS THE TORAH GIVEN?

A Galilean scholar expounded on the giving of the Torah on Mount Sinai in the following words: "May the Holy One be blessed for giving a triple Torah, to a triple people, by the hand of a third son, in the third month."

"A triple Torah," because the holy book is composed of three parts: the Pentateuch, the Prophets, the Writings.

"A triple people," because the people of Israel comprises three groups: the Kohanim (the priests), the Levites (the servants of the Temple), and *Shear Yisrael* (the rest of Israel).

"By the hand of a third son," because Moses was the third son of his father Aram.

"In the third month," because God appeared to Israel in the month of Sivan, the third month in the Hebrew calendar.[376]

14 / SINAI AND THE UPROOTER OF MOUNTAINS

Owing to the sacred memories rooted in God's own mountain, its name became a symbol of scholarship and learning in Jewish lore; a scholar well-versed in Jewish law and tradition and possessing a comprehensive knowledge of them is called "Sinai."

The one who is more skillful in dialectics—the logical disputation and discussion of the text of the Holy Scriptures— is entitled *Oker Harim*, Uprooter of Mountains.

The rabbis make a clear distinction between these two

FIG. 62 THE ISRAELITES IN FRONT OF MOUNT SINAI
From a Mahzor (prayer book) for the Feast of Shevuot, printed in
Prague, 1854.

dispositions, and there was once a dispute as to which of the two was superior to the other. One view was that it was the Sinai—the erudite savant—who was superior and the other that it was the keen dialectician.

"Rabbi Joseph was a well-read scholar. Rabbah was a keen dialectician. An inquiry was sent up to Eretz-Israel as to which of these should take precedence. They sent them word in reply: a well-read scholar is to take precedence."

Rabbi Shimon ben Yohai, of the second century, to whom is attributed the Holy Zohar, the book of the mystics, was granted the title "Sinai"; and in the annual pilgrimage to his tomb in Upper Galilee the crowds sing fervently while dancing: "Sinai, Sinai, thus we shall call the lion among the fellows,/From him comes Torah, our Master, the son of Yohai."[377]

15 / A LAW FROM MOUNT SINAI

Talmudic scholars used the expression, *"halakha le-Moshe me-Sinai"*—a ruling of Moses [who received it] on Mount Sinai—when they wished to emphasize the importance of an ancient traditional usage.

They were wont to add, *"All* the Torah is a tradition that was handed to Moses at Sinai."

But if one is lax in the fulfilling of a religious precept, one argues, *"Ein zu Torah me-Sinai"*—This is not a commandment from Mount Sinai![378]

16 / THE BROKEN PIECES OF THE HOLY TABLETS

*"On the seventeenth day of the month of Tammuz
were the Holy Tables broken."*

The Book of Exodus records: "And Moses turned, and went
down from the mount, with the two tables of the testimony
in his hand. . . . And the tables were the work of God, and
the writing was the writing of God, graven upon the tables.
. . . And it came to pass, as soon as he came nigh unto the
camp, that he saw the calf and the dancing; and Moses' anger
waxed hot, and he cast the tables out of his hands, and broke
them beneath the mount."

The ancients conjectured: If the original Tables of the Law
had not been broken the Holy Law would not have been
forgotten by Israel, and no people and no nation could have
subjugated them. For in the above passage of the Holy Texts,
when you reach the words "the writing of God *graven* upon
the tables," you should read not graven (Hebrew, *harut*) but
herut, meaning "liberty." If the Holy Tables had not been
destroyed Israel would have known everlasting liberty!

What was the destiny of the broken fragments? "Two
chests went with Israel in their wanderings. One contained
the Torah and the other the fragments of the Holy Tablets.
The one with the Torah remained in the Tabernacle. The
one with the fragments of the Holy Tablets went in and out,
following the Israelites in all their movements." (This last one
also went out with them to war.)

In Sinai, there rises a mountain named, in Arabic, *Ras
a-Zafzafa*—the Head of the Willow Tree. It commands a
beautiful view of a wide valley known as *a-Rakha*—the Rest
Place—for here it is believed the Israelites halted on their
way to Canaan.

According to a belief widespread among the monks and
the bedouin of the vicinity, the broken fragments of the Holy

Tables of the Law are concealed at the foot of the mount, on the margin of this very valley.[379]

17 / WHERE DID THE BURNING BUSH GROW?

The Greek monastery of St. Catherine, built in the sixth century, stands among the mountains of Sinai between two impressive rocky peaks. Its holiest spot is the "Room of the Burning Bush"—the site, according to Christian tradition, where the Almighty first revealed Himself to Moses.

When Moses was tending his flocks in the wilderness of Sinai, "the angel of the Lord appeared unto him in a flame of fire out of the midst of a bush; and he looked, and, behold, the bush burned with fire, and the bush was not consumed. And Moses said: 'I will turn aside now, and see this great sight, why the bush is not burnt.' And when the Lord saw that he turned aside to see, God called unto him out of the midst of the bush, and said: 'Moses, Moses!' And he said: 'Here am I.' And He said: 'Draw not nigh hither; put off thy shoes from off thy feet, for the place whereon thou standest is holy ground.'"

It was asked: Why did the Almighty choose to adress himself to Moses from amidst a bush? To prove that there is no place upon this earth free from the presence of the *Shekhinah*—the Divine Providence—not even the branches of an ordinary shrub.

Further, it was said, "As the bush is small and weak among the trees of the world, so was Israel lowly and feeble beside the Egyptians."

"The bush has thorns harder and sharper than all other trees, and any bird caught in its thicket can not make its escape without losing some of its feathers.

Likewise, the subjugation in Egypt was more difficult than all other slavery in the world."

"Shrubs of the same species are used to fence in gardens, similarly Israel is a hedge to the world."

"The bush grows thorns and also flowers. So does Israel produce righteous men and wicked ones, too."

The sages said, "O bush! O bush! Not because thou art the tallest of all trees didst the Almighty, blessed be He, rest His Divine Presence among thy branches but because thou art the lowliest."[380]

18 / MOSES—THE GOOD SHEPHERD

"Now Moses was keeping the flock of Jethro, and he led the flock to the farthest end of the wilderness, and came to the mountain of God, unto Horeb."

The ancient rabbis relate: "When Moses, our teacher, peace be upon him, was tending the flock of Jethro in the wilderness, a little kid escaped from him. He ran after it until it reached Hasit. When it reached Hasit, there appeared in view a pool of water, and the kid stopped to drink. When Moses approached it, he said, 'I did not know that you ran away because of thirst; you must be weary!' So he placed the kid on his shoulders and walked away.

"Thereupon, God said, 'Because thou hast mercy in leading the flock of the mortal, thou wilt assuredly tend my flock Israel!'"[381]

19 / THE CAVE OF MOSES AND ELIJAH IN SINAI

"There is no Holiness but Sinai."

Legend tells of a cavern in Mount Sinai, also known as Mount Horeb, wherein sojourned Moses, the Man of God, and Elijah the Prophet. Elijah fled to this cave from the wrath of the King of Israel: "And he arose, and did eat and drink, and went in the strength of that meal forty days and forty nights unto Horeb the mount of God. And he came thither unto a cave, and lodged there; and, behold, the word of the Lord came to him."

The sages of Israel mention "ten things which were created on the eve of the Sabbath in the twilight," and one of them is "the cave where Moses and Elijah stayed."

"The Divine Presence never moves from the cavern of Sinai. If an aperture the size of a needle-hole were made in the wall of the cave where Moses and Elijah stood, the light that would pour through that opening would be so dazzling that the human eye would not be able to bear it."[382]

20 / KORAH WAS SWALLOWED UP IN THE SINAI MOUNTAINS

A popular tradition identifies in the mountains of Sinai the spot where Korah and his people were swallowed up by the earth during Israel's wanderings.

"And," writes the Bible, "the earth opened her mouth, and swallowed them up, and their households, and all the men that appertained unto Korah, and all their goods. So they, and all that appertained to them, went down alive into the pit; and the earth closed upon them, and they perished from among the assembly. And all Israel that were round about them fled at the cry of them; for they said: 'Lest the earth swallow us up.' "

Legend tells that among the ten marvels which were created on the Sabbath eve, in the twilight, there was also "the opening of the earth's mouth to swallow up the wicked."

Rabbi Bar Hanna, of about the third century, renowned for his fanciful tales, relates how a vagabond bedouin named Taya led him to Mount Sinai:

"Said to me the same Taya: 'Come and I shall show thee Mount Sinai!' I went and I saw scorpions the size of white asses standing around him.

"I heard an echo say: 'Woe to me that I have vowed not to redeem Israel before the prescribed time! And now that I have sworn thus, who is going to release me from my oath?'

"Said to me the same Taya: 'Come and I shall show thee the place where Korah was swallowed up by the earth.' I went and saw two cracks on the surface of the earth and smoke was coming out of them. I dipped two pieces of wool in water, fixed them at the head of a lance, and introduced them there (inside the cracks). And when I took them out, they were scorched.

"Said Taya: 'Lend thine ear, what dost thou hear?' [And I heard] 'Moses and his Torah are truth and we are impostors!' "*383

21 / THE SEAT OF MOSES

On their way to Mount Sinai, the Children of Israel fought the Amalekites in Raphidim. The Torah relates: "And it came to pass, when Moses held up his hand, that Israel prevailed; and when he let down his hand, Amalek prevailed. But Moses' hands were heavy; and they took a stone, and put it under him, and he sat thereon."

The learned rabbis wondered: "Why did Moses choose to sit upon a stone? Would not a cushion have been better suited?" And they added, "As long as Israel was in danger the Man of God would not accept comfort. Happy is the man who participates in his own people's sorrows."

The sages of Israel were acquainted with the rock of Moses, and they instructed: "Whoever sees the stone whereon sat Moses, the Man of God, while Joshua fought Amalek, must return thanks and praise the Lord!"

In the mountains of Sinai, at the bottom of one of the passes, named, in Arabic, *Wadi a-Sheikh*—the Ravine of the

* See *Legends of Jerusalem*, p. 241, "Where Does the Cave Head?"

Venerable Old Man—there stands out a lofty rock known to the Arabs as *Makad en-Nebi Musa*—the Seat of the Prophet Moses. They tell that here sat Moses, the Holy Man, while he commanded the tribes of Israel who were fighting their enemies.[384]

FIG. 63. SEAT OF MOSES

22 / THE HEALING ROCK OF MOSES

In the mountains of Sinai, in the dry bed of a brook named, in Arabic, *Wadi e-Leja*—the Ravine of the Shelter—there lies, at the foot of a stony hill, a big rock called by the Arabs,

Hajar Musa—the Rock of Moses. It is about three-and-a-half-meters high, and is carved with inscriptions in the ancient Sinaitic script, as well as more recent engravings made by pilgrims of past generations.

The Rock of Moses is sacred to the bedouin, the inhabitants of Sinai. They often come to worship it, bringing with them their sick; they lay them against the rock in the belief that the contact with the holy stone will cure them of all their ills.[385]

FIG. 64. MOSES STRIKES THE ROCK
This medieval illustration shows the Israelites running to the water pouring from the rock.

23 / THE ROCK THAT SPOKE TO MOSES

"He cleaved rocks in the wilderness."

Along Wadi Bara, one of the stony dry riverbeds in the Sinai mountains, there stands a big rock, named by the Arabs *Hajar al-Laghwa*—the Talking Stone—and this is the story that is related: "Moses, the Holy Man, once walked within the depths of this ravine. A big rock stood in his way and barred his passage. Suddenly, a voice spoke from within the rock calling out 'Moses! Moses! Lay thy hand upon me!'

"Moses did so, and the stone cleaved itself open in front of him, and he stepped through and continued his way in peace.

"After Moses had passed, the two parts of the rock joined again, and the stone resumed its former appearance. Since then it has been named 'The Talking Rock.' "[386]

FIG. 65. MOSES STRIKES THE ROCK
This ancient mosaic shows an Israelite drinking the water pouring from the rock.

24 / A STONE FROM SINAI IN JERUSALEM

Legend tells of the precious and magnificent utensils of the Great Temple in Jerusalem, which were carried away from the destroyed capital and secreted in various hiding places in Eretz Israel and the Diaspora. Among the many vessels there was a stone from Sinai: "One precious stone valuable and excellent, which Moses on Mount Sinai carved out from under the Divine Throne of Sapphire."

"All is put away and concealed in the source of Zedekiah. And they shall remain unrevealed until dawns the day when Israel shall regain its former glory and the esteem of the world anew, when a man will be found named David the son of David [the Messiah], and all the silver and gold shall be revealed unto him, and all Israel shall gather together and go up as one people to Jerusalem."*

Today, in the great Armenian Church of the Old City of Jerusalem, there is kept a stone, which, according to the monks, was brought from Mount Sinai. Its holiness is great in the eyes of the Armenians.[387]

* A stone from Sinai was preserved in a church on Mount Zion. The Russian pilgrim Daniel of the year 1106 C.E. describes the altar of this church, and adds: "And there is a sacred stone that was brought thither from Mount Sinai, by angels."

XXX
THE WONDERS AT THE RED SEA

1 / HOW ISRAEL CROSSED THE RED SEA

"And He rebuked the Red Sea, and it was dried up;
And He led them through the depths,
as through a wilderness."

Said the Almighty, blessed be He, to Moses: "Moses! Stretch thy hand over the sea and cleave its waters asunder!"

And Moses lifted his hand over the sea and the waters did not defer to his command and did not open in front of him. And he showed them the coffin of Joseph, and the Holy Rod engraved with the "Ineffable Name," and still the sea did not comply.

Then Moses faced the Almighty again and said, "Lord of the Universe, the sea does not obey me!"

Forthwith, the Almighty, blessed be He, revealed Himself in all His glory over the sea. And the sea retreated, and its waters stormed angrily, and they shivered and trembled and went down into the abyss. As it is said: "The waters saw Thee, O God;/ The waters saw Thee, they were in pain;/ The depths also trembled."

At the same time as the waters opened, they froze into twelve paths for the number of the tribes, and they stood like walls on both sides, and between one path to another there were openings. And one tribe could see the other crossing.

And the Almighty, blessed be He, lighted the way in front of them, but His footprints were not to be seen and not to be known. As the psalmist sang: "Thy way was in the sea,/ And Thy path in the great waters,/ And Thy footsteps were not known."[388]

2 / THE DIVIDING OF THE RED SEA

"To Him who divided the Red Sea asunder,
For His mercy endureth for ever."

The opening of the waters of the Red Sea in front of the tribes of Israel is one of the most important events of the Exodus. Hebrew folklore delves repeatedly into this miraculous episode; it has permeated Jewish consciousness so thoroughly that it emerges in everyday thought and action.

Ke-kriat Yam-suf—like the dividing of the Red Sea—is a common Hebrew expression to describe any arduous task.

Offering his prayer, the Jew repeats his trust in the Almighty, and says, "Whoever answered your fathers at the Red Sea shall answer you now and hear your cry."

The sages instructed: "When uttering the *Shma*—the basic declaration of faith of Judaism—'Hear, O Israel, the Lord our God, the Lord is One'—the worshiper must mention the splitting of the Red Sea."

And why verily and truly must one recall the opening of the Red Sea? Because then "Israel saw the great work which the Lord did upon the Egyptians, and the people feared the Lord; and they believed in the Lord and in His servant Moses.

"And thanks to their belief and to their faith, he [Moses] was found worthy to sing the praises of the Almighty, and the Divine Presence rested upon them."

FIG. 66. OPENING OF THE RED SEA
To the left, the ranks of the Israelites, with shields and banners, march over the dry bed of the sea with its fish and shells. To the right, Moses points his staff against the drowning Egyptians. The hands of the Divine Providence stretch over Moses and the Israelites.

Said the Almighty, blessed be He: "The sun and the moon bear witness that I divided the sea for My children."

"When the Red Sea was divided for Israel, it was heard from one end of the world to the other."

The sages also taught: "Whoever sees the fords of the Sea must return thanks and sing the praises of the Lord."[389]

3 / THE MIRACLES AT THE RED SEA

Extolling the wonders performed by the Almighty on behalf of His chosen people, the psalmist sang: "God . . . who had done great things in Egypt . . . terrible things by the Red Sea."

וינער ה את מצרים בתוך הים   ובני ישראל הלכו ביבשה בתוך הים

FIG. 67. ISRAELITES AND EGYPTIANS IN THE RED SEA
The Hebrew caption to the left reads: "But the children of Israel walked upon dry land in the midst of the sea" (Exodus 14:29); the caption on the right reads: "And the Lord overthrew the Egyptians in the midst of the sea (Exodus 14:27).

Ten miracles were performed for Israel at the Sea:

The sea was broken through and made like a vault. It was divided into two parts. It became a sort of clay. It crumbled into pieces. It turned into rocks. It was cut into several parts. It was piled up into stacks. It formed a sort of heap. [God] extracted for them [Israel] sweet water from the salt water.

The sea congealed on both sides and became a sort of glass crystal.[390]

4 / THE ALMIGHTY ON THE RED SEA

"And God led the people through the desert
of the Red Sea, in order to perform
for them miracles and great deeds."

Our rabbis relate: "Because the Holy One, blessed be He, appeared on the sea as a mighty warrior, therefore it is written: 'The Lord is a man of war, the Lord is His name.'"

"When the Almighty, blessed be He, revealed himself on the Red Sea in order to wage the war of His sons and to take revenge on the Egyptians, He appeared in the guise of a young man, for battles befit the young."[391]

5 / THE PROPHET JONAH IN THE RED SEA

"And the Lord prepared a great fish to swallow up Jonah; and Jonah was in the belly of the fish three days and three nights."

This succint biblical narrative has fired the imagination of the people, and legend dwells lengthily on Jonah's sojourn within the bowels of the fish—*leviathan,* in Hebrew—and on all that befell him there:

"And Jonah entered within the mouth [of *leviathan*] as a man enters into a large synagogue.

"And the two eyes of the fish were like open windows that illuminated the depths for Jonah. A pearl in the entrails of the fish lighted the darkness for Jonah as the sun in the glory of midday. And Jonah saw all that was in the sea and in the abyss. And he was shown the paths of the Red Sea where the sons of Israel crossed."[392]

THE ANCIENT SOURCES

THE BIBLE. It is divided into three parts: Torah or Pentateuch, Nebiim (Neviim) or Prophets, and Ketubim (Ketuvim) or Writings (Hagiographia); hence the Hebrew name of the Bible: *Tanakh*. The English translation used in the series The Sacred Land is by The Jewish Publication Society of America, Philadelphia.

RASHI. The most popular commentator on the Bible. Rashi is the acronym taken from his full name: *R*abbi *Sh*elomo *I*zhaki. He lived at the end of the eleventh century in France.

RADAK. Another commentator on the Bible. Radak is contracted from *R*abbi *Da*vid *K*imchi. He lived in the thirteenth century in Narbonne, France.

JOSEPHUS. The Jewish historian Joseph ben Mattiahu Hacohen. He was born in Jerusalem about 38 C.E. and took part in the revolt against Rome. His various treatises on the history of the Jews have survived in Greek and have been widely translated. His main works are *Antiquities of the Jews* and *Wars of the Jews against the Romans*.

MISHNAH. From the Hebrew *shano,* "to study." This is a literary creation written in Hebrew, mainly in the second century, and compiled in Galilee in 200 C.E. The Mishnah, sometimes called in the plural Mishnayot, is divided into six orders (Hebrew *Sh*isha Sedarim, which gave rise to the contracted name: *Shas).* Each order *(seder)* contains various tractates *(masekhot),* sixty-three tractates in all. The English translations used here are by H. Danby (Oxford, 1933) and P. Blackman, (New York, 1965).

TOSEFTA. The Aramaic form of the Hebrew *tosefet,* which means "supplement." It is an addition to the Mishnah, which was compiled and edited in Eretz-Israel at the end of the fourth century.

TALMUD. From the Hebrew *lamod,* "to learn"; Talmud-learning. A vast collective literary creation to which hundreds of sages contributed during the course of several generations. There are two Talmuds, each produced by a different school of study, one in Eretz-Israel and the other abroad:

Talmud Yerushalmi was compiled in Eretz-Israel, mainly in Galilee; it is named Yerushalmi (Jerusalemite) as an expression of longing for the capital then held by foes. It is sometimes called the Palestinian Talmud. It was completed at the end of the fourth century, under Byzantine rule. Mainly written in Aramaic, it is about one-third the size of the Talmud Babli. The only existing translation was by M. Schwab into French, eleven volumes, published in 1871–89, Paris.

Talmud Babli (or *Bavli),* the Babylonian Talmud, was compiled in Babylon (Hebrew *Babel* or *Bavel)* at the end of the fifth century. Written in Aramaic and Hebrew, it is a comprehensive treatise of Judaic laws and a treasury of Jewish folklore. The English translation of the whole Babylonian Talmud was done by a number of scholars under the editorship of I. Epstein and published in 1935–52 by Soncino Press, London.

ABOTH DE-RABBI NATHAN. A collection of folk tales concerning the forefathers, *aboth* or *avot* in Hebrew, and named after its compiler, Rabbi Nathan, who lived in the third century. There are two versions of the work, A and B. They were published by S. Schechter in 1887. The English translation of version A was published by A. Goldin in 1955, New Haven.

MECHILTA DE-RABBI ISHMAEL. *Mechilta* is Hebrew-Aramaic for "collection." This *mechilta* is named for the sage mentioned in its opening sentence: "Rabbi Ishmael says. . . ." It is a collection of interpretations of the Book of Exodus, written in approximately the eighth century. An English translation by J. Z. Lauterbach was published by The Jewish Publication Society in 1933–35, Philadelphia (reprinted [paperback] in 1976).

MECHILTA DE-RABBI SHIMON BAR-YOHAI. A collection of commentaries on Exodus compiled about the fifth century and attributed to the famous rabbi of the second century who lived in Eretz-Israel. His tomb, in Galilee, is venerated to this day.

MIDRASH TANAIM. The Hebrew word *midrash* is derived from *darosh,* to inquire, to investigate. *Tanaim* (singular *tana*) is the title accorded to the sages of the Mishnah period. *Midrash Tanaim* is a collection of exegeses to Deuteronomy.

TANHUMA. A collection of legendary explanations to the Torah (Pentateuch), written by Tanhuma son of Abba in the fourth and fifth centuries.

PESIKTA DE-RAB KAHANA. *Pesikta* is Hebrew-Aramaic for "portion." This was written in the sixth and seventh centuries and attributed to Rabbi Kahana. The English translation by W. G. Braude, published in New Haven, was used here except where otherwise indicated; The Jewish Publication Society's English translation by Braude was published in 1975.

MIDRASH RABBA. *Rabba* is similar to *Rabbati.* This is a large collection of various homiletics on Torah quotations (Five Books of Moses) and the Five Scrolls. It was composed by various rabbis who lived from the fourth to the twelfth centuries.

Its first five volumes deal with the Five Books of Moses: *Bereishith Rabba* is about Genesis, approximately fifth century; *Shemot Rabba* is about Exodus, approximately tenth century; *Va-Yikra Rabba* is about Leviticus, approximately seventh-ninth centuries; *Ba-Midbar Rabba* is about Numbers, approximately eighth-ninth centuries; *Debarium Rabba* is about Deuteronomy, approximately eighth-ninth centuries.

The next five volumes deal with the Scrolls: *Shir ha-Shirim Rabba* is about the Song of Songs, approximately seventh-eighth centuries; *Ruth Rabba* is about the Book of Ruth, approximately seventh-tenth centuries; *Eicha Rabba* is about the Book of Lamentations, approximately fifth century; *Koheleth Rabba* is about the Book of Ecclesiastes, approximately seventh century; *Esther Rabba* is about the Book of Esther, approximately fifth century.

An English translation was prepared under the editorship of H. Freedman and M. Simon and published in ten volumes, in 1939, by Soncino Press, London.

MIDRASH TEHILLIM. Relates to the Book of Psalms (Hebrew *Tehillim*) *Shoher Tov* (Hebrew for "seeketh good") is another name of *Midrash Tehillim* because it opens with the following verse: "He that diligently seeketh good seeketh favor" (Proverbs 11:27). *Midrash Tehillim* was composed in the ninth-tenth centuries approximately, probably in Eretz-Israel. The English translation was prepared by W. G. Braude and published in two volumes in 1957, New Haven.

PIRKE RABBI ELIEZER. *Pirke* is Hebrew for "chapters." This is attributed to Eliezer son of Hyrcanos, a prominent sage. It is a collection of homiletics and tales and was written about the ninth century in Eretz-Israel. The English translation by G. Friedlander appeared in 1916, London.

ZOHAR. Hebrew for "splendor." This is a collection, written partly in Aramaic and partly in Hebrew, of mystical commentaries on the five books of the Torah, the Pentateuch. It is attributed to the above-mentioned Rabbi Shimon bar-Yohai, although in fact it was composed in Spain, in the thirteenth century, by Rabbi Moses de Leon, probably from earlier sources.

The *Zohar* is the fundamental book of the Cabala Jewish mysticism. Its adepts are called Cabalists. *Cabbala* is Hebrew for "reception." Every generation was supposed to receive the secrets of mysticism from the preceding generation. The English translation of the *Zohar* was done by H. Sperling and M. Simon and published in five volumes by Soncino Press in 1931–34, London.

YALKUT SHIMONI. A comprehensive collection (in Hebrew, *yalkut*) of legendary commentaries and rabbinical sayings covering all the books of the Bible. It was edited by Rabbi Shimoni, "chief of the preachers" of Frankfurt, Germany, in the thirteenth century.

BEIT HA-MIDRASH. Hebrew for "the house of study"; the name of a modern publication of various small Hebrew tractates of later periods, edited by A. Yellinek. The six volumes of *Beit ha-Midrash* were originally published in 1853–77, Germany.

ABBREVIATIONS

JJS—Journal of Jewish Studies

JPOS—Journal of the Palestine Oriental Society

JQR—Jewish Quarterly Review

MGWJ—Monatsschrift für Geschichte und Wissenschaft des Judentums

MPCC—Migne, Patrologiae Cursus Completus

PEQS—Palestine Exploration Fund, Quarterly Statement

PPTS—Palestine Pilgrims Text Society

QDAP—Quarterly of the Department of Antiquities in Palestine

REJ—Revue des Études Juives

ZDMG—Zeitschrift der Deutschen Morgen Ländischen Gesellschaft

ZDPV—Zeitschrift des Deutschen Palästina Vereins

"The Travel of Reb Haim ben Attar," *Tarbitz*, 7, 1932, p. 93.

9. *THE MAD MAID IN THE CAVE OF ELIJAH:* Told in *Amud Hayira*, the Jerusalemite paper, 1879.

10. *THE CAVE OF ELIJAH AND JESUS OF NAZARETH:* L. Ginzberg, *Genizah Studies*, 1928, pp. 332–336.

11. *THE ALTAR OF ELIJAH ON MOUNT CARMEL:* Yerushalmi, Taanith 2:8. I Kings 18:19–42.

12. *HIEL HID IN THE ALTAR OF BAAL: Debarim Rabba*, supplement (ed. Lieberman), 1940, p. 132. *Shemot Rabba* 15:15. *Pesikta Rabbati*, 1880, p. 13a. Amos 9:3.

13. *THE MELONS THAT TURNED TO STONE:* I heard this story in Haifa, in my youth. F. Goujon, *Histoire et Voyage de la Terre Sainte*, 1671, p. 64.

14. *THE MAGIC STONE OF MOUNT CARMEL:* Antoninus Martyr; *PPTS II*, 1897, p. 4. Babli, Shabbath 66b.

15. *THE GOD OF CARMEL:* Tacitus, *The Histories*, II, LXXXVIII, translated by C. H. Moore, p. 287. Tosefta, Abodah Zarah 6:8.

16. *TABOR AND CARMEL ENVY SINAI: Bereishith-Rabba* 99:1. Jeremiah 46:18.

17. *THE ARROGANCE OF TABOR AND CARMEL: Midrash Tehillim* 68:9. *Yalkut Shimoni, Shoftim* 42.

18. *THE TEMPLE WILL BE BUILT ON CARMEL AND TABOR:* Isaiah 2:2. *Pesikta de-Rab Kahana*, p. 147b. The name "Hermon" appears in the Carmoli manuscript, *Midrash Tehillim*, 68:9.

19. *THE WISE MEN OF MOUNT CARMEL:* Talmud Sanhedrin 104a. This legend also appears in *Midrash Eicha Zuta* 4 (ed. Buber), 1894, p. 60, and is entitled "Two Children of the Land of Israel."

20. *THE GORGE OF THE CYCLAMEN:* A tale current among the children of Haifa and its surroundings.

21. *REINCARNATION: Itinerary of Rabbi Benjamin of Tudela* (ed. Asher), p. 62.

22. *ZEBULUN INHERITED THE SEA OF HAIFA:* Genesis

SOURCES OF THE LEGENDS

1. *WHY WAS IT CALLED HAIFA?*: Astori ha-Parhi, *Kaftor Va-Perah*, XI (ed. Berlin), p. 47. Wildebrandi de Oldenborg, *Itinerarium Terrae Sanctae* (ed. Laurent), 1875, p. 24. "The Voiage and Trauaile of Syr John Maundevile Knight."
2. *THE PRONUNCIATION OF THE JEWS OF HAIFA:* Babli, Megillah 24b. Yerushalmi, Berachoth 3:4. Leviticus 22:2. Isaiah 8:17.
3. *AMONG THE ROCKS ON THE HAIFA SEASHORE:* Pesikta de-Rab Kahana, 1868, p. 137a.
4. *WHO WAS HAIFA'S BITTEREST FOE?*: Song of Songs 2:2. Lamentations 1:17. *Shir ha-Shirim Rabba* 2:2.
5. *THE MARTYR OF THE HOLY WAR:* I heard this story many times from the Arabs of Haifa, where I spent my childhood.
6. *"THY HEAD UPON THEE IS LIKE CARMEL":* Song of Songs 7:6. *Shir ha-Shirim Rabba* 7:6.
7. *THE PROPHET ELIJAH ON MOUNT CARMEL:* I Kings 18:42–45.
8. *THE CAVERN OF THE PROPHET ELIJAH:* J. Mann,

49:13. Babli, Baba Bathra 122a. *Ba-Midbar Rabba* 2:7.
23. *THE SEA OF HAIFA—A SILVER BOWL:* Numbers 7:24–25. *Ba-Midbar Rabba* 13:17.
24. *THE SEA OF HAIFA IN THE DAYS TO COME:* Deuteronomy 33:19. *Midrash Tanaim,* 1909, p. 219.
25. *THE DISCOVERY OF GLASS:* Plinius, *Naturalis Historia,* XXXVI, 6:5.
26. *THE SONS OF ZEBULUN WERE GLASSMAKERS:* Deuteronomy 33:19. *Ba-Midbar Rabba* 13:17. *Midrash Tanaim,* 1909, p. 219.
27. *THE SAND THAT TURNS INTO GLASS:* Flavius Josephus, *Wars,* II, 10, 2.
28. *HOW PURPLE WAS DISCOVERED:* G. W. Tyron, *Manual of Conchology,* 1880, vol. II, p. 43. S. Bochart, *Hierozoicon* (ed. 1663), vol. II, p. 74.
29. *ZEBULUN WERE PURPLEMAKERS:* Deuteronomy 33:19. *Sifri Berakha,* 355, 1862, p. 226. Jeremiah 52:16. Babli, Shabbath 26a. *Midrash Tanaim,* p. 219. *Vezot Haberakha,* p. 147. *Shir ha-Shirim Rabba* 4a. Exodus 26:1–37, 28:4–5.
30. *THE CHILDREN OF ZEBULUN WERE TRADESMEN:* Genesis 49:13. Babli, Baba Bathra 122a. Deuteronomy 33:18. *Ba-Midbar Rabba* 2:7.
31. *THE BOND BETWEEN ZEBULUN AND ISSACHAR:* Deuteronomy 33:18. *Bereishith Rabba* 99:13. *Ba-Midbar Rabba* 13:17. Chapter Zedakot: *Batei Midrashot* (ed. Wertheimer), A, 1950, p. 235. Proverbs 3:18.
32. *THE RIVER KISHON—THE ANCIENT RIVER:* Judges 5:3, 19, 20–26. Talmud, Pesahim 118b. *Sifrei, Ekeb.*
33. *WHY WAS IT CALLED ACCO?:* H. Relandus, *Palestina ex Monumentis Veteribus Illustrata,* 1714, p. 536, which cites the book *Etimologicum magnam,* written at the beginning of the twelfth century. Job 38:11. Yerushalmi, Shekalim, 6a. *Bereishith Rabba* 23:7.

34. *FAMOUS SAGES OF ACCO:* Yerushalmi, Shevuot 6:-11. Mishnah, Abodah Zarah 3:4.
35. *THE FATE OF NAKDIMON'S DAUGHTER IN ACCO:* Song of Songs 1:8. *Eicha Rabba* 1:48.
36. *MIRIAM THE DAUGHTER OF TANHUM IN ACCO:* *Eicha Rabba* 1:49.
37. *THE SYNAGOGUE OF KING ATTAB IN ACCO:* B. Klar, *Haim ben Attar,* 1951, p. 131. Mishnah, Para 8:11.
38. *TO BRING FISH TO ACCO: Bereishith Rabba* 13:16.
39. *THE PRECIOUS TREASURE IN THE MOSQUE OF ACCO:* S. M. Zwenser, "Hairs of the Prophet": *Ignace Goldziher, Memorial Volume,* 1948, pp. 48–54.
40. *THE SPRING OF THE OX:* Nasir Khosrau, *Sefer Nameh,* 1881, p. 49. Yakut, *Mujam al-Buldan* III, p. 758. *QDAP,* VI, 1938, p. 95.
41. *THE SPRING THAT OBSERVES THE SABBATH: Sibub Rabbi Petahia.*
42. *THE RIVER NAAMAN AND THE WALL OF ACCO:* I heard this story during my childhood in Haifa.
43. *THE RIVER NAAMAN AND THE SERPENTS:* Ludolphus of Suchem (Sudheim), *De Itinere Terrae Sanctae.*
44. *ROCK OF THE THREE CONTINENTS: Joinville Chronicle: Memoirs of the Crusades,* 1888, p. 112.
45. *THE PALM GROVES OF ACCO:* I heard this story during my childhood from the Arabs of Acco.
46. *THE GRAVE OF ABU-ATABAH:* Ibn-Battuta, *Tuhfat an-nuzzar fi gharaib al-amsar wa'ajaib al-as far* (ed. Defremery), 1853. Anonymous Jewish Traveller, 1522, note 48, p. 18; repeated in *Hibat Yerushalaim,* Horowitz, note 45, p. 19b.
47. *ABRAHAM AT THE LADDERS OF TYRE:* Genesis 12:7. *Bereishith Rabba* 39:8.
48. *THE REVIVING OF THE LION AT THE LADDERS OF TYRE: Ba-Midbar Rabba* 18:22.
49. *ALEXANDER THE GREAT IN ROSH-HANIKRA:* Yakut, *Mujam al-Buldan* I, 816. *Kaftor Va-Perah* (ed. Berlin), p. 32.

50. *THE CAVE OF SIGHS:* This story was told to me by an Arab while I was traveling from Acco to Tyre in 1936. U. J. Seetzen, *Reisen durch Syrien, Palestine, etc.*, II, 1854, p. 111.
51. *KING SOLOMON'S POOLS NEAR TYRE:* Dimashki, *Nuhbat ed-Daher fi Ajaib el-Bar wael-Bahr* (ed. Mehreen), 1886. Song of Songs 4:15.
52. *HIRAM, KING OF TYRE, BUILT HIM SEVEN HEAVENS:* Midrash Hagadol, Shemot, va-Ere, 1918, p. 57. *Yalkut Shimoni, Yehezkel* 367:28. *Beit Eked ha-Agadoth* (ed. Horowitz-ha-Levi), II, 1882, pp. 28–31. H.Horowitz,*Hibat Yerushalaim*, 1844, p. 8b. M. Reisher, *Shaarei Yerushalaim*, 1879, p. 10.
53. *"TYRE IS THINE":* Plutarchi Vitae Parallelae, III, XXIV, p. 306.
54. *TYRE AND THE COMING OF THE MESSIAH:* Sefer *Eliyahu. Beit ha-Midrash* (ed. Yellinek), III, p. 71.
55. *THE WESTERN VALLEY OF JEZREEL WENT TO ZEBULUN: Bereishith Rabba* 97. *Birkat Yaacov: Beit ha-Midrash*, II, p. 70.
56. *THE CENTRAL VALLEY OF JEZREEL WENT TO ISSACHAR:* Joshua 19:17–18. Genesis 49:14–15. *Bereishith Rabba* 99:12.
57. *THE SONS OF ISSACHAR WERE MEN OF LEARNING:* I Chronicles 12:33. *Midrash Tanaim*, p. 218. *Ba-Midbar Rabba* 13:15.
58. *THE TEMPLE IN THE LAND OF ISSACHAR:* Deuteronomy 33:18–19.
59. *WHY NABOTH PERISHED FROM THE EARTH:* I Kings 21:1–19. *Pesikta Rabbati* 25, 1880, p. 127a.
60. *THE PROPHET ELISHA IN SHUNEM:* II Kings 4:8. *Shir ha-Shirim Rabba* 2:5. Babli, Berachoth 10b. *Kaftor Va-Perah* (ed. Berlin), p. 43.
61. *SHEIKH ABREIK AND THE HEALING MARSH:* J. Schwarz, *Tevuot Haaretz*, 1900, p. 203.
62. *FROM NAHALAL TO JERUSALEM:* Joshua 19:14. Psalms 23.2. Isaiah 49:10. Yerushalmi, Megillah 1:1. Maaser Sheni 8:2.

63. *RABBI LEVI AND THE INHABITANTS OF SIMONIA:* *Bereishith-Rabba* 81:2. Yerushalmi, Yebamoth 12:6.

64. *THE ACACIA SHRUBS ON THE HILL OF SHIMRON:* Quarterly Statement, 1873, p. 58. A. Aronson, *Bulletin de la Société Botanique de France,* XIII, 1913, p. 498. W. Ahlwardt, *Die Arab. Handsh. der König. Bibliothek zu Berlin,* VII, 1869, nos. 9251–9292.

65. *THE HUMBLE MAN FROM HAVRAYA:* Yerushalmi, Megillah 1:1. Babli, Holin 12b. *Bereishith-Rabba* 13.

66. *THE TOWN OF DOBRATH AND THE PROPHETESS DEBORAH:* Joshua 19:10–12. Micah 2:12. Henri Maundrell, *Journey from Aleppo to Jerusalem.* S. S. Buckingham, *Travels in Palestine,* 1822, p. 159.

67. *THE CAVE OF THE TRAITRESS:* Warren-Conder, *The Survey of Western Palestine,* I, 1881, p. 412.

68. *WHY THE TEACHER IN TABERNETH WAS DISMISSED:* Yerushalmi, Megillah 4.

69. *TEL KEIMON—JOSHUA'S BATTLEFIELD:* G. J. Juynboll, *Chronicon Samaritanum,* 1848, pp. 26–35.

70. *YOKNEAM—THE MOUNT OF CAIN:* "Burchard of Mount Sion," *PPTS,* XII, 1897, p. 45.

71. *THE BATTLE OF ARMAGEDDON:* Revelation 16:14, 16–18. *Encyclopaedia Britannica:* Armageddon.

72. *NEBUZARADAN IN THE VALLEY OF MEGIDDO:* II Kings 25:8–9. *Midrash Zuta* (ed. Buber), p. 68. *Yalkut Shimoni, Eicha* 1027. Babli, Gittin 57b.

73. *EIN-IBRAHIM—SPRING OF ABRAHAM:* Ibn el-Fakih, *Kitab al-Buldan,* 1885, p. 117. Yakut, *Mujam al-Buldan,* IV, p. 351.

74. *RABBI PINHAS AND THE RIVER GINNAI:* Babli, Holin 7a. Yerushalmi, Demai 1:3. Josephus, *Antiquities* XX, 6:1.

75. *EIN-HAROD—THE SPRING OF GIDEON:* Judges 7. *Tanhuma* (ed. Buber), p. 138. *Yalkut Shimoni* II, *Shoftim* 62.

76. *THE VALLEY OF JEZREEL—THE BATTLEFIELD OF DAVID AND GOLIATH:* J.J. Rivlin, *Sipur David ve-Goliat, Zion,* IV, 1930, p. 110.

77. *THE HILL OF MOREH—LITTLE HERMON:* Psalms 89:13.
78. *BEIT-SHEAN IS THE GATE OF EDEN:* Genesis 49:-22–25. *Bereishith-Rabba* 88:25. Babli, Eirubin 19a.
79. *THE PARADISIAL SPRING IN THE VALLEY OF BEIT-SHEAN:* Yakut, *Mujam al-Buldan,* I, p. 788. Mujir ed-Din, *Kitab al-Uns ej-Jalil be-Taarikh al-Kuds wal-Khalil.*
80. *THE PRONUNCIATION OF THE JEWS OF BEIT-SHEAN:* Babli, Megillah 24b. Yerushalmi, Berachoth 3:4.
81. *IF THE PALMS OF BEIT-SHEAN SHOULD DIS-APPEAR:* Yakut, *Mujam al-Buldan,* I, p. 788; II, p. 954.
82. *WHERE WAS SATAN BANISHED TO?:* al-Masudi, *Muruj ad-Dahab wa-Ma'adin al-Jawhar,* I, 1871, p. 60.
83. *WHERE DID THE PALACE OF MELCHIZEDEK STAND?:* Genesis 14:18. John 3:23. "Pilgrimage of Saint Silvia," *PPTS* I, 1896, p. 30. Corpus Christianorum: Itinerarium Egeriae, 1965, p. 55.
84. *THE CURSE ON MOUNT GILBOA:* I Samuel 31:1–6. II Samuel 1:19.
85. *TO BRING HAY TO OFRAIM:* Babli, Minahoth 88a. Mishnah, Minahoth 9:1. *Shemet Rabba* 9:7.
86. *THE BRIDGE OF MEETING:* This story was told to me by a bedouin sheikh in 1928. *The Survey of Western Palestine,* III, 1882, p. 132.
87. *THE RIVERS JORDAN AND YARMUK:* Psalms 24:-1–2. Babli, Baba Bathra 74b. *Midrash Tehillim* (ed. Buber), 24:6. Yerushalmi, Ketuboth 12:3. Kelim 9:4. *Yalkut Shimoni, Tehillim* 697.
88. *WHO BUILT HAMAT-GADER?:* Antoninus Martyr, *PPTS,* II, 1896, p. 7. Yakut, *Mujam al-Buldan,* III, p. 509. Kazwini, *Athar al-Buldan,* II, p. 145.
89. *ON A ROCK OF HAMAT-GADER:* Midrash Tanaim, 1909, p. 282.
90. *A CUSTOM PRACTICED IN GOVAT-SHAMAI:* Yerushalmi, Yoma 4:1. *Bereishith-Rabba* 34:15.

91. *THE ORIGIN OF THE NAME NAZARETH:* Isaiah 11:1. Matthew 1:1–16; 2.23.

92. *THE PRIESTLY FAMILY IN NAZARETH:* I Chronicles 24:3–15.

93. *THE SYNAGOGUE-CHURCH OF NAZARETH:* Luke 4:16. Antoninus Martyr, in *PPTS,* II, 1897, p. 4. Ludolphus of Suchem (Sudheim), *PPTS,* XII, 1895, p. 65. E. Webbe, "The rare and most wonderful things . . . in the cities of Jerusalem," 1590.

94. *THE CHURCH THAT SAILED IN THE AIR:* L. de Feis, *La Santa Casa di Nazaret e il Santuario di Loreto,* 1905. A. Patirgnani, *La Santa Casa di Loreto e la Dalmazia: Arch. Stor. per la Dalmazia,* XIII, 1932, p. 158. Hueffer, Loreto, 1903, p. 21. Luke 1:26–32.

95. *THE COLUMN OF ST. MARY:* Luke 1:30–31.

96. *THE LEAP OF THE LORD—MOUNT OF THE PRECIPICE:* Luke 4:16–30. Ludolphus of Suchem, *PPTS,* XII, 1895, p. 125.

97. *MENSA CHRISTI—TABLE OF CHRIST:* Franciscus Quaresmi, *Historica, Theologica et Moralis Terrae Sanctae Elucidatio,* 1626.

98. *A MOSLEM TRAVELER IN NAZARETH:* al-Masudi, *Muruj ad-Dahab wa-Ma'adin al-Jawhar,* I, 1872, p. 123.

99. *THE PRIESTLY FAMILY IN KEFAR-KANNA:* I Chronicles 24:3–12. John 2:1–11. Antoninus Martyr, *PPTS,* II, 1897, p. 4.

100. *THE CAVE OF MELCHIZEDEK ON MOUNT TABOR:* A.M. Kropp, *Ausgewählte Koptische Zaubertexte,* III, 1931, p. 113, no. 3. E.R. Goodenough, *Jewish Symbols,* II, 1954, p. 165. Genesis 14:18.

101. *THE TOWN OF ZIPPORI:* Babli, Megillah 6a. Yerushalmi, Maaser Sheni 8:2.

102. *PROSPEROUS ZIPPORI:* Babli, Sanhedrin 109a. Baba Bathra 78b.

103. *RABBI JUDAH HA-NASI IN ZIPPORI:* Yerushalmi, Kelim 9:4. Genesis 47:28. Psalms 145:9. *Tanhuma, Va-Yehi,* p. 108

104. *RABBI YOSSI IN ZIPPORI:* Deuteronomy 16:20. Psalms 84:4. Babli, Sanhedrin 109a.
105. *PRIESTLY FAMILIES IN ZIPPORI:* I Chronicles 24:7. Nehemiah 12:7. Yerushalmi, Taanith 4. Kelim 9:4. Proverbs 27:8.
106. *THE VENDOR OF THE PHILTER OF LIFE IN ZIPPORI: Va-Yikra Rabba* 16:2. Psalms 34:13. Proverbs 21:23.
107. *THE FATE OF A TAILOR FROM ZIPPORI: Shir ha-Shirim Rabba* 6:12.
108. *MAGICIANS IN ANCIENT ZIPPORI:* Yerushalmi, Sanhedrin 7:19.
109. *RUMA—THE ABODE OF ANTONINUS CAESAR:* M. Alsheikh, *Shoshanat Haamakim* 7:6.
110. *RUMA—WHERE MESSIAH WILL APPEAR:* Yerushalmi translation of Exodus 12:42. Yerushalmi, Gittin 6. Babli, Sanhedrin 98a.
111. *THE REAPER IN THE VALLEY OF BEIT-NETOFA: Va-Yikra Rabba* 22:4. In this text, the name of Beit-Netofa has been altered to Beit-Shufre. *Ba-Midbar Rabba* 18:22. *Midrash Tanhuma, Hukot,* II, p. 98.
112. *HOW RABBI JOSHUA DISSUADED THE REBELS:* Ezra 4:13. *Bereishith Rabba* 64:10.
113. *THE ROCK OF NAILS:* Yerushalmi, Hagigah 3:1.
114. *THE TWO GALILEES:* Mishnah, Shebiit 9:2.
115. *USHA—THE SEAT OF THE DIVINE PROVIDENCE:* Babli, Rosh ha-Shanah 31:9b. B. Klar, *Rabbi Haim ibn Attar,* 1951, p. 137.
116. *THE WONDROUS CAVERN OF CABUL:* Y. Sofer, *Edut be-Yosef.* H. Horowitz, *Hibat Yerushalaim,* 1844, p. 27a.
117. *WHY WAS CABUL DESTROYED?:* Joshua 19:24. I Kings 9:11. I Chronicles 24:11. Flavius Josephus, *Antiquities,* VIII, 5, 3. Yerushalmi, Shabbath 5:2. Babli, Shabbath 54a. *Eicha Rabba* 2:4.
118. *THE FERTILITY OF ANCIENT SIKHNIN:* Deuteronomy 32:13. *Sifri, Haazinu,* 316, p. 105. Yerushalmi, Peah 7:3. *Midrash Tanaim,* p. 174.

119. *WHY WAS SIKHIN DESTROYED?:* I Chronicles 24:-13. Yerushalmi, Hagigah 1. Taanith 4:5. Peah 7:3. *Eicha Rabba* 2:7.
120. *THE STONE OF HANINAH: Koheleth Rabba* 1:1. Babli, Taanith 24b. Sottah 49a. Yerushalmi, Sottah 9:17.
121. *THE PIOUS WOMEN OF TIRAN: Shir ha-Shirim Rabba* 6:4.
122. *FROM YAMA TO TIGNI (TIGNA):* Babli, Nedarim 57b. Kidushin 44a. Rabbi Hananel in Rashi Commentary. Yerushalmi, Gittin 6b, and Commentary Penei Moshe.
123. *WHY IS BEIT-KESHET SO NAMED?:* II Samuel 1:18.
124. *WHY IS IT CALLED KINNERET?:* Babli, Megillah 6a. *Pirke Rabbi Eliezer* II. Yerushalmi, Megillah 1.1. Deuteronomy 11:10–12.
125. *HOW THE SEA OF GALILEE WAS CREATED:* Several versions of this legend appear in O. Dahnhardt, *Natursagen* I, 1907, p. 44.
126. *THE TASTE OF THE FISH OF KINNERET: Pesikta de-Rab Kahana* (ed. Buber), p. 188b.
127. *WHO HAD FISHING RIGHTS IN LAKE KINNERET?:* Deuteronomy 33:23. *Midrash Tanaim*, 1907, p. 220. Tosefta, Baba Kama 8:17–18. Babli, Baba Kama 81b. Rambam (Maimonides), *Nezakei Mamon* 8.
128. *THE WELL OF MIRIAM IN THE KINNERET:* Exodus 17:3–6. Numbers 21:16–18. Tosefta, Sukkah 3:11. Yerushalmi, Kelim 9:4. *Tanhuma, Hukot* (ed. Buber) 2, p. 128. *Midrash Tehillim* 24:6. Babli, Pesahim 54a.
129. *THE MERITS OF MIRIAM'S WELL: Va-Yikra Rabba* 22:4. H. Vital, *Pri Ez Haim*, 1782. Y. Zemah, *Nagid Umezave*, 1798, p. 4. Babli, Shabbath 35b.
130. *MIRIAM'S WELL WANDERS IN THE DIASPORA:* Israel ben Yizhak, *Esser Zahzahot*, 1910, p. 69. M. Buber, *Or Haganuz*, 1947, p. 397.
131. *THE BUCKET OF MIRIAM:* S. Asaf, *Yerushalaim* (in memory of A.M. Lunz), 1928, pp. 51–61 (Hebrew).
132. *FROM THE HOLY OF HOLIES TO THE SEA OF*

GALILEE: Zechariah 14:8. Ezekiel 47:8. Yerushalmi, Shekalim 6:2. Tosefta, Sukkah 3:9.

133. *THE ARCH OF THE COVENANT IN LAKE KIN-NERET:* Mujir ed-Din, *Kitab al-Uns ej-Jalil be-Taarikh al-Kuds wal-Khalil.*

134. *THE ROCK OF THE ANTS:* The Arabic name of this rock is mentioned in 1690 by the Arab traveler Abed el-Ghani. A. Noroff, *Meine Reise nach Palästina,* II, 1862, p. 203. *ZDMG* XXXVI, 1882, p. 390. Genesis 31:45. *Bereishith Rabba* 74:13.

135. *WHEN WILL LAKE KINNERET BE DRIED UP?:* *Sefer Eliyahu. Beit ha-Midrash* (ed. Yellinek), III, p. 72. Yakut, *Mujam al-Buldan,* I, p. 515. II, p. 934.

136. *THE MIRACULOUS STREAM OF THE JORDAN:* *Bereishith Rabba* 4:5. *Mivhar Kitvei Naftali Imber,* 1929, p. 116.

137. *THE BLUE HEARTS OF GALILEE:* I heard this story in 1928 while I was rambling over the mountains of Galilee.

138. *THE REDEMPTION OF ISRAEL IS LIKE THE MORNING STAR:* Yerushalmi, Berachoth 1:1. *Shir ha-Shirim Rabba* 6:10.

139. *THE VALLEY OF ARBEL IN OLDEN DAYS:* Yerushalmi, Peah 7:3. Sottah 1. Taanith 2. Babli, Ketuboth 112a. *Pesikta de-Rab Kahana,* p. 114a.

140. *THE MESSIAH IN THE VALLEY OF ARBEL:* Yerushalmi, Berachoth 2:4. Yoma 3:2. *Esther Rabba* 10:14.

141. *WHY WAS IT CALLED GINNOSAR?:* *Bereishith Rabba* 98:21.

142. *THE FRUIT OF GINNOSAR AND JERUSALEM:* Babli, Pesahim 8b.

143. *GINNOSAR WAS IN THE LAND OF NAPHTALI:* Babli, Baba Bathra 122a.

144. *NAPHTALI, SATISFIED WITH FAVOR:* *Ba-Midbar Rabba.* Deuteronomy 33:23.

145. *NAPHTALI, A HIND LET LOOSE:* Genesis 49:21. Babli, Megillah 8b.

146. *EIN KAHAL—THE HIDING-PLACE OF THE TREA-SURES:* Naftali Elhanan, *Emek Hamelech*, p. 14, Mishnah 10. H. Horowitz, *Hibat Yerushalaim*, 1844, p. 22. M. Reisher, *Shaarei Yerushalaim*, 1879, p. 56.

147. *NAPOLEON AND THE TREASURES IN EIN KAHAL:* M. Reisher, *Shaarei Yerushalaim*, 1879, p. 56. M. M. Rabin, *Masa Meiron*, 1919.

148. *JOB ON THE SHORES OF LAKE KINNERET:* Bereishith Rabba 57:4. J.S. Buckingham, *Travels in Palestine*, 1822, p. 341. Z. Biever, *Conférences de Saint Étienne*, 1909–10, p. 135.

149. *THE MIRACLE OF THE LOAVES AND FISHES:* Matthew 14:15–21. Theodosius, in *PPTS*, II, 1896, p. 8. Antoninus Martyr, in *PPTS*, II, 1896, p. 8.

150. *CAPERNAUM ON THE SHORE OF LAKE KINNERET:* Ecclesiastes 7:26. *Koheleth Rabba* 1:8. Matthew 11:23.

151. *THE SPRING IN CAPERNAUM:* Flavius Josephus, *Wars*, III, X, 8.

152. *CHORAZIM NEAR CAPERNAUM:* Matthew XI, 21–22. Petrus Diaconus (ed. Geyer), p. 113.

153. *CHORAZIM—BETHSAIDA—CAPERNAUM:* Matthew XI, 21; XVI, 18. John I, 44.

154. *BETHSAIDA'S GIFT TO EMPEROR HADRIAN:* Deuteronomy 8:9. Yerushalmi, Shekalim 6. *Koheleth Rabba* 2:8.

155. *WHEREFORE THE NAME KURSI?:* Yakut, *Mujam al-Buldan*, III, p. 260.

156. *GOG AT THE SHORES OF LAKE KINNERET:* Ezekiel 39:11–15. *Midrash Zuta, Shir ha-Shirim*, 1894, p. 13.

157. *THE NAME TIBERIAS:* Psalms 49:7–12. *Bereishith-Rabba* 23:1. Babli, Megillah 6a.

158. *WHEREFORE THE NAME RAKKATH?:* Joshua 19:35. Babli, Megillah 6a. Eirubin 19a. *Shir ha-Shirim* 4:3.

159. *THE INHABITANTS OF RAKKATH—LOVERS OF REMAINS: Kaftor Va-Perah* 7. *Tanhuma, Va-Yehi* 3.

Yerushalmi, Kelim 9:4. Babli, Megillah 6:1. For a description of the holy tombs in Tiberias, see: Zev Vilnay, *Holy Shrines in the Land of Israel,* 1951 (Hebrew).

160. *HOW TIBERIAS WAS PURIFIED:* Josephus, *Antiquities,* XVIII, 2, 3. Babli, Shabbath 34a. Rosh ha-Shanah 31a. Yerushalmi, Shebiit 9:1.

161. *THE REDEMPTION WILL BEGIN IN TIBERIAS:* Zephaniah 1:11. Babli, Rosh ha-Shanah 31b. Rambam, *Hilkhot Sanhedrin* 14:12.

162. *THE MESSIAH'S ROD IS CONCEALED IN TIBERIAS:* Psalms 110:2. *Sefer Zerubbabel, Beit ha-Midrash* (ed. Yellinek), II, p. 55.

163. *THE PEOPLE OF TIBERIAS GIVE GOOD WORDS:* Genesis 49:21. *Sefer ha Yeshub,* II, p. 14.

164. *THE TWELVE MONTHS IN TIBERIAS:* Al-Mukaddasi, *Ahsan al-Takassim fi Muarif al-Akalim,* 1906, pp. 161, 185.

165. *THE BLACK STONES OF TIBERIAS:* Moses Bassola, *Massaoth Eretz Israel,* p. 71.

166. *PURIM OF TIBERIAS:* J. Beirav, *Zimrat Haaretz,* 1745, p. 9.

167. *THE HOLY ARI IN TIBERIAS:* Naftali ben Yitzchak Elhanan, *Emek Hamelech,* 1644, p. 11a. Habakkuk 2:-11.

168. *WHEN THE WALL OF TIBERIAS IS REBUILT:* Hamabit, *Sheelot ve-Teshuvot,* 1629, p. 31b.

169. *THE EMPEROR AND RABBI JUDAH THE PRINCE:* Babli, Abodah Zarah 10a.

170. *THE OLD PLANTER AND THE EMPEROR: Koheleth Rabba* 1:12.

171. *THE MIRACULOUS HERB OF TIBERIAS: Va-Yikra Rabba* 22:4.

172. *WHAT DID DANIEL DO IN TIBERIAS?:* Daniel 1:-3-6. *Shir ha-Shirim Rabba* 5:5. Babli, Sanhedrin 93a.

173. *EARLY TIBERIAS AND LATE ZIPPORI:* Babli, Shabbath 118b.

174. *FROM TIBERIAS TO SUSSITA:* Lamentations 1:17. *Eicha Rabba* 1:20. *Bereishith Rabba* 32:9. Job 39:7.

175. *TIBERIAS AND ZEFAT BENEFIT FROM EACH OTHER:* Simha ben Yehoshua, *Ahavat Zion,* 1790.

176. *THE HOT SPRINGS STREAM PAST HELL:* Babli, Megillah 6a. Shabbath 39a. Sanhedrin 108a. Pesahim 8b. Genesis 7:11.

177. *WHY ARE THERE NO HOT SPRINGS IN JERUSALEM?: Sifri, Ba-Midbar* 89.

178. *A MIRACLE AT THE HOT SPRINGS OF TIBERIAS:* Yerushalmi, Sanhedrin 7:19.

179. *STEAM BATHS IN TIBERIAS ON THE SABBATH:* Babli, Shabbath 40a.

180. *THE CURE-SEEKERS AT THE HOT SPRINGS:* J. Mann, *The Jews in Egypt and in Palestine,* II, 1922, pp. 193, 197.

181. *WHO HEATS THE SPRINGS OF TIBERIAS?:* Ecclesiastes 2:8. *Koheleth Rabba* 2:9. Nasir Khosrau, PPTS, IV, 1893, p. 17.

182. *THE PALACE OF BERENICE, DAUGHTER OF THE KING:* Tosefta, Bikurim 2:10. *The Life of Josephus,* 13.

183. *THE PALACE OF THE EMPEROR'S DAUGHTER:* Babli, Berachoth 57b. Abodah Zarah 11a. Holin 123a. Moses Bassola, *Massaoth Eretz Israel.*

184. *THE BLESSING OF THE RAIN IN MIGDAL:* Yerushalmi, Berachoth 9:14a. *Bereishith-Rabba* 13:15.

185. *THE PRIESTLY FAMILY OF MIGDAL-NUNIA:* I Chronicles 24:16.

186. *HANDICRAFTS IN ANCIENT MIGDAL-ZOVIM: Eicha Rabba* 2. Yerushalmi, Taanith 4:8.

187. *FROM MIGDAL-ZOVIM TO JERUSALEM:* Yerushalmi, Maaser Sheni 5:2.

188. *THE ACACIA TREES IN MIGDAL-ZOVIM:* Yerushalmi, Pesahim 4. Taanith 1. Exodus 26:15; 25:10; 27:1; 25:23–30.

189. *MAZKA—THE PLEASANT HAMLET: Bereishith-Rabba* 34:15.

190. *THE NAME "ZEFAT":* Numbers 15:38. Leviticus 19, Deuteronomy 6:8.
191. *FIRE SIGNALS ON THE MOUNT OF ZEFAT:* Yerushalmi, Rosh ha-Shanah 2:8. Mishnah, Rosh ha-Shanah 2:4. Tosefta, Rosh ha-Shanah 2:2.
192. *THE PRAISE OF HOLY ZEFAT:* A. Azulai, *Hesed Le-Abraham* (ed. Amsterdam), p. 32b.
193. *ZEFAT DESTROYED BY AN EARTHQUAKE:* Y. Sofer, *Edut be-Yosef,* 1763.
194. *ZEFAT SHALL BE SUDDENLY REBUILT:* Israel of Sheklov: *Yerushalaim* (ed. Lunz), IX, 1911, p. 198.
195. *THE HOLY ARI—LEADER OF THE ZEFAT CABALISTS:* D. Conforti, *Kore Hadorot,* p. 38b. *Emek Hamelech,* pp. 10b, 13a, 33a.
196. *THE SEPHARDIC SYNAGOGUE OF THE ARI: Emek Hamelech,* p. 13a. *Etz Hayim,* introduction, p. 2b.
197. *THE SYNAGOGUE OF ELIJAH THE PROPHET: Travels of Moshe Bassola.*
198. *THE ARI'S SEAT IN THE SYNAGOGUE:* Simha ben Yehoshua, *Ahavat Zion.* Reisher, *Shaarei Yerushalaim,* p. 50.
199. *THE ASHKENAZIC SYNAGOGUE OF THE ARI:* Shivhei Haari, *Behinat Hadat,* 1629, p. 38b. *Shulhan Arukh le-Ari,* 1859, p. 19b.
200. *THE FIELD OF APPLES:* Song of Songs 2:3. Babli, Shabbath 88a. Exodus 24:7. *Zohar,* II, 1895, p. 284. *Otzar Hatefilot,* 1928, pp. 320–321.
201. *THE ABODE OF THE HOLY ARI IN ZEFAT:* Simha ben Yehoshua, *Ahavat Zion.* Reisher, *Shaarei Yerushalaim,* p. 50.
202. *OSTRICH EGGS IN THE SYNAGOGUES OF ZEFAT:* Menahem Mendel, *Koroth ha-Itim* (ed. Kressel), p. 60. Sidur Beit-Yaacov, *Shaar Shamaim,* I, 1745, p. 208a.
203. *THE RITUAL BATH OF THE HOLY ARI: Shulhan Arukh le-Ari,* 1859, p. 17b. *Sefer Hagilgulim,* p. 45b. Y. Zemah, *Nagid Umezave.* Simha ben Yehoshua, *Ahavat Zion.* Horowitz, *Hibat Yerushalaim,* 1844, p. 14b. Ezekiel 36:25.

204. *THE SYNAGOGUE OF ABUAB IN ZEFAT:* Simha ben Yehoshua, *Ahavat Zion.* Horowitz, *Hibat Yerushalaim,* 1844, p. 14a. M. Reisher, *Shaarei Yerushalaim,* p. 18.

205. *THE CITADEL ON MOUNT ZEFAT:* Simha ben Yehoshua, *Ahavat Zion. Otzar Massaoth,* p. 243. Reisher, *Shaarei Yerushalaim,* p. 143.

206. *RABBI ABRAHAM HALEVY IN THE STREETS OF ZEFAT:* Babli, Berachoth 5a. Levi Hirsch Kaidnover, *Kab ha-Yashar,* chapter 93. *Kobetz al-Yad,* III, 1940, p. 123.

207. *A DESCENDANT OF KING DAVID IN ZEFAT:* Simha ben Yehoshua, *Ahavat Zion,* p. 24.

208. *"TASHLICH DAY" IN ZEFAT: Hibat Yerushalaim,* p. 15. Micah 7:18–19. *Shaarei Yerushalaim,* p. 43.

209. *THE CAVERN OF THE DAUGHTERS OF JACOB:* Menahem Mendel, *Koroth ha-Itim.* L.A. Mayer, QDAP, II, 1935, p. 127.

210. *THE STUDY HOUSE OF SHEM AND EVER:* Menahem Mendel, *Koroth ha-Itim.* Genesis 10:21. *Bereishith Rabba* 63:6.

211. *ZEFAT—THE BIRTHPLACE OF QUEEN ESTHER:* N.C. Radzvill, *Hierosolymitana Peregrinato,* 1601. E. Roger, *La Terre Sainte,* 1646. Jean de Thévenot, *Relation d'un Voyage Fait au Levant,* 1664, p. 685.

212. *HOW FIREFLIES HELPED THE JEWS OF ZEFAT:* I heard this in 1947 from David Canaani, a member of Kibbutz Ayelet-Hashahar.

213. *THE SULTAN'S PRAYER:* I heard this in 1940 from M. Lunz, director of Bank Leumi in Haifa.

214. *THE RIVALRY BETWEEN JERUSALEM AND ZEFAT:* The eulogy delivered by Moshe Sofer is printed in his commentary to the Bible: *Torat Moshe* (ed. 1906), p. 57b.

215. *ON THE WAY TO EIN-ZEITIM:* Naftali ben Yitzchak Elhanan, *Emek Hamelech,* 1644, pp. 11a–12a.

216. *WHERE DO THE WATERS OF EIN-ZEITIM FLOW*

FROM?: *Kobetz al-Yad*, XIII, 1940, p. 125. *Ahavat Zion, Otzar Massaoth*, p. 246.

217. *THE COCKEREL SAINT:* I heard this tale in Zefat. It is first mentioned by Simha ben Yehoshua in 1744. See his *Ahavat Zion* (The Love of Zion) or *Sippurei Eretz Hagalil* (The Stories of the Hand of Galilee) in *Otzar Massaoth*, note 8; p. 246.

218. *THE SPRING IN NAHAL HATAHANOT:* Y. Hagiz, *Hilkhot Kettanot*, 1704, p. 71a. Dimashki, *Nuhbat ed-Daher fi Ajaib el-Bar wael-Bahr*, 1886.

219. *"LIKE THE PEOPLE OF MEIRON":* Mishnah, Rosh ha-Shanah 1.2. Tosefta, Rosh ha-Shanah 1.11. Babli, Rosh ha-Shanah 18a. Isaiah 40:26.

220. *THE LINTEL AND THE MESSIAH: Otzar Massaoth*, p. 127. Masudi, *Muruj ad-Dahab*, p. 271. Yakut, *Mujam al-Buldan*, II, p. 175. "Nistaroth Rabbi Shimon," *Beit ha-Midrash* (Yellinek), III, pp. 79, 82.

221. *THE TOMB OF RABBI SHIMON BAR YOHAI: Shemot Rabba* 3. *Yalkut Shimoni, Mishlei* 964. *Bereishith Rabba* 38:2. Yerushalmi, Berachoth 9.

222. *THE REBELLIOUS RABBI SHIMON:* Babli, Shabbath 33b. Abodah Zarah 2b.

223. *THE GRAVE OF RABBI ELEAZAR:* Babli, Baba Mezia 84b. *Koheleth Rabba* 11:2. *Pesikta de-Rab Kahana* 94.

224. *THE HOLY ARI AND HIS FRIENDS AT MEIRON:* Zohar, Haidrot. H. Vital, *Sefer Hahizionot*, 1954, p. 153.

225. *THE PILGRIMAGE TO MEIRON:* Z. Vilnay, *Holy Shrines in the Land of Israel*, 1951 (Hebrew).

226. *THE PRIESTLY FAMILY IN MEIRON:* I Chronicles 24:7, 19. Babli, Makhirin 11a. Psalms 94:22–23. *Tosefta, Taanith* 4:9. Yerushalmi, Taanith 4:5.

227. *THE CAVERN OF THE PRIESTS NEAR MEIRON:* B. Klar, *Rabbi Haim ibn Attar*, 1951, p. 45.

228. *THE THRONE OF ELIJAH THE PROPHET:* Malachi 3:23. Elijah 27:13. M. Yerushalmi, *Yedei Moshe*, 1938. Reisher, *Shaarei Yerushalaim*, 1879, p. 78.

229. *THE BATH OF THE PROPHETESS DEBORAH:* Reisher, *Shaarei Yerushalaim,* p. 50.

230. *TEKOA IS FIRST FOR OIL:* II Samuel 14:2. Babli, Minahoth 85b. Baba Bathra 145b. Pesahim 53a.

231. *HOW WAS TEKOA BUILT?* Tosefta, Eirubin 8:6. Babli, Minahoth 72a.

232. *WHY DOES HANUKKAH LAST EIGHT DAYS?:* Babli, Shabbath 21b. J. Musafio, *Teshuvot ha-Geonim,* 1864, p. 33. D. M. Levin, *Otzar ha-Geonim,* II Shabbath, 1930, pp. 23, 163.

233. *THE CAVE OF SHIMON BAR YOHAI.* Beit ha-Midrash (Yellinek), IV, p. 122. Babli, Shabbath 33b. *Pesikta de-Rab Kahana* (ed. Buber), p. 88b. *Koheleth Rabba* 10:8.

234. *THE PRAYER IN THE CAVE OF RABBI SHIMON BAR YOHAI:* M. Reisher, *Shaarei Yerushalaim,* 1879, p. 58.

235. *ELIJAH AT THE CAVE OF RABBI SHIMON:* Babli, Sanhedrin 98a. Psalms 95:7.

236. *HOW THE ZOHAR WAS FOUND:* A. Azulai, *Or Hahama,* I, 1816, at the end of the introduction.

237. *THE SAINT OF THE MILLS:* I heard this story in Pekiin, in 1936.

238. *THE MESSIAH WILL APPEAR IN UPPER GALILEE:* Mishnah, Sottah 9:15. *Zohar* I, *Bereishith,* p. 119a. II, *Shemot,* p. 7b. *Beit ha-Midrash* (Yellinek), IV, p. 122. *Lekah Tov,* Balak, p. 258. Saadia Gaon, *ha-Emunot va-Hadeot,* chapter 8.

239. *THE PRAISE OF GALILEE IN THE OLDEN DAYS:* Mishnah, Massaoth 2:3. Babli, Baba Bathra 25:2. Exodus 26:35. Yerushalmi, Ketuboth 4:15.

240. *THE FAULTY PRONUNCIATION OF THE GALILEANS:* Babli, Eirubin 52a. Yerushalmi, Shabbath 47b.

241. *MAY A LION DEVOUR THEE!:* Babli, Eirubin 53a.

242. *WHAT CAUSED THE RUIN OF UPPER GALILEE?:* Mishnah, Baba Kama 7:7. Babli, Sukkah 29:1. Yerushalmi, Sottah 9:10. Tosefta, Baba Kama 8:14. Babli, Baba Kama 90:1.

243. *THE INHERITANCE OF ASHER IN GALILEE:* Genesis 49:20. *Tanhuma, Va-Yehi* 13. *Bereishith Rabba* 71:-13. Deuteronomy 33:24. *Midrash Tanaim,* p. 220. Babli, Minahoth 85b. I Chronicles 12:37.
244. *THE TWO RIVAL VILLAGES:* Moses Bassola, *Massaoth Eretz Israel,* p. 70.
245. *DO NOT BRING POTTERS TO KEFAR HANANIAH:* Babli, Shabbath 122b. *Bereishith Rabba* 86:3. Yerushalmi, Peah 7:4.
246. *THE AFFLUENCE OF ANCIENT GUSH-HALAV:* Babli, Minahoth 85b. *Midrash Tanaim,* 1909, p. 220.
247. *WHAT DID THE EMPORER RECEIVE FROM GUSH-HALAV?:* Deuteronomy 8:9. *Koheleth Rabba* 2:8.
248. *THE CHAIN OF KING DAVID AT GUSH-HALAV:* Al-Mukaddasi, *Ahsan al-Takassim fi Muarif al-Akalim.*
249. *THE CAVERN OF THE BABYLONIANS:* Moshe Yerushalmi, *Yedei Moshe* (ed. Haberman), 1938.
250. *THE STRANGE INSCRIPTION IN KEFAR-BIRAM:* Moses Bassola, *Massaoth Eretz Israel.*
251. *THE WONDER-CHILD OF KEFAR-BIRAM:* Y. Zemah, *Nagid Umezave,* 1798.
252. *THE CITY OF REFUGE:* Joshua 19:32, 37. Mishnah, Arakhin 9:6. Tosefta, Makkoth 3:8. Babli, Makkoth 10:2. *Midrash Tehillim* (ed. Buber), p. 107.
253. *WHAT DID THE EMPEROR RECEIVE FROM NIZHANA?:* Deuteronomy 8:9. *Koheleth Rabba* 2:8. Babli, Yoma 81b.
254. *AYELET-HASHAR—THE MORNING STAR:* I heard this in 1925 from S. Shechter, a member of Kibbutz Ayelet-Hashahar.
255. *JOSEPH'S PIT IN UPPER GALILEE:* "Shemuel son of David": H. Y. Gurland, *Ginzei Israel,* 1865. Simha ben Yehoshua, *Ahavat Zion.*
256. *THE BRIDGE OF THE DAUGHTERS OF JACOB:* William of Tyre, XVIII, 13. Yakut, *Mujam al-Buldan,* I, p. 775. Bassola, *Massaoth Eretz Israel,* p. 65.
257. *THE TEARS OF THE DAUGHTERS OF JACOB:* I. L. Burckhardt, *Travels in Syria and the Holy Land,* 1822.

258. *YESOD-HAMAALAH—WHY WAS IT SO CALLED?:*
Ezra 7:9. Mishnah, Sottah 9:15.

259. *RABBI MEIR IN KEFAR-MAMLA: Bereishith Rabba*
59. I Samuel 2:31, 33. *Midrash Shemuel* 8. *Yalkut Shimoni, Bereishith Rabba* 103.

260. *THE ORIGIN OF THE NAME HULA:* Yakut, *Mujam al-Buldan.* Genesis 10:22, 23.

261. *FROM JERUSALEM TO HULA:* Tosefta, Sukkah 3:9.
Yerushalmi, Shekalim 6.

262. *A TRADE OF THE SONS OF NAPHTALI: Bereishith Rabba* 94:6.

263. *THE SOURCES OF THE JORDAN:* Babli, Berachoth 58a. Eusebius Hieronymus (Saint Jerome), *Onomastikon* (ed. Klostermann), 1904, p. 77.

264. *DAN WAS FORMERLY NAMED LESHEM:* Babli, Berachoth 55a. Judges 18:26–29, and Rashi's commentary. Joshua 19:47.

265. *THE SYMBOL OF DAN:* Exodus 28:15–19. Genesis 49:-17. *Ba-Midbar Rabba* 2:7. Rashi's Commentary to Deuteronomy 33:22.

266. *DAN IS A LION'S WHELP:* Proverbs 30:30.
Deuteronomy 33:22. *Sifrei, Vezot Haberakha* 355. I Chronicles 12:36.

267. *THE HILL OF THE JUDGE:* D. Kimhi: *Ahdut,* 1911, No. 6.

268. *THE GOLDEN CALF IN DAN:* Judges 18:30. I Kings 12:28–29. *Travels of Rabbi Benjamin of Tudela,* 1840.

269. *MAY THE WATERS OF PANIAS BE TURNED INTO BLOOD:* Babli, Sanhedrin 98a. William of Tyre, XIX, 10. Dimashki, *Nuhbat ed-Daher fi Ajaib el-Bar wael-Bahr,* 1886.

270. *THE SUFFERING OF PANIAS: Bereishith Rabba* 63:5.
Yerushalmi, Shebiit 9:2. Numbers 6:24. *Ba-Midbar Rabba* 11:3.

271. *THE MIRACULOUS STATUE IN BANIAS:* Matthew 9:20–22. Eusebius Hieronymus (Saint Jerome) VII, 18.
Sozomenus V, 21. *Itinerarium Saint Willibaldi.*

272. *MOUNT HERMON:* Babli, Holin 60b. Deuteronomy 3:9. *Targum Yerushalmi* 1:2, and Rashi's commentary. *Shir ha-Shirim Rabba* 4:3. *Midrash Agadah* (ed. Buber), p. 118.

273. *MOUNT HERMON—SNOW MOUNT:* Babli, Sanhedrin 106a. Shabbath 152b.

274. *THE ANGELS ON MOUNT HERMON:* Genesis 5:18–22. Enoch 1:6.

275. *THE PLACE OF THE PROMISE:* Genesis 15:1–18. *Shemot Rabba* 2:4. Rashi, on Exodus 12:41. *Mechilta, Masekhet de-Pesah* 14, p. 113. *Yedei Moshe* (ed. Haberman). Y. Sofer, *Edut be-Yosef.*

276. *THE SNOW-CAPPED HERMON:* A tale, current among the children of Galilee, based on the legend about Tabor and Carmel. See legend II:16.

277. *MOSES AND MOUNT HERMON:* Deuteronomy 32:-52. *Debarim Rabba* (ed. Liberman), p. 48.

278. *JERUSALEM WILL BE BUILT ON MOUNT HERMON:* Isaiah 2:2. *Sefer Zerubbabel. Beit ha-Midrash* (ed. Yellinek), II, p. 57.

279. *THE HIVITES ON MOUNT HERMON:* Joshua 11:3; 9:1–27. Judges 3:3. Babli, Shabbath 85a. *Bereishith Rabba* 26:7. Yerushalmi, Kidushin 4:1.

280. *WATER FLOWS FROM MOUNT HERMON TO PERSIA:* J. Green, *A Journey from Aleppo to Damascus,* 1736, p. 60.

281. *THE FORTRESS OF NIMROD:* Genesis 10:8–9.

282. *FROM RAM TO PANIAS:* Babli, Berachoth 55a. Josephus, *Wars,* III, 10:7.

283. *MOSES AND THE TUNNEL OF CAESARION:* *Midrash Tanaim,* 1909, p. 19. *Mechilta,* II, p. 152.

284. *HOW THE LAKE OF RAM CAME INTO BEING:* I heard this story in 1926 from a Druze inhabitant of the town of Majdal-Shams.

285. *THE BIG EYE OF RAM:* Genesis 8:2. Babli, Sanhedrin 108a. *Bereishith Rabba* 33:4.

286. *WHERE WAS THE LAND OF TOB?* Judges 11:3–6. Yerushalmi, Shebiit 10:1.

287. *THE TOMBS OF THE ISRAELITES IN GOLAN:* G. Shumacher, *Across the Jordan,* 1886, p. 68.

288. *EDREI—THE CAPITAL OF KING OG:* Psalms 136:-18–20. Numbers 21:33–35. Deuteronomy 3:1. *Debarim Rabba* 1:64. Babli, Berachoth 54a.

289. *HOW KING OG FOUGHT THE ISRAELITES:* Yalkut Hamachiri on Psalms, III, 1900, p. 26. Psalms 3:8. *Midrash Temura; Batei-Midrashot* (ed. Wertheimer), 1953, p. 199.

290. *THE LAND OF THE PROPHET JOB:* Job 1:1. *Midrash Iyov: Batei-Midrashot* (ed. Wertheimer), II, 1953, p. 157a. Ashtori ha-Parhi, *Kaftor Va-Perah* (ed. Berlin), p. 49. Yakut, *Mujam al-Buldan,* II p. 645. Job 2:13.

291. *KARNAIM—THE BIRTHPLACE OF JOB:* Job 1:15. *Ruth Rabba* 2:10. *Pesikta de-Rab Kahana,* p. 66a. Eusebius, *Onomastikon,* p. 112. Joanni Chrysostomi, *Homilae XXI—Carnea;* English translation Pusey, Library of the Fathers, 1842, p. 92. *Batei-Midrashot* (ed. Wertheimer), II, 1953, p. 161.

292. *WHEREFROM CAME THE WICKED HAMAN?:* Babli, Megillah 97a. *Pesikta de-Rab Kahana* 8 (ed. Buber), p. 72b. *Pesikta Rabbati* 18 (ed. Ish-Shalom), p. 93b. *Va-Yikra Rabba* 28:7. *Esther Rabbati* 4. *Yalkut Shimoni, Esther* 1058. *Midrash Abba Gurion* 6; *Beit ha-Midrash* (ed. Yellinek) 1, p. 16.

293. *WHEREFORE THE NAME ASHTAROT-KARNAIM?:* Genesis 14:5. Joshua 13:12. Babli, Sukkah 2a.

294. *THE STONES ON THE EASTERN BORDER OF ERETZ-ISRAEL:* Tosefot to Babli, Ketuboth 112a. *Tanhuma* (ed. Buber), p. 96. Yerushalmi, Shebiit 4:9. Psalms 102:15.

295. *THE INHERITANCE OF GAD:* Genesis 49:19. *Bereishith Rabba* 97:19. Deuteronomy 33:20. *Sifri, Debarim* 355, p. 226. I Chronicles 12:9.

296. *THE BANNER OF GAD: Midrash Agadah* (ed. Buber), p. 79. *Ba-Midbar Rabba* 2:7. Genesis 49:19.

297. *WHY IT WAS CALLED MAHANAIM:* Genesis 32:2.

Tanhuma, Vayishlah 3, p. 82. *Bereishith Rabba* 74:17.

298. *KING DAVID IN MAHANAIM:* II Samuel 17:27–29. *Midrash Tehillim* (ed. Buber), p. 18. *Yalkut Shimoni, Samuel* 151.

299. *THE FLAG OF REUBEN:* Genesis 30:14. *Ba-Midbar Rabba* 2:7.

300. *IN THE INHERITANCE OF GAD AND REUBEN:* Numbers 32:1–5. *Midrash Agadah,* 1894, p. 163.

301. *THE TOWN OF REFUGE IN THE LAND OF REUBEN:* Deuteronomy 4:41. *Debarim Rabba* (ed. Liberman), p. 59. Genesis 37:22. Proverbs 28:17.

302. *BEIT-GERES—THE GATE OF EDEN:* Babli, Eirubin 43b. Deuteronomy 33:14. Stephanus Byzantium.

303. *THE ORIGIN OF THE NAME BALKA:* Yakut, *Mujam al-Buldan,* I, p. 728. Ashtori ha-Parhi, *Kaftor Va-Perah,* p. 77.

304. *AMMONITES AND MOABITES IN JERUSALEM:* Deuteronomy 23:4. *Eicha Rabba, Petihta* 9:1, 38.

305. *THE CLOUDS OVER AMMON AND MOAB:* Deuteronomy 23:4. Babli, Taanith 25a. *Eicha Rabba, Petihta,* 1.

306. *IN THE WILDERNESS OF AMMON AND MOAB:* *Sefer Zerubbabel. Bereishith Rabba* 53:13. Psalms 120:2–4.

307. *ISRAEL IN THE DESERT OF AMMON AND MOAB:* Yehuda Eben Shemuel, *Midrashei Geulah,* 1943, p. 313. Job 30:4. Babli, Kidushin 66a. *Bereishith Rabba* 53:13; 98:19. Yerushalmi, Peah 1:1.

308. *REDEMPTION SHALL BEGIN IN THE DESERT OF MOAB:* Isaiah 16:4. Jeremiah 48:47. *Midrash Zuta* (ed. Buber), 1894, p. 33.

309. *THE ISRAELITE VICTORY IN TRANSJORDAN:* Numbers 21:28. Babli, Rosh ha-Shanah 3a. Baba Bathra 78b.

310. *KING SOLOMON IN THE LAND OF AMMON:* I Kings 14:21. *Emek Hamelech,* p. 14b. *Beit ha-Midrash* (ed. Yellinek), II, p. 86.

311. *THE THEATER OF KING SOLOMON IN RABAT-AMMON:* Al-Mukaddasi, *Ahsan al-Takassim.* Yakut, *Mujam al-Buldan,* III, p. 760.

312. *WHEN THE PALM TREES OF RABAT-AMMON PERISH:* Yakut, *Mujam al-Buldan,* II, p. 934

313. *THE POOLS OF HESHBON:* Song of Songs 7:5, and Rashi's commentary. B. Klar, *Rabbi Haim ibn-Attar,* 1951, p. 30. Joshua 13:24.

314. *THE CAVE OF RAKIM:* Koran, The Cave 15:8. Guy le Strange, *Palestine under the Moslems,* 1890, p. 274; 292–300.

315. *THE THORN-PALMS OF THE IRON MOUNT ARE VALID:* Mishnah, Sukkah 3:1.

316. *JACOB AT THE BURNING WATERS:* Genesis 32:12. Mishnah, Shabbath 22:8. Yerushalmi, Shabbath 3. *Agadath Bereishith* 46. *Bereishith Rabba* 76:8. Isaiah 43:2.

317. *BAARA—THE SPRING OF BURNING WATERS:* Flavius Josephus, *Wars,* VII, 6, 3.

318. *WHO HEATS THE HOT BATHS OF IBN HAMMAD?:* A. Musil, *Arabia Petraea* I, "Moab," 1907, p. 158.

319. *THE SNEEZING GOATS IN THE MOUNTAINS OF MACHOR:* Mishnah, Tamid 3:8. Babli, Yoma 39b. Yerushalmi, Sukkah 8:3. *Midrash Zuta* (ed. Buber), p. 127.

320. *WHEREFORE THE NAME "MOUNTAINS OF AVARIM"?:* Numbers 33:47. Deuteronomy 32:48, 49. Midrash Tenaim p. 206 (ed. Talpiot, p. 175). *Zohar, Ba-Midbar Rabba.* Isaiah 40:9.

321. *MOSES ON MOUNT NEBO:* Numbers 27:12. Deuteronomy 34:1. *Sifrei, Debarim, Shelah,* p. 109.

322. *THROUGH THE GRACE OF PRAYER:* Midrash Agadah Va-ethanan, 2, p. 181. Babli, Sottah 14a. *Ba-Midbar Rabba* 21:12. *Midrash Tanaim,* p. 17.

323. *MOSES WISHED TO ENTER THE HOLY LAND:* Aboth de-Rabbi Nathan (ed. Shechter), p. 156. *Midrash Tanaim,* 1909, p. 67.

324. *MOSES' EYE AND THE TEMPLE'S PORTAL:* Yalkut *Shimoni, Va-yalekh,* 940. Yerushalmi, Hagigah 2:2.
325. THE TREASURES HIDDEN ON MOUNT NEBO: *Book of the Maccabees,* II, 2:4–9.
326. *MOSES, THE MAN OF GOD, AND BETH-PEOR:* Deuteronomy 3:29, 4:44–46, 34:6.
327. *WHEREFORE THE NAME BETH-PEOR?:* Numbers 25:3. Joshua 22:17. Hosea 9:10. Babli, Sanhedrin 64a. *Shir ha-Shirim Rabba* 4:6. Mishnah, Sanhedrin 7:6.
328. *THE CULT OF PEOR:* Yerushalmi, Abodah Zarah 3:4. Babli, Sanhedrin 64a. *Sifri, Ba-Midbar* 131.
329. *ABEL-SHITTIM—THE PLACE OF FOLLY:* Numbers 28:1; 33:49. Babli, Sanhedrin 106a. Berachoth 5b. *Sifrei, Balak,* 1866, p. 80.
330. *WHY WAS IT CALLED SHITTIM?:* Tanhuma, 1875, p. 110. Exodus 27:1; 37:1. *Shemot Rabba* 50:13.
331. *THE FOUNTAIN AND THE RIVER OF SHITTIM:* Joel 4:18.
332. *KORAH AND HIS PEOPLE AT THE RIVER SHITTIM: Sefer Zerubbabel* (ed. Constantinople), 1509.
333. *MATTANAH, NAHALIEL, BAMOTH, HAGAI:* Numbers 21:18–20. Mishnah, Aboth 6:2. Babli, Nedarim 55a.
334. *THE HORITES—THE ANCIENT EDOMITES:* Genesis 14:6. Deuteronomy 2:12. Babli, Shabbath 85.
335. *THE BOON OF RAIN ON MOUNT SEIR:* Deuteronomy 2:5. Genesis 27:38. *Aboth de-Rabbi* Nathan (B), 77. *Beit Eked ha-Agadoth* (Horowitz ha-Levi), II, 1912, p. 6. Genesis 36:31.
336. *IN THE MOUNTAINS OF GEBAL:* Psalms 83:2–8 (Aramaic translation). Babli, Ketuboth 112a.
337. *THE TORAH WAS OFFERED TO THE SONS OF ESAU:* Deuteronomy 33:2 (Aramaic translation). *Pesikta Rabbati,* 1880, p. 99b.
338. *MOSES AND AARON ON MOUNT HOR:* Numbers 20:23–29. Z. Vilnay, *Holy Shrines in the Land of Israel,* 1951 (Hebrew).

339. *THE SHRINE OF AARON THE PRIEST:* Masudi, *Muruj ed-Dahab,* I, 1861, p. 94.

340. *THE SPRING OF MOSES IN EDOM:* Yakut, *Mujam al-Buldan,* IV, p. 879. Koran, II, 57. Josephus, *Antiquities* IV, 4, 6.

341. *PETRA AND ITS INHABITANTS: JPOS* IX, 1929, p. 216.

342. *THE TREASURE OF PHARAOH IN PETRA:* A current tale among the bedouin of Petra which I heard on several occasions while visiting the ruins.

343. *THE PALACE OF PHARAOH'S DAUGHTER:* G. Dalman, *Neue Petra Forschungen,* 1912, p. 16. A. Musil, *Arabia Petraea,* II, 1917, p. 10. *JPOS,* IX, 1929, p. 145.

344. *THE WILDERNESS OF SNAKES AND SCORPIONS:* Deuteronomy 8:15. *Midrash Tehillim* 22:11 (ed. Buber), p. 186.

345. *MOSES SET THE TIME FOR MEALS:* Exodus 16:8. Babli, Yoma 75b.

346. *THE MANNA—THE FOOD OF ISRAEL:* Exodus 16:-14–35. Joshua 5:12. *Alpha-Beitha de-Rabbi Akiva: Beit ha-Midrash* (ed. Yellinek), III, p. 27. Psalms 78:23. Babli, Horayoth 12a. Yerushalmi, Shekalim 6:1. Babli, Hagigah 12b. Pesahim 54a.

347. *THE MANNA-CARRYING TAMARISK BUSH:* Exodus 16:14. *Alpha-Beitha de-Rabbi Akiva: Beit-Midrash* III, p. 27.

348. *THE QUAIL IN THE DESERT OF SINAI:* Numbers 11:31–32. Babli, Yoma 78b. Shabbath 148b.

349. *IN THE WILDERNESS OF SHUR: Exodus Rabba* 24:4. Exodus 15:22. Ezekiel 30:5.

350. *THE NAME "DESERT OF SHUR."* Ba-Midbar Rabba 24:4. Isaiah 64:9. Zechariah 2:9.

351. *ISRAEL IN THE DESERT OF PARAN:* Habakkuk 3:3. Babli, Shabbath 89b. Abodah Zarah 2b. Deuteronomy 33:2.

352. *HE APPEARED ON MOUNT PARAN:* Deuteronomy 33:2, and Rashi's commentary.

353. *BAAL-ZEPHON—A STATION IN THE WANDER-INGS:* Exodus 14:2, 10. Numbers 33:7. *Mechilta de-Rabbi Ishmael,* I, 1933, Tractate *Pisha* XIII, pp. 98, 190.

354. *PI-HAHIROTH—A STATION IN THE WANDER-INGS:* Exodus 14:9. Numbers 33:7. *Mechilta de-Rabbi Ishmael,* I, 1933, Tractate *Beshallah* II, p. 188.

355. *MARAH—A STATION ON THE WAY OF ISRAEL:* Exodus 15:22–25. *Tanhuma* (ed. Buber), II, p. 33. *Yalkut Shimoni,* I, p. 256. Babli, Rosh ha-Shanah 23a.

356. *MITHKAH AND MARAH:* Numbers 33:8:28.

357. *ALOSH—A STATION IN THE WANDERINGS:* Genesis 18:6. Exodus 16:4, 15. *Bereishith Rabba* 49:12. *Shemot Rabba* 25:5.

358. *REPHIDIM OF THE SINAI DESERT:* *Bereishith Rabba* 48:12. *Sheimoth Rabba* 25:8.

359. *TOPHEL—LABAN—DI-ZAHAB:* Deuteronomy 1:1. Numbers 21:5. Exodus 16:31. Babli, Berachoth 32a. *Debarim Rabba* (ed. Liberman), p. 6.

360. *EL-ARISH—THE CAPITAL OF SINAI:* *Otzar Massaoth:* "Meshullam from Volterra," p. 96. Yakut, *Mujam al-Buldan,* III, p. 660. Zakaria Kazwini, *Athar al-Buldan* (ed. Wüstenfeld), 1849, p. 147. Genesis 33:-17.

361. *A BIGGER TRAITOR THAN THE GOVERNOR OF EL-ARISH:* Kazwini, *Athar al-Buldan,* p. 147. According to Tabari, in his book *Taarich el-Russul wael-Muluk,* I, p. 393, this incident occurred in the town of Kulzum, today the site of Suez.

362. *RHINOCORURA—ANCIENT EL-ARISH:* Strabo XVI, 2, 31.

363. *WHO SAVED THE TOWN PELUSION?:* Herodotus, *History,* II, p. 141. Josephus, *Antiquities,* X, 1, 4.

364. *THE VARIOUS NAMES OF MOUNT SINAI:* Exodus 32:15; 19:20. Babli, Shabbath 89b.

365. *SINAI IS ALSO NAMED BASHAN:* Babli, Megillah 29b. *Va-Yikra Rabba* 21:20. Psalms 68:16–17. Leviticus 21:18–21. Proverbs 16:19.

366. *WHEREFORE THE NAME SINAI?:* Pirke Rabbi *Eliezer* 41. M. Narboni's commentary to *More Hane-vukhim,* I, 66. Stanley, *Sinai and Palestine,* 1877, p. 17.
367. *WHEREFROM CAME MOUNT SINAI?:* Psalms 87:1. *Midrash Tehillim* 87:3.
368. *WHY WAS THE LAW GIVEN FROM SINAI?:* Exodus 19:20. *Midrash Aseret Hadibrot: Beit ha-Midrash* (ed. Yellinek), I, p. 66.
369. *WHY WAS THE HOLY LAW GIVEN IN A WILDER-NESS?:* Exodus 19:2. *Pesikta de Rabbi Shimon bar Yohai, Yithro* II, 1905, p. 93.
370. *MOSES ON THE HEIGHTS OF MOUNT SINAI:* Exodus 19:20; 33:17–23. Babli, Megillah 19b.
371. *SINAI UNITES ISRAEL: Mechilta de Rabbi Shimon bar Yohai, Yithro* II, 1905, p. 94. Exodus 19:2. Numbers 33:15–16.
372. *HOW DID THE LORD APPEAR ON SINAI?:* Pesikta *Rabbati* 21. Job 12:12.
373. *THE DIVINE PRESENCE EXALTED MOUNT SINAI:* Exodus 34:3. Babli, Taarith 21b.
374. *A VOICE FROM MOUNT SINAI: Eicha Rabba, Pe-tikhta,* Mishnah, Aboth 6:2.
375. *ISRAEL'S REWARD ON MOUNT SINAI: Pesikta Rab-bati* 5:6. Exodus 24:7. Ezekiel 16:14.
376. *WHEN WAS THE TORAH GIVEN?:* Babli, Shabbath 88–89.
377. *SINAI AND THE UPROOTER OF MOUNTAINS:* Babli, Horayoth 14a. Berachoth 64a.
378. *A LAW FROM MOUNT SINAI:* Babli, Nidah 45a.
379. *THE BROKEN PIECES OF THE HOLY TABLETS:* Exodus 32:15–19. Babli, Eirubin 54a. Aboth 6:2. Tosefta, Sottah 7:18. *Sifri, Behaalotkha* 82. Yerushalmi, Sheka-lim 6a. Sottah 8:3.
380. *WHERE DID THE BURNING BUSH GROW?* Exodus 3:2–5. *Shemot Rabba* 2:8. Babli, Shabbath 67a.
381. *MOSES—THE GOOD SHEPHERD: Shemot Rabba* 2:2, and the commentary of Matanot Kehura.

382. *THE CAVE OF MOSES AND ELIJAH IN SINAI:* I Kings 19:8–9. *Yalkut Shimoni, Tehillim* 785. Babli, Pesahim 54a. *Midrash Tanaim,* p. 219.

383. *KORAH WAS SWALLOWED UP IN THE SINAI MOUNTAINS:* Numbers 16:32. Babli, Baba Bathra 74a. Pesahim 54a.

384. *THE SEAT OF MOSES:* Exodus 17:11. *Mechilta de-Rabbi Ishmael,* Tractate *Beshallah* 17. Babli, Berachoth 54a. *Eliyahu Zutta,* p. 196.

385. *THE HEALING ROCK OF MOSES:* Koran, II, 57:6, 160. In *Ahsan al-Takassin,* p. 151, Al-Mukaddasi mentions the Rock of Moses without telling its site.

386. *THE ROCK THAT SPOKE TO MOSES:* Psalms 78:15. Charles Wilson, *Picturesque Palestine,* VI, 1884.

387. *A STONE FROM SINAI IN JERUSALEM:* Naftali ben Yitzchak Elhanan, *Emek Hamelech,* pp. 3, 14. "The Pilgrimage of the Russian Abbot Daniel: PPTS, 1888.

388. *HOW ISRAEL CROSSED THE RED SEA:* Psalms 106:9; 77:17–20. *Pirke Rabbi Eliezer* 42.

389. *THE DIVIDING OF THE RED SEA: Exodus 14:21. Melchilta* 163b.

390. *THE MIRACLES AT THE RED SEA:* Psalms 106:22. *Mechilta de-Rabbi Ishmael* (ed. Lauterbach), I, 1933, pp. 223–224.

391. *THE ALMIGHTY ON THE RED SEA: Mechilta, Masekheth de-Shurta* 4.

392. *THE PROPHET JONAH IN THE RED SEA: Tanhuma, Va-Yikra* 8. *Yalkut Shimoni, Yoma* I. *Midrash Yoma: Beit ha-Midrash* (ed. Yellinek) I, p. 96.

DATE DUE			

Vilnay   177757